Sounding the Color Line

Series Editors
Jon Smith, Simon Fraser University
Riché Richardson, Cornell University

Advisory Board
Houston A. Baker Jr., Vanderbilt University
Leigh Anne Duck, The University of Mississippi
Jennifer Greeson, The University of Virginia
Trudier Harris, The University of North Carolina, Chapel Hill
John T. Matthews, Boston University
Claudia Millian, Duke University
Tara McPherson, The University of Southern California

Sounding the Color Line

Music and Race in the Southern Imagination

ERICH NUNN

THE UNIVERSITY OF GEORGIA PRESS   *ATHENS AND LONDON*

"Country Music and the Souls of White Folk" originally appeared in *Criticism: A Quarterly for Literature and the Arts* 51.4 (Fall 2009): 623–649, and is reprinted here by permission of Wayne State University Press.

Set in Sabon MT Pro by Graphic Composition, Inc.
Printed and bound by Thomson-Shore
The paper in this book meets the guidelines for permanence and durability
of the Committee on Production Guidelines for Book Longevity of the
Council on Library Resources.

Most University of Georgia Press titles are available from popular e-book vendors.

Printed in the United States of America
19 18 17 16 15 P 5 4 3 2 1

Library of Congress Cataloging-in-Publication Data
Nunn, Erich, author.
    Sounding the color line : music and race in the southern imagination /
Erich Nunn.
        pages cm — (The new southern studies ; 6)
    Includes bibliographical references and index.
ISBN 978-0-8203-4736-3 (hardcover : alk. paper) —
ISBN 978-0-8203-4737-0 (pbk. : alk. paper) —
ISBN 978-0-8203-4835-3 (ebook)
    1. Music and race—Southern States—History—20th century. 2. Music and race—
Southern States—History—21st century. 3. Popular music—Southern States—
History—20th century. 4. Popular music—Southern States—History—21st century.
5. Folk music—Southern States—History—20th century. 6. Folk music—Southern
States—History—21st century. 7. Toomer, Jean, 1894-1967. Cane. 8. Faulkner,
William, 1897-1962. Sanctuary. I. Title.
    ML3551. N86 2015
    780.89'00975—dc23   2014036313

British Library Cataloging-in-Publication Data available

Contents

Acknowledgments

While this book grew out of my doctoral dissertation and several years of post-dissertation research, it speaks to questions that I began to ask many years ago, before I knew that such things as dissertations or graduate school existed. After school, my friend Ron Franklin and I would pore over my father's record collection, listening to LPs by Blind Willie McTell, Jimmie Rodgers, Robert Johnson, and Bob Wills and the Texas Playboys. We had little context to help us make sense of what we heard, but gradually we were able to piece together an understanding of these records as artifacts of a history of popular music that assigned McTell and Johnson to a blues tradition that was more or less discrete from the hillbilly or country and western canon that Rodgers and Wills belonged to. Even then I think we intuited that this taxonomy was not quite right, that it obscured as much as it revealed about the musical performances that captivated us. Ron has spent the last quarter-century exploring this music through performance, whereas this book represents my attempt to think through the questions those records raised in a scholarly context. While our perspectives have diverged over the years, Ron has remained a valuable interlocutor and collaborator.

This project has benefited immeasurably from the advice, criticism, and encouragement of teachers, scholars, and colleagues. I never would have been in a position to even consider a career in academia without the patient mentoring of Jefferson Hendricks, David Havird, and Steven Shelburne at Centenary College of Louisiana. At the University of Florida, Susan Hegeman helped me corral my initial inchoate thoughts into an early version of chapter 2. Eric Lott, Jennifer Wicke, and Anna Brickhouse provided timely criticism, sage advice, and emotional support as I worked to complete the dissertation at the University of Virginia. Richard Will kept me honest as the project veered into musicology. Rainer Plaschka and John Mahoney offered their keen ears and help with musical transcriptions. Wesley King, Nathan Ragain, David Sigler, and Omaar Hena provided hours of friendly and collegial criticism and counsel. Karl Hagstrom Miller read an early draft of the manuscript and prompted me to think through questions of audience, style, and tone. Correspondence with Nolan Porterfield was instrumental to my thinking about Jimmie Rodgers. Similarly, Christopher Ballantine shared both his expertise on South African vernacular music and rare recordings of South African blue yodels, neither of which would have been available to me without his generosity.

This project would not have been possible without the resources and support provided by a number of fellowships and archives. I am grateful in particular for the support of an Appalachian Sound Archives Fellowship at Berea College (with particular thanks to Harry Rice and John Bondurant), a Lillian Gary Taylor Fellowship in American Literature at the University of Virginia's Albert and Shirley Small Special Collections Library, an Andrew W. Mellon Foundation Research Fellowship at the University of Texas's Harry Ransom Center, and a Formby Research Fellowship at the Southwest Collection / Special Collections Library at Texas Tech. I owe additional thanks to the staffs of the Orwig Music Library at Brown University, the Center for American History at the University of Texas at Austin, and the American Folklife Center at the Library of Congress. Perhaps most significantly, a year-long residential fellowship at Emory University's Bill and Carol Fox Center for Humanistic Inquiry was invaluable and afforded me the time, intellectual space, and support I needed to finish the manuscript. Thanks are also due to the English Department at Auburn University; Hilary Wyss, Susana Morris, and Sunny Stalter have been particularly supportive. I owe a debt of gratitude as well to my research assistants, Grace Moss and Benjamin Arnberg.

I received valuable feedback on much of this book's material from audience members and seminar participants at meetings of the Society for the Study of Southern Literature, Modern Language Association, Modernist Studies Association, Society for American Music, Louisville Conference on Literature and Culture, American Comparative Literature Association, and the "Southern Sounds / Out of Bounds" conference sponsored by the Center for Global Initiatives and the Center for the Study of the American South at the University of North Carolina at Chapel Hill. My thinking about the relationship between African American culture and Ireland owes much to a symposium on Ireland and African America sponsored by the Clinton Institute for American Studies at University College Dublin; I owe particular thanks to Louise Walsh and Liam Kennedy for organizing it. Chapter 1 grew out of a paper I presented at the "Transatlantic Routes of American Roots Music" conference at the University of Worcester, where I had the remarkable opportunity to exchange ideas with Tony Russell and Elijah Wald, among others. Material from that chapter subsequently appeared in *Transatlantic Roots Music* (University Press of Mississippi); I am grateful to Neil Wynn and

Jill Terry for inviting me to contribute to that volume. Portions of chapters 2 and 6 appeared in *Criticism* and *The Faulkner Journal*, respectively, and I am grateful for permission to present that material here in revised and expanded form.

Finally, I am delighted that this project found a home in the University of Georgia Press's New Southern Studies series. While it has benefited from the support of scholars across a range of fields, the southern studies community has been essential to my project's development. Scott Romine, Andy Crank, Amy Clukey, Leigh Anne Duck, Adam Gussow, Gina Caison, Cole Hutchison, Debra Rae Cohn, Martyn Bone, Jesse Karlsberg, and too many others to list have provided intellectual camaraderie, criticism, and support every step of the way. Jon Smith, Walter Biggins, and Rebecca Norton at the University of Georgia Press have been a pleasure to work with. I'm thrilled to be part of the conversation.

Sounding the Color Line

Introduction

In 1986 New York–based punk band–turned–rap group the Beastie Boys released *Licensed to Ill*, their critically acclaimed and commercially successful debut album.[1] It went to number one on the *Billboard* pop charts, and the next year the single "(You Gotta) Fight for Your Right (To Party!)" reached number seven on the *Billboard* Hot 100. Its success, along with that of contemporaneous releases by Run DMC and LL Cool J, marked an important stage in rap's crossover success. Much of that success is due to rap music expanding its audience beyond the urban Northeast, where the music developed in the late 1970s, to other markets, including those in the rural South. *Licensed to Ill* was produced by Rick Rubin, who, after helping define the sound of commercial rap music in the 1980s, would later helm the albums that led to Johnny Cash's late-career renaissance. Rubin's sonic signature in the 1980s involved overlaying hard rock guitars onto hip-hop breakbeats, a technique epitomized by Run DMC's 1986 collaboration with Aerosmith on "Walk This Way."[2] The tracks he produced for the Beastie Boys' first album incorporate samples from Led Zeppelin, Black Sabbath, Aerosmith, and the Clash, among other rock acts.

When *Licensed to Ill* came out, I was a twelve-year-old junior high school student in rural Louisiana, just across the Texas border, and was afflicted by an early adolescent's dubious taste in music and general insecurity. The Beastie Boys' record precipitated a moment of crisis among my peers, who responded with pleasure to the distorted guitar riffs, straight-ahead 4/4 drum tracks, and petulant adolescent lyrics of songs like "Fight for Your Right" and "No Sleep Till Brooklyn," the latter of which features a heavy guitar riff played by Kerry King of the thrash metal band Slayer. Those sonic ingredients—the hallmarks of Rubin's productions—marked these recordings as generically acceptable to us rural southern white kids: they sounded like what we would have described as heavy metal or hard rock, sonic signifiers of a particular form of white masculinity to which we aspired and attempted to conform.

The crisis arose for me and my peers once we discovered that the Beastie Boys, despite their distorted guitars and nasal, shouted vocals on tracks like "Fight for Your Right," were not a rock band but rather a rap group, a fact that we discovered in the album's more straightforward hip-hop tracks, like "Paul Revere" and "Rhymin' and Stealin'." The problem was not that we didn't like what we heard—we did—but we somehow felt that we weren't supposed to like it, that doing so violated an unspoken protocol. In retrospect, it is clear that this protocol was a racial one: for us, certain sounds, styles, and genres had become coded as white, others as black, and that difference was fraught with significance. Moreover, the generic significance of these sounds were bound up not only in codes of race but also of gender and sexuality. It is perhaps noteworthy that the Beastie Boys had originally proposed to title their album *Don't Be a Faggot*. Thankfully, their record label vetoed that idea, and the band latter apologized "to the entire gay and lesbian community for the shitty and ignorant things [they] said on [their] first record."[3] The explicit homophobia of the record's proposed title and the juvenile lyrical content for which the band later apologized gave voice to an anxiety about heteronormative masculinity that we listeners shared with the music's creators. That anxiety about gender and sexuality was in turn amplified by the racial confusion that resulted from the music's generic hybridity. We experienced the racial anxieties that this generically confusing music elicited in terms of gender while at the same time translating gender anxieties into racial terms.

The phenomenon of cultural segregation along racial lines is a familiar one, with a long history. As W. E. B. Du Bois famously predicted in *The Souls of Black Folk* in 1903, "[t]he problem of the twentieth century is the problem of the color-line," and the encoding of "rock" as white and "rap" as black is just one among innumerable examples of the color line's manifestations in the realm of popular culture.[4] At the same time, the rap/rock hybrid music that Rubin and the Beastie Boys made is but one of similarly innumerable instances of the process Ralph Ellison describes, whereby juxtaposed "traditions . . . tend, regardless of what we do to prevent it, irresistibly to merge."[5] Writing at midcentury, Ellison is referring specifically to the traditions of classical music and African American vernacular music. "One learns," he continues, "by moving from the familiar to the unfamiliar. . . . Those who know their native culture and love it unchauvinistically are never lost when encountering the unfamiliar."[6]

We might ask, though, what would have constituted a "native culture" for rural southern middle-schoolers in the mid-1980s, as opposed to Ellison growing up in Oklahoma a half-century earlier. For his part, Ellison confidently lays claim to "the blues, the spirituals, and jazz" as key parts of his musical patrimony, but his affinities for those cultural forms are not a given. They are in an important sense elective, and they both speak to a sense of aesthetic discernment on his part and provide an example of musical affiliation as an act of self-fashioning. By contrast, the dismissive response to these musical traditions that he experiences as a child in Oklahoma City attests to a chauvinism (to borrow Ellison's term) on the part of cultural gatekeepers who fear musical contamination and erect sonic barriers to prevent it. For my classmates and me, the irony in our confusion about how to understand what we heard on the Beastie Boys album is that, unlike Ellison, as relatively isolated rural southern boys, we did not "know" our "native culture" and were therefore in no position to "love it unchauvinistically." Rather, we had adopted as key components of our shared cultural identity the music from which Rubin sampled the sounds that we responded to as familiar and generically safe. The bands whose records Rubin sampled for *Licensed to Ill* were from such faraway places as Boston (Aerosmith) and England (Black Sabbath, Led Zeppelin, the Clash). By the mid-1980s, for us at least, any idea of a local, "native" musical culture had been supplanted by one transmitted via the radio, LPs, cassette tapes, and compact discs.

This phenomenon, too, is not a new one; the story of popular music in the twentieth century is inextricably bound with the history of technological mediation and reproduction. Karl Hagstrom Miller, in *Segregating Sound: Inventing Folk and Pop Music in the Age of Jim Crow*, carefully and compellingly outlines the ways in which recording technologies transformed scholarly and popular understandings of the relationships between race and musical forms between the 1880s and the 1920s.[7] Thomas Edison's phonograph, he argues, "changed the way people conceived sound. The metaphysical marvel separated the voice from the body and enabled music to travel independently of musicians."[8] The effects of this technological and metaphysical innovation intersect with other contemporaneous developments in thinking about the subjects of music and race and the relationships between them. Du Bois instantiates one such intellectual tradition, which Ellison would later develop, laying the groundwork for current work on these subjects.

Critics such as Ronald Radano and Guthrie P. Ramsey Jr., for example, have considered how ideological investments in racial difference condition contemporary understandings of vernacular musical forms. Both interrogate the idea of "black music" and reveal the role that ideological discourses of race play in producing what Radano describes as "a sound form expressive simultaneously of both the difference of blackness and the relation of black to white."[9] While Ramsey investigates how ideas of racial difference work to produce musical difference, Radano emphasizes how such notions obscure "the sameness that accumulates in American sound forms."[10] By reconsidering the equation of racial identifications and musical forms, Radano and Ramsey demonstrate the limitations that racial categories pose in delimiting musical spheres. Echoing Du Bois and Ellison, these and other contemporary scholars explore the "unresolved dialectical relationship" that "black" culture maintains with "white America, in a kind of stability in instability."[11]

Such rethinkings of the relationships between racial identities and vernacular musical forms have informed other recent work that questions long-held notions about such key figures in twentieth-century popular music as Robert Johnson and "Mississippi" John Hurt.[12] Elijah Wald's systematic unraveling of the romantic racialist mythology surrounding Johnson, for example, undermines the seemingly intuitive notion that the blues is the exclusive product of an African American folk culture by focusing on the music's interracial and commercial aspects. Such recent revisions of long-held ideas concerning the "blackness" of vernacular musical forms reveal how ideas of racialized folk purity risk being pressed into the service of racist tautologies (e.g., that "authenticity in music is an attribute of race and that southern musical reality matched the 'hillbilly' and 'race' distinctions invented by the record industry in its early years," as Bill Ivey puts it).[13] These new studies of "black" music have recast our understanding of the subject in terms of hybridity and reciprocal interracialism.

At the same time, as Ivey's invocation of "southern musical reality" suggests, "the South," both actual and imagined, provides a crucial organizing idea for thinking about the interrelations of music and race. In focusing on what I term "the southern imagination," my approach in this book reflects the work of such scholars as Jon Smith, Scott Romine, Leigh Anne Duck, Houston Baker, Michael Kreyling, and Adam Gussow, who have all worked to interrogate and reconfigure studies of the literature and culture of the American South. These scholars understand the South as heterogeneous rather than as monolithic and situate it within networks of exchange—of people, of languages, of capital, and of cultural representations. They situate discussions of race and region in the United States within a global framework. Kreyling sums up this approach concisely: "'New' southern studies surrenders its traditional claim to regional and historical distinctiveness, finds a common language in public debates over globalization of identities, and takes its chances in the dangerous, new, postmodern world where construction replaces essence."[14]

Most often, these questions of cultural representation are framed through the circulation of images. Scott Romine, for example, describes how in the twenty-first-century U.S. South, "local differences are relentlessly absorbed and reproduced by a commodifying regime of spectacle and simulacra."[15] Romine's understanding of "the South" as a product of circulating media representations resonates with Arjun Appadurai's work on global media formations' impacts on modern subjectivity. For Appadurai, "[e]lectronic media give a new twist to the environment within which the modern and the global often appear as flip sides of the same coin. . . . [T]hese media . . . are resources for experiments with self-making in all sorts of societies, for all sorts of persons."[16] *Sounding the Color Line* draws on the approaches exemplified by Romine's and Appadurai's work but shifts the focus from the circulation of images to the circulation of sound. My goal here is simple: by focusing on aural media (e.g., records, radio broadcasts, and live performances as well as their textual representations) rather than on visual media like photography and film, we can begin to dissociate the meaning of media representations from the visual logic of racial signification in which they are so deeply embedded.

My approach in this book is likewise indebted to Karl Hagstrom Miller's elaboration of the ways folkloristic practice and the economic imperatives of the culture industry worked continually to segregate sounds in the twentieth century. At the same time, I want to shift the emphasis from Miller's exploration of the role of institutions (both academic and commercial) in shaping the ways in which listeners ascribe racial significance to music. Instead, I want to focus on the individual emotional or affective negotiations of race through which individuals experience music as possessing, producing, or reinforcing racial attributes. As my anecdote about processing the racial meanings of the Beastie Boys' records and Ellison's recollection of his own childhood encounter with racialized understandings of both popular and classical music both illustrate, the commercial, academic, and ideological institutions that together work to racialize musical forms do so only imperfectly. Sounds constantly leak through the racial barriers such institutions place around and between them. Consequently, focusing on these institutions only tells part of the story. I am concerned, therefore, with working through some of the myriad ways that individuals—including musicians, folklorists, song collectors, scholars, and writers—have understood, engaged, reproduced, and resisted the racialized meanings of musical sounds in response to these institutional pressures. In other words, my focus is less on material structures of production and commodification and their attendant ideological effects than on what Raymond Williams defines as "structure[s] of feeling"—the individual affective responses to culture (music, in this case) through which ideology is experienced.[17]

Leigh Anne Duck, elaborating on another of Ellison's essays, has rightly observed that "southern segregation was notable less for the ways in which it lingered than for the ways in which it was continually reproduced."[18] Similarly, Diane Pecknold, in the introduction to a recent collection of essays considering the role of African American performers in country music, describes "an obvious paradox: that country music includes a long-standing tradition of black participation and contribution but remains nonetheless 'white' music."[19] Both Duck and Pecknold point to a fundamental contradiction animating twentieth-century (and to some extent twenty-first-century) understandings of race and culture. While musicians, writers, and scholars have long identified and explicated the fundamental interracial character of American culture, in the face of this manifest interracialism we nevertheless continue to hear, feel, and experience race and racial difference. There is, in other words, a critical disjuncture between actual interracial musical and cultural forms, on the one hand, and racialized structures of feeling on the other. Like Jim Crow segregation in general, it has taken enormous energy to maintain the separation of musical forms along racial lines.

The agents of this century-long endeavor to define and maintain racially segregated understandings of American vernacular music include folklorists, record collectors, and record company executives, as Miller, Benjamin Filene, Marybeth Hamilton, and others have discussed at length.[20] Filene, in his influential *Romancing the Folk: Public Memory and American Roots Music*, observes that "historically the vast majority of folk canonizers have been male" and argues that the men whose stories serve as his case studies "are intended to illuminate the work of other brokers, both male and female."[21] This near-exclusive emphasis on men is an attribute shared by much work on folk and vernacular music. My examples—whether focused on musicians, folklorists, critics, or literary figures—likewise involve men primarily. I want to make a significantly different claim from Filene's, however. Throughout this book I aim to illustrate how the relationships between and among men (e.g., the Lomaxes and their folk informants, Jimmie Rodgers and his musical peers, the characters in Jean Toomer's and William Faulkner's fictions, and others) are significant as negotiations not only of race and region but also of masculinity, that is to say, of gender and sexuality.

In the first half of the book I emphasize the musical archive and musicological record, while in the latter half I shift my focus to literary engagements with these musical concerns. The two sections should not be understood as discrete, however. Figures such as W. E. B. Du Bois and John and Alan Lomax appear in both sections, and the self-conscious elaborations of the workings of race and desire in the literary works shed light on the less-examined ways these ideas circulate in the musicological archive. The first three chapters examine the contradictions inherent in the work of folklorists like John Lomax and his son Alan as they worked to catalog, classify, and popularize the folk music first of cowboys in the Southwest and later African Americans throughout the Southeast. The first chapter explores how folklorists and performers associated particular genres, like cowboy songs and mountain ballads, with a transplanted European racial ancestry, a choice that strongly registers contemporaneous anxieties about interracial cultural exchange in the rural South and Southwest. I begin by examining the work of John Lomax, whose collections of folk songs profoundly influenced twentieth-century thinking about the relationships between racial identities and musical forms, in light of folklorists' ideological investments in mapping vernacular musical traditions along racial lines. I read Lomax's 1910 *Cowboy Songs and Other Frontier Ballads* and the work of musician/folklorist Bradley Kincaid as exemplars of a way of thinking about "ballads" that ascribed to them a racial significance produced by cultural isolation and ancestral connections uncomplicated by the cross-racial social and musical blendings that have long characterized American popular culture. At the same time, I argue that these same texts and artifacts bear witness to precisely such interracial exchanges—whether by evincing the legacy of minstrelsy or by documenting African Americans' participation in ostensibly "white" (i.e., English, Scottish, or Anglo-Saxon) cultural practices.

Moving from folklore to the products of the recording industry, chapter 2 focuses on the invention of country music in the late 1920s as a case study in the effects of the twentieth-century culture industry's imperative to organize musical expression along racial lines. The music listed as "hillbilly" in record company catalogs was in fact steeped in African American traditions and shared by whites and blacks, yet it became coded as white through the workings of academic folklorists on the one hand and the culture industry on the other, both of which worked to delimit separate white and black musical spheres. This chapter argues that the construction of country music as white emerges as a response to the threat that the potential permeability of the racial sound barrier poses to the cultural logic of segregation. Focusing on Jimmie Rodgers, "the father of country music," this chapter examines country music's origins in blackface minstrelsy and the blues, and traces its path back into an ostensibly African American folk tradition and its racial transformations as the recording industry disseminates it worldwide in the 1920s and '30s.

Chapter 3 moves from the commercial recording studio to the real and imagined spaces of the southern plantation. For folklorists like the Lomaxes, twentieth-century plantations represented bastions of musical and racial purity. The Lomaxes, for example, sought out singers from communities that had supposedly been isolated from members of other racial and ethnic groups and, ideally, from the modern world and its culture industries. In searching for African American folk singers, John and Alan Lomax deliberately searched for "the Negro who had had the least contact with jazz, the radio, and with the white man."[22] The Lomaxes found what they were looking for on working plantations and in segregated prison farm camps such as Angola and Parchman Farm. The musicians discovered on the Lomaxes' scouting trips included Lead Belly and Muddy Waters, whose subsequent careers evince a fraught relationship between folkloristic conceptions of musical and racial purity born of isolation and the modern, cosmopolitan aspirations of the musicians themselves. The figure of the bluesman arises from this contradiction. This chapter argues that the plantation and prison music the Lomaxes recorded gives voice not only or primarily to the legacy of slavery but to the modern sounds of Jim Crow.

Chapter 4 considers African American writers' and intellectuals' engagements with and challenges to both folkloristic endeavors like those of the Lomaxes and those of the culture industry. This chapter reads Alain Locke's *The New Negro* (1925), a cornerstone text of the Harlem Renaissance, as an intervention into debates engendered by the intersections of African American vernacular culture (often read as rural and southern) and the emerging technologies of the culture industry. Locke and other African American literary authors and intellectuals in the first decades of the twentieth century manifest an uneasy relationship with the nascent popular culture derived from both the commercial and folk cultures of the preceding decades. Locke grounds African American cultural expression in a racialized, pre-industrial folk culture born of slavery. At the same time, working to legitimate African American musical and literary expression under the shadow of nearly a century of minstrelized appropriations of black culture, Locke is deeply suspicious of the uses to which the actual folk—black and white—put this wellspring of folk purity and creativity. This chapter argues that Locke's writings and those of contemporaries such as James Weldon Johnson and Zora Neale Hurston defended the ostensible integrity of folk forms against the challenges produced by the culture industry's appropriation, mediation, and transformation of these materials.

The final two chapters examine the connection between music, sex, and racial violence in key works of twentieth-century southern literature. Scenes linking music with racial and sexual violence appear with unnerving frequency in the literature of the twentieth-century South, from James Weldon Johnson's *The Autobiography of an Ex-Colored Man* (1912) and Jean Toomer's *Cane* (1923) to William Faulkner's *Sanctuary* (1931), as well as in key works by Wright and Ellison (discussed in the next section). In these and other texts, music both gives voice to cross-racial sexual desire and renders audible the violent histories that such desires so often elicited. Toomer's *Cane* and Faulkner's *Sanctuary* reveal the workings of segregation's cultural logic and the stress points at which it breaks down, demonstrating an ambivalence toward the passing of the agrarian, slave-based social economy of the old South from opposing sides of the color line. I suggest that by paying attention to the connections between sexual desire and music in literary works that engage with the history of racial violence in the South, we can not only forge new understandings of American writers' engagements with the South's history of sexual transgression and racial violence but also gain a new perspective on music's role in documenting and giving voice to this history.

To this end, chapter 5 examines how technological mediations of folk musical expression mark transformations of racial identities in Toomer's *Cane*. Such transformations are not only existential or conceptual; they are actualized by the book's many acts of racialized violence and death, which are marked by songs or other musical fragments. These instances of musical performance both enforce a logic of racial difference and elicit cross-racial affective responses that potentially undermine this logic. I argue that music in *Cane* plays a number of contradictory roles: it serves as a marker of racial difference, gives voice to cross-racial desire, and commemorates the insistent reinstantiation of the color line through acts of racial violence. Likewise, in the final chapter, I read instances of musical performance in Faulkner's *Sanctuary* as alternately articulating, destabilizing, reconfiguring, and affirming racial identities. *Sanctuary* depicts the technologies of radio and the phonograph, and the musical forms of blues and jazz, as among the modern forces undermining the old South's social and racial orders. Faulkner's novel enacts ambivalence toward this transformation and loss as well as the musical performances that catalyze and commemorate it.

The book's coda returns to the scene where we began, as the mass-mediated, commercial sounds of hip-hop, a genre that emerged from African American neighborhoods of the urban North, spread to communities in the rural South. In the past three decades, hip-hop has achieved global popularity. Nevertheless, despite this global scope, the genre's concerns remain inextricably tied to performances of particular forms of African American masculinity rooted in the urban spaces in which the music originated. What happens to hip-hop, though, as it migrates from north to south, from the inner city to rural small towns? How do listeners and performers in places that are radically dissimilar from, say, the Bronx or Brooklyn negotiate the genre's insistence that its practitioners "keep it real"? From hip-hop's origins in the Bronx, this imperative has accompanied its move to the West Coast and to the "Dirty South." The book's conclusion briefly considers the work of such southern rappers as Georgia-born Bubba Sparxxx; Gadsden, Alabama, native Yelawolf; and Mississippian Big K.R.I.T., who engage the imperatives of authenticity and the complications of gender, race, and region that inform their hip-hop styles. What, finally, can we learn from these twenty-first-century rappers' negotiations of these complications, and how does this knowledge reflect on the previous century's engagements with questions of music, race, and region?

To illustrate some of the stakes and contours of this argument, I'd like to open by briefly considering fictional works by Richard Wright and Ralph Ellison. Both writers have been instrumental in laying bare the complex interrelations of race, sex, culture, and region in the twentieth-century United States. For Wright and Ellison, as for many others in the first half of the twentieth century, the technology of the phonograph is invested with racial significance. For them, as for us, the experience of mass-mediated recorded sound is overdetermined by what Lisa Gitelman calls "the *visuality of music*, the sum of visual experiences that bolster and accompany musical practice and that extend to the societal norms of visually apprehending racial and other differences."[23] Both Wright's "Long Black Song" and Ellison's *Invisible Man* engage this constellation of racial identification, affect, and technological mediation. Together, these two texts attest to the importance of the idea of the phonograph's racial significance to American literary production while conveying different understandings of that significance; at the same time, they help lay out the concerns that I will explore throughout this book.

Richard Wright's short story "Long Black Song," published in *Uncle Tom's Children* in 1938, begins with a musical epigraph that telegraphs the action of the story:

> Go t sleep baby
> Papas gone t town
> Go t sleep, baby
> The suns goin down

Go t sleep, baby
Yo candys in the sack
Go to sleep, baby
Papas comin back. . . .[24]

The first sentence of the narrative proper opens with a woman named Sarah singing to her baby, whose "wail [drowns] out the song." In Wright's story, folk song is organically linked with the land through language: "Sky sang a red song. Fields whispered a green prayer. And song and prayer were dying in silence and shadow."[25] The world thus represented seems at first literally to be timeless; the old clock in the cabin is broken, and Sarah gives it to her baby to use as a drum, explaining, "We git erlong widout time."[26] Superficially, Sarah and her family resemble what Jean Toomer describes as the "back-country Negroes" he encountered in "the valley of 'Cane.'"[27] Toomer laments the passing of the folk culture of such "Negroes" and bemoans the fact that "[t]hey had victrolas and player-pianos." For Wright, too, the technologies of mechanical reproduction destroy the unity of racialized folk culture, but at the same time his narrative reveals that its characters are modern subjects whose lives are not confined to a hermetic folk-world, but rather implicated with and affected by the forces of modernity. We learn, for example, that Tom—Sarah's former lover—has just returned from fighting in World War I, and that "white folks" had "beat up a black soljer" for "sass[ing] a white woman."[28] The phonograph in particular is symptomatic of the impact of modernity on the characters' lives in Wright's story.

Superficially, the plot of Wright's story is simple. A white salesman appears at Sarah's door while her husband, Silas, is in town selling his cotton crop. He first attempts to sell her a "graphophone" (a type of phonograph) with a built-in clock. The conversation that ensues makes it clear that both the phonograph and the clock are unwelcome and unnecessary intrusions into the world that Sarah inhabits. "Havent you ever had a clock?" the salesman asks.[29] "Mistah, we don need no clock," Sarah replies. "'But you need a clock,' the white man insisted. 'Thats what Im out here for. Im selling clocks and graphophones. The clocks are made right into the graphophones, a nice sort of combination, hunh? You can have music and time all at once.'" The salesman shows Sarah the graphophone, to which she responds in a way that is both erotic and maternal: "Slowly she slid a finger over a beveled edge; she wanted to take the box into her arms and kiss it."[30] He puts on a record and enjoins her to listen to it.

Sarah responds to this command and to the music in a visceral way: "There was a sharp, scratching noise; then she moved nervously, her body caught in the ringing coils of music."

The song the salesman plays is a gospel hymn, "When the Roll Is Called Up Yonder," published by James M. Black in 1894. The song was popular among Methodist congregations. In 1913 Black wrote of his composition: "It is the common consent of all people everywhere that 'When the Roll is Called Up Yonder' is the greatest song that has ever been written for the past twenty-five years. I am of that opinion myself. It goes into more books than any other one gospel song in the English language."[31] This composed gospel hymn, written by a white northerner and distributed via songbook and phonograph record, at first seems an intrusive, alien presence in the rural folk sound-world of the story. Sarah's response to it, however, complicates this assessment. Wright interweaves the song's lyrics with lyrical descriptions of Sarah's ecstatic response to the record:

> *When the trumpet of the Lord shall sound . . .*
> She rose on circling waves of white bright days and dark black nights.
> *. . . and time shall be no more . . .*
> Higher and higher she mounted.
> *And the morning breaks . . .*
> Earth fell far behind, forgotten.
> *. . . eternal, bright and fair . . .*
> Echo after echo sounded.
> *When the saved of the earth shall gather . . .*
> Her blood surged like the long gladness of summer.
> *. . . over on the other shore . . .*
> Her blood ebbed like the deep dream of sleep in winter.
> *And when the roll is called up yonder . . .*
> She gave up, holding her breath.
> *I'll be there . . .*[32]

This scene, in which the salesman forces Sarah to listen to the graphophone, in turn eliciting an evocative if ambiguous affective response, sets the stage for the story's pivotal event, when the salesman rapes Sarah. If the presumed whiteness of the gospel hymn registers on an unconscious level in Sarah's response, the salesman's whiteness is paramount: "White arms were around her, tightly. She was still. But hes a *white* man. A *white* man."[33] The language the narrator uses to evoke Sarah's response to the trauma of the rape directly echoes the descriptions through which her response to the music is figured: "A liquid metal covered her and she rode on the curve of white bright days and dark black nights and the surge of the long gladness of summer and the ebb of the deep dream of sleep in winter. . . ."[34] That Sarah's response to the sound of the graphophone so closely mirrors her response to the assault by the salesman points to a significant connection between the two events. The salesman matter-of-factly tells Sarah after raping her: "I'm leaving that clock and graphophone."[35] The phonograph serves as a concrete reminder of his power over her and propels the rest of the narrative, which details a predictable, if tragic, series of events. Silas returns home, sees the graphophone and other evidence of the salesman's presence, vows to kill him, does so, and is lynched in return. Before killing the white man, though, Silas smashes the graphophone, which clearly symbolizes the technologies of racial and sexual domination that the story dramatizes. The symbolic violence represented by the demolished graphophone anticipates the racialized violence that will take the life both of the salesman and of Silas.

In the prologue to *Invisible Man*, Ralph Ellison, too, structures a narrative of racial and sexual violence around the central image of a phonograph. While in Wright's story the dynamic is almost exclusively coercive and the mode tragic, Ellison's is instead saturated with ambiguity and ambivalence. While listening to a recording of Louis Armstrong's "(What Did I Do to Be So) Black and Blue?" on his phonograph, the narrator finds himself "hearing not only in time, but in space as well." He "not only enter[s] the music but descend[s], like Dante, into its depths."[36] The narrator's experience in the depths of Armstrong's recording takes him back in time. First, he encounters "an old woman singing a spiritual as full of Weltschmerz as flamenco," then "a beautiful girl the color of ivory pleading in a voice like [his] mother's as she stood before a group of slaveowners who bid for her naked body," and finally a sermon on "the 'Blackness of Blackness.'"[37] Warned to flee by "a voice of trombone timbre," he again encounters "the old singer of spirituals," who, asked what is wrong, replies, "I dearly loved my master, son."[38] Pressed, she explains that she both loved and hated her master, with whom she had several sons: "[B]ecause I loved my sons I learned to love their father though I hated him too." "I too have become acquainted with ambivalence," the narrator replies, "that's why I'm here."

Though he tells the old woman that "ambivalence" is "[n]othing, a word that doesn't explain it," the term is in fact key to the scene's negotiation of music's relationship to fraught histories of interracial domination and filiation. The narrator's vision in Ellison's prologue invokes a number of themes, including slavery and spirituals, interracial consanguinity, and racial and sexual violence. In Wright's story, the technology of the phonograph intrudes on a racialized folk-world and operates in concert with the violent imposition of white privilege through Sarah's violation. In Ellison's narrative, by contrast, the narrator's experience with the phonograph provides a key for interpreting the history of which this violence is a product and a symptom.

Louis Armstrong recorded "(What Did I Do to Be So) Black and Blue?" in July 1929 for the OKeh record label. It was composed by Fats Waller with lyrics by Andy Razaf for *Hot Chocolates*, a Broadway musical with an African American cast (Armstrong was a cast member). In Armstrong's hands, the song becomes a satirical, tragicomic lament not only about racism and discrimination but about the process of racialization itself. Armstrong's rendition begins: "Old empty bed, springs hard as lead / Feel like ole Ned. Wish I was dead / All my life through, I've been so black and blue. // Even the mouse ran from my house / They laugh at you and scorn you too / What did I do to be so black and blue?"[39] These verses are followed by a vocal bridge that breaks from the verses' structure, and makes a peculiar claim: "I'm white inside, but that don't help my case / 'Cause I can't hide what is in my face." The final verse sums up with: "How will it end? Ain't got a friend / My only sin is in my skin / What did I do to be so black and blue?" The song's lyrics proclaim the superficiality of visible racial difference, proposing an understanding of race as skin-deep. While calling attention to the arbitrary significance of skin color in the verses, however, the song's bridge ironically points to a normative racial whiteness: "I'm white inside, but that don't help my case." Armstrong's lyrical reworking of "Black and Blue" balances the relative frivolity of the Broadway show tune genre with social satire and critique.

Significantly, though, with the exception of the song's refrain, Ellison's narrator does not refer to any of the song's lyrics, either as written by Razaf or as reworked by Armstrong. Rather, he responds to the meanings he hears in the instrumental voices on Armstrong's recording. Armstrong's orchestra plays through three full choruses and the bridge before Armstrong starts singing, and these instrumental choruses spark the narrator's "surreal but illuminating descent into the racial past."[40] At the end of the sermon on "the blackness of blackness," for example, the trombone of Fred Robinson, Armstrong's accompanist, screams at him, "*Git out of here, you fool! Is you ready to commit treason?*"[41] The "racial past" thus revealed is not one of racial purity but rather one of mixture—albeit one that is the product of coercion and wildly unequal power relations of gender and race. Below the racialized form of the spirituals, the narrator encounters slave owners bidding to possess a female slave "the color of ivory"—herself evidently the product of an earlier coercive cross-racial coupling.[42] That the woman has "a voice like [the narrator's] mother" reveals his filial connection to this interracial past. Below that lies "the blackness of blackness"; lower still the singer of spirituals, her sons, and their white slave owner father.[43] In each instance, blackness and whiteness are inextricably bound. The genealogical and cultural lineage that the narrator imagines complicates and frustrates racial boundaries.

While in Wright's story (as in Toomer's anecdote) the phonograph represents the technological intrusion of a white-identified culture industry into a rural, southern, African American folk culture, Ellison tells a different story. For Ellison, American culture is always already interracial. Armstrong's recording of "Black and Blue" is a paradigmatic product of the culture industry—written to spec, performed on Broadway, commercially recorded and distributed by a white-owned record label. While writers from Du Bois to Wright argue that such products of the culture industry pose a threat to a racially defined folk culture, the narrator's experience in Ellison's prologue suggests otherwise. He hears in the grooves of Armstrong's record a history both of racial exploitation and consanguinity. The ambivalence toward this history expressed by "the old singer of spirituals" is of a piece with the narrator's own vexed affective response to the music he hears. The mechanically reproduced nature of this music is not incidental; rather, it is key to the narrator's experience. Significantly, his vision of the racial past is enabled by the experience of listening to a phonograph record, not to a live performance. At the moment, he tells us, he has one phonograph, but he plans to have five, all playing at once. Mechanical reproduction enhances the cultural significance of the listening experience rather than detracting from it. In Wright's story, the phonograph functions as a symbol of racial and sexual domination—a violent imposition of industrial modernity on a racialized folk-world. Ellison's narrative, by contrast, suggests a different mode of listening. The invisible man's narrative does not treat the products of the culture industry as corruptions of or threats to racially specific vernaculars but rather as avatars of the complex interracial exchanges—often violent or coercive—that define not only the contemporary historical moment from which his narrator is speaking but also the long history of the music itself.

CHAPTER ONE

American Balladry and the Anxiety of Ancestry

In *Cowboy Songs and Other Frontier Ballads* (1910), John Lomax writes: "Out in the wild, far-away places of the big and still unpeopled west . . . yet survives the Anglo-Saxon ballad spirit that was active in secluded districts in England and Scotland even after the coming of Tennyson and Browning. This spirit is manifested both in the preservation of the English ballad and in the creation of local songs."[1] Lomax's identification of "the Anglo-Saxon ballad spirit" among his cowboy informants anticipates Cecil Sharp's later expeditions into the Appalachian hills in search of remnants of an Anglo-Saxon ballad tradition. Describing the informants from whom he collected the texts and tunes published in *English Folk Songs from the Southern Appalachians* (1917), Sharp writes: "[T]hese mountain people, albeit unlettered, have . . . one and all entered at birth into the full enjoyment of their racial heritage." Their songs, like other elements of their culture, "are merely racial attributes which have been gradually acquired and accumulated in past centuries and handed down generation by generation."[2] Sharp offers as evidence of this racial inheritance his having heard sung in Appalachia thirty-seven so-called Child ballads (the texts of which had been recorded in Francis James Child's *English and Scottish Popular Ballads*, which was published in ten volumes between 1882 and 1898).[3]

For ballad collectors like Lomax and Sharp, cultural forms such as the ballad function as the means through which a racial heritage—white Englishness, in this case—is expressed and transmitted. So pervasive was this racialist logic that collectors like Lomax would at times record performances of ballads and other songs by African American singers while simultaneously insisting on the ballads' white racial provenance, eliding or flatly denying any African American contribution to such song traditions. The converse of this understanding of folk music along racially segregated lines—that some musical forms are intrinsically "black" or "Negro," regardless of their immediate provenance—obtains as well. As John Greenway observed in 1957, commercial songs composed and/or recorded by the white singer Jimmie Rodgers (arguably hillbilly music's first superstar) showed up, with no evident intentional irony, for nearly three decades after Rodgers's death in 1933 as examples of "Negro" music in printed collections.[4] Lomax himself was keenly interested in the music of African Americans, although for him (as for most of his contemporaries) "black" and "white" folk music constituted discrete, mostly non-overlapping areas of interest.

Key examples from Lomax's own work, however, complicate this notion of strictly segregated traditions, and at times he seems to be aware of these complications. At one point in his introduction to *Cowboy Songs*, for example, he observes that "[t]he range community consisted usually of the boss, the straw-boss, the cowboys proper, and the cook—often a negro." While Lomax acknowledges the presence of the "negro" cook here, he remains apart from "the cowboys proper." A couple of pages later, Lomax goes a step further, noting that "[i]t was not unusual to find a Negro who, because of his ability to handle wild horses or because of his skill with a lasso, had been promoted from the chuck-wagon to a place in the ranks of the cowboys."[5] In fact, as Lomax recounts in a later edition of *Cowboy Songs*, he collected "Home on the Range," the most famous song in the collection, from an African American informant.[6] He explains: "Some one told me that in San Antonio, Texas, lived a Negro singer and cook, who had first plied the latter art in the rear of a chuck wagon which followed many a herd of long-horned cattle up the trail from Texas to Fort Dodge, Kansas. I found him in 1908 leaning against a stunted mulberry tree at the rear of his place of business, a low drinking dive."[7] While the white cowboys' singing reflects "the freedom and the wildness of the plains,"[8] the "Negro singer" is as debased as his surroundings: "'I'se too drunk to sing today. Come back tomorrow,' he muttered."[9] Lomax perseveres despite this inauspicious initial encounter, extracting "Home on the Range" from the African American inebriate and publishing it in the first edition of *Cowboy Songs*.

In a more detailed account published in 1945, Lomax elaborates on the process through which "Home on the Range" achieved popular currency. Apparently, despite his drunkenness at their first meeting, the saloonkeeper kept his word, as Lomax reports that he "spent all the next day under the mesquite with this Negro. Among the songs he sang for me was 'Home on the Range,' the first time I had heard the melody."[10] Lomax recorded the song of "this Negro" onto a cylinder using a portable recording device. "From the record I made that day down in the Negro red-light district," he reports, "Henry Leberman, a blind teacher of music at the State School for the Blind in Austin, a few weeks afterwards set down the music. Leberman used earphones and played the record over and over again until he felt sure that he had captured the music as the Negro saloonkeeper had rendered it."[11] Lomax points out with justified pride that his arrangement of the song, published in *Cowboy Songs*, became popular around the world. "The original cylindrical record of the song has crumbled into dust," he observes, "but the music that Henry Leberman set down from the record I made still survives."[12]

The agents of the song's preservation credited in this final sentence include Lomax, who produces the cylinder recording, and Henry Leberman, who (remarkably, it would seem, given that Lomax describes him as blind) provides the transcription. The "Negro saloonkeeper," who is never named, plays a subordinate role. In the structure of Lomax's narrative, he, like Lomax's cylinder recording or Leberman's transcription, plays the role of a passive recording technology that facilitates the song's preservation rather than an agent actively involved in this project. He serves, in other words, as a conduit between the folk tradition that Lomax sets out to document and the world at large, but not as a contributor to that tradition. Rather, he appears in the narrative as a resource to be mined, with "Home on the Range" as the valuable commodity he possesses and that Lomax seeks to appropriate. By the end of the 1945 article, Lomax makes this relationship explicit, as he refers to the singer as "*my* San Antonio Negro saloon-keeper."[13]

This language equating "negro" singers with recording technologies appears even more explicitly elsewhere in Lomax's writing. In a 1912 letter to a correspondent, for example, Lomax explains the reason for his delay in sending records he had promised: "I shall send you records of the three negro songs that you want *as soon as I find a negro with a good voice to use as a transmitter.* My own records, while entirely adequate for my purpose, I think would not be as suggestive for your work as others I believe I can get."[14] In this instance, as with "Home on the Range," the singer's racial identification dictates his suitability for sufficiently recording a given song. Just as Lomax's voice could serve merely as a placeholder for the more "suggestive" voice of a negro singer, so too does the voice of his "Negro saloon-keeper" substitute for the racially authentic voice of the cowboy.

"Home on the Range" derives at least in part from Dr. Brewster Higley's 1873 poem, "My Western Home," though its origins had become obscure by the time Lomax encountered it.[15] A 1909 issue of *The Journal of American Folk-Lore* prefaces a version of the song credited to one "Mr. Otis Tye of Yucca, N[orth] Dak[ota]" with the note that "[n]o information could be obtained as to its origin, but after questioning a number of older cowboys it seems that it is almost universally known in the northwest, though most of the men knew but a few verses."[16] That Mr. Tye of North Dakota and Lomax's anonymous informant from San Antonio provide similar versions of the song attests to its popularity; that Tye is named as a participant in the cowboy culture with which the song was identified while Lomax's "Negro singer" is neither named nor given such credit is symptomatic of the racial logic that structures the folklore scholarship of Lomax and many of his contemporaries.

"Home on the Range" is hardly unique as an instance in which an African American musician is instrumental in Lomax's search for cowboy songs. He wrote to Harvard's Barrett Wendell in 1907: "The people who know [cowboy songs] are very sly and suspicious of one's object. Professor [George Lyman] Kittredge will be interested to know that my best success thus far has been with negroes who can neither read nor write, who got the songs from the cowboys when they (the negroes) were cooks on the trail to Montana, twenty-five or thirty years ago. They seem to have kept the words in some virginal freshness, and they sing the songs with a spirit and dash that I wish you might hear."[17] Later in the same letter, however, he avers that "the person who gets the ballads will have to go out on the plains and down the canyons and among the camps to meet and know the men who, true to their Anglo-Saxon impulses, are still fond of expressing their emotions in the ballad form." The "negroes" are secondhand informants who, though they sing with "spirit and dash," do not possess the "Anglo-Saxon impulses" of the cowboy songs' rightful practitioners.

In much the same vein, Lomax wrote to the trustees of the Carnegie Foundation in 1908: "The three men who have been most helpful to me in Texas are illiterate negroes with a talent for music. Since childhood they have lived among the cattle camps, and the songs and stories they have heard are their sole literary possessions. They have not forgotten them."[18] Such a situation obtains as well in Lomax's "Cowboy Songs of the Mexican Border" (1911), in which he notes that "[a] number of the most interesting songs were obtained from four negroes who have had experience in ranch life."[19] He goes on to conclude that these songs are products of "the ballad instinct of the race, temporarily thrown back to primitive conditions, again actively at work. How much relationship really exists between these songs and the ballads in the great collection of Professor Child of Harvard University, I am not ready to surmise about."[20] The "race" in question here is white; despite African American singers' value as sources of interesting songs, they, like Lomax's "Negro San Antonio saloonkeeper," serve as passive conduits, not as active participants in the ballad tradition.

The paradox at work in Lomax's assertion illustrates what Werner Sollors has identified as "the conflict between contractual and hereditary, self-made and ancestral, definitions of American identity—between *consent* and *descent*," which Sollors posits as "the central drama in American culture."[21] Approaches to vernacular musical traditions like Lomax's and Sharp's link cultural forms to racial or ethnic identities and articulate what Sollors describes as an ideology of descent, which "emphasizes . . . our hereditary qualities, liabilities, and entitlements."[22] Such hereditary qualities define Lomax's cowboy informants; they evince "the gallantry, the grace, and the song heritage of their English ancestors."[23] These hereditary traits, in turn, are reflected in the ballads the cowboys sing. "Thrown back on primal resources and for entertainment and for the expression of emotion," they "express themselves through somewhat the same character of songs as did their forefathers of perhaps a thousand years ago."[24] The homology between the hereditary qualities of the singers and the character of their songs emphasizes an ostensibly heritable racial song heritage. The song culture of the cowboys is both transatlantic and transhistorical, spanning two continents and "a thousand years."

At the same time, Lomax's model leaves little room for musical traditions that cross racial lines. In other words, the possibility of a culture of consent, to borrow Sollors's vocabulary—in which the "Negro singer" would count as a full participant—is short-circuited by the logic of descent that structures Lomax's thinking. The "Negro" cannot share the song tradition of the cowboys because he does not share their hereditary qualities. This tautological idea accounts for the seeming paradox that "Home on the Range" represents. Though Lomax collects the song from an African American source, the racial logic that undergirds his project obviates the possibility that this source participates in the song culture being documented. According to this logic, "Home on the Range," like the other material in *Cowboy Ballads*, expresses a white racial inheritance, from which "the Negro singer" is by definition excluded. While the "Negro" may ventriloquize this inheritance, his racial status prevents him from being a part of it.

At the same time, despite Lomax's decision—conscious or otherwise—not to name him or credit him with any degree of agency, without the "Negro singer," there is no "Home on the Range," at least not in the form that Lomax made famous. While it is true that the understanding of folk music that informed Lomax's project held that cowboy songs were the collective product of a folk culture rather than the creations of individuals, such a conception didn't prevent Lomax from naming individual sources. In "Hunting Cowboy Songs," chapter 3 of his 1947 *Adventures of a Ballad Hunter*, for example, Lomax provides another account of his encounter with the source of "Home on the Range," who, as in the 1945 article, is referred to by his race and occupation but never by name (as before, Henry Leberman does receive credit for his transcription).[25] In this same chapter, Lomax gives detailed accounts of named individuals whose songs he recorded. He spends two pages, for example, discussing his interactions with a source named Tom Hight: "Tom knew more cowboy melodies than any other person I have ever found."[26]

If the presence of the "Negro singer" poses a problem for Lomax's model of a racially defined ballad tradition that had taken root in the American Southwest, the idea of ancestry provides a solution. Faced with the prospect of acknowledging a multiracial culture of consent being forged among cowboys of diverse ethnic origins, he instead posits a racially homogeneous musical heritage that insulates from the influence of their nonwhite neighbors "many a young Virginia aristocrat; many sons of Alabama, Mississippi, and Georgia planters; many a coon hunter from Kentucky; roving and restless young blades from all over the South." "From such a group, given a taste for killing in the Civil War, in which Southern feeling and sentiments predominated," he continues, "came the Texas cowboy and the cowboy songs."[27] Lomax does not explain precisely what he means by "Southern feeling and sentiments," though the structure of feeling he describes is born of a collective identity that transcends divisions of social class and geography under the sign of a shared racial inheritance. "These boys," who "came mainly from the Southern states," Lomax maintains, "brought the gallantry, the grace, and the song heritage of their English ancestors."[28] While an understanding of folk songs as products of a culture of consent would lead to a consideration of how cowboys of diverse geographic, racial, and ethnic backgrounds might forge a shared musical culture, Lomax's descent model instead seeks continuity with ancestors real and imagined, proposing a relatively static musical culture whose racial character has remained unchanged for "perhaps a thousand years."

This conception of musical cultures as racially bound depends on a logic of cultural, social, and often physical segregation; Lomax and other proponents of descent-oriented understandings of ballad and song traditions sought out singers from communities that had supposedly been isolated from members of other racial and ethnic groups and, ideally, from the modern world and its culture industries. Lomax recounts a conversation with Theodore Roosevelt (to whom he dedicated his *Cowboy Songs and Other Ballads*), for example, during which the president observed of the cowboy songs Lomax was collecting that "[t]here is something very curious in the reproduction here on this continent of essentially the conditions of ballad growth which obtained in mediaeval England."[29]

Such ideas of ethnic isolation not only inform Lomax's understanding of an English-derived cowboy culture; they also structure dominant conceptions of Appalachian identity in the first decades of the twentieth century. An influential articulation of this idea is William Goodell Frost's "Our Contemporary Ancestors in the Southern Mountains," published in the *Atlantic Monthly* in 1899, which maintained that "the 'mountain whites'" lived "to all intents and purposes in the conditions of the colonial times."[30] Working in part to counter stereotyped depictions of mountain residents as backwards, "poor white trash," Frost defined "'Appalachian America' . . . as a unique and distinct social and cultural entity" that represented a transplanted English (or "Saxon") culture uncorrupted by industrial American modernity.[31]

Song collector and radio performer Bradley Kincaid, billed as "The Kentucky Mountain Boy," echoes this idea in his popular songbooks, in one of which he maintained that "the mountain folks were isolated from the rest of America for about one hundred years."[32] In Kincaid's self-presentation, the idea of Appalachian isolation serves as a marker of racial and cultural purity. Kincaid was one of the most popular and successful early commercial "hillbilly" singers, though he resisted that label, arguing that his songs were "folk songs," not the degraded dilutions of commercial-minded hillbilly performers. As such, Kincaid serves as a prime example of the ways in which the concerns of folklorists like Lomax and Sharp about ancestry have influenced understandings of popular music based in vernacular folk traditions.[33] Kincaid's career as a radio and recording artist began in 1927, the same year that Jimmie Rodgers and the Carter Family made their first records, jump-starting "hillbilly" music as a commercial genre. Though he did not sell records on the scale of the Carters or Rodgers, Kincaid was hugely popular through his radio broadcasts: first on WLS in Chicago, and then on a number of other stations, culminating in a stint with WSM's Grand Ole Opry in Nashville in 1944.

More so than either the Carters or Rodgers, Kincaid insisted on the folk provenance of his material and denied a pecuniary motivation for his musical activities. "I tried for many years," Kincaid explained in a 1943 interview, "to preach the difference between ballads and hillbilly songs and said I never would sing a hillbilly song. . . . But I gave up when a radio magazine came out with a long story which was titled: Bradley Kincaid, King of the Hillbillies."[34] Nonetheless, he pioneered the marketing of folk-based music through his radio broadcasts, recordings, and songbooks, twelve volumes of which were eventually published, the first in 1928, the last in 1941. Kincaid undertook yearly collecting trips in rural Kentucky, North Carolina, and Georgia to gather ballads and folk songs, combining the roles of collector, scholar, interpreter, and popularizer of a body of songs that he understood to represent a unified folk tradition. Though his repertoire was diverse—including Child ballads, nineteenth-century parlor songs, novelty tunes, and songs derived from minstrelsy and Tin Pan Alley—Kincaid took pains to distinguish the folk songs of the mountains from the hillbilly songs of his fellow recording artists. He wrote in 1928: "I have tried earnestly to bring to you a true picture of the people of the mountains as manifested in the songs they sing. To me there is character and dignity to be found in the old mountain ballads: they represent a certain type, and are just as distinctive as the Negro Spirituals. They are truly American Folk Songs, born out of the life and experiences of the mountain people. Therefore, I have tried to bring to the radio audience, only those songs that are truly representative of these people."[35]

Kincaid rooted this folk tradition in a specific locale—the mountains of eastern Kentucky—but he also insisted that it constituted an ancestral racial inheritance. In doing so, Kincaid seems to be responding, somewhat defensively, to W. E. B. Du Bois's claim in "The Sorrow Songs" that "the Negro folk-song—the rhythmic cry of the slave—stands to-day not simply as the sole American music, but as the most beautiful expression of human experience born this side of the seas."[36] Kincaid maintained that the songs he collected, sang, broadcast, and published were "just as distinctive" as Du Bois's sorrow songs, and embodied an ancestral whiteness that had rooted itself in the Kentucky hills. As a promotional piece from 1928 explains, "Bradley Kincaid was born in Garrard County, Kentucky, in the edge of the mountains and very near the Blue Grass. His parents were both native Kentuckians. His great-grandfather was a full-blooded Scotchman, coming to Virginia from Scotland. So Bradley is Scotch, but he says he was born in this country to save transportation."[37] Its attempt at humor aside, the "[g]enerational rhetoric" of this piece, as Werner Sollors explains the phenomenon in general, "confers . . . a sense of kinship and community upon the descendants of heterogeneous ancestors."[38] While the piece's author invokes a legitimate genealogical fact (that Kincaid's great-grandfather emigrated from Scotland), this "supposedly pure descent definition" (the identification of Kincaid as "Scotch") is "far from natural, being largely based on a consent construction."[39] In point of fact, for example, if we consider only the evidence Kincaid presents concerning his Scottish great-grandfather, Kincaid is precisely as Scottish as fellow Kentuckian Muhammad Ali is Irish, as both men are descended from immigrant great-grandfathers. (Ali's maternal great-grandfather, Abe Grady, emigrated from County Clare to Kentucky in 1862.)[40] That, in twentieth-century Kentucky, Kincaid could self-identify as "Scotch" while Ali could not plausibly self-identify as "Irish" reveals how consent masquerades as descent in such ethnic identifications. In Ali's case, the descent logic of ancestral Irishness is superseded by the binary racial logic of Jim Crow.

The ethnic affiliation by which Kincaid is "Scotch" by virtue of having a "full-blooded Scotch" grandfather extends to the songs he sings as well. The foreword to the first volume of *Favorite Mountain Ballads and Old Time Songs*, published in Chicago in 1928, for instance, maintains: "To those who live in the mountains this little booklet will represent a group of familiar songs. To those who live outside of the mountains it will represent the life and spirit of a people in whose veins runs the purest strain of Anglo-Saxon blood to be found anywhere in America. These mountain ballads are songs that grew out of the life and experiences of hardy Scotch, Irish, German, English and Dutch natives."[41] This passage conflates various national and ethnic terms, revealing an ideological investment in ancestral whiteness that supersedes any intraracial national or ethnic distinctions. According to the then-current racial logic from which this terminology derives, though, of these groups, only the English could plausibly be characterized as "Anglo-Saxon." The Scotch and Irish, rather, were Celts; the Germans and Dutch were Teutons.[42] The very racial logic from which Kincaid's claim to ancestral purity derives renders nonsensical the idea that Appalachian residents possessed "the purest strain of Anglo-Saxon blood."

Kincaid's emphasis on ancestry echoes the claims of Sharp and Lomax, who held that the ballad tradition in America provided a racial link with English (or Scottish or Anglo-Saxon) forebears. Historian Bill C. Malone, one of the first scholars to examine critically and begin to dismantle the romantic racialism that has long structured discussions of country music, observes that the idea of American folk music as English or Anglo-Saxon has largely waned, but thinly veiled claims to an ancestral whiteness infusing vernacular music forms persist. As Malone puts it, "[m]ercifully, no one speaks of 'Anglo-Saxon' roots any longer, but a disquieting attribution of 'celticism'" persists, particularly regarding bluegrass. "As in the days of Bradley Kincaid," he continues, "visions of musical, cultural, and ethnic purity have been revived to distinguish a form of country music from its presumably inferior and more commercial competitors."[43] Elsewhere he observes that "Appalachian ballad hunters spoke rhapsodically about the Anglo-Saxon or Elizabethan nature of southern mountaineers (without understanding that the two labels were not synonymous)."[44]

Kincaid's Anglo-Saxonist investments were not unique or unusual; instead, they were very much of the moment in both scholarly and popular discussions of Appalachian music. As folklorist Archie Green observes, "[a]lthough careful scholars today do not assert Teutonic [*sic*; presumably he means Anglo-Saxon or Elizabethan] ancestry for American balladry, Kincaid's view was a key intellectual assumption in the discovery of Appalachian folksong between 1900 and 1925."[45] In fact, such ideas persisted well beyond the 1920s. In the preface to the inaugural 1932 issue of *The Cumberland Empire*, a journal whose professed "aim [was] to mirror the mountains so that the world may see and know us, not as the novelist and feature writer pictures us to be, but as we really are," publisher James Taylor Adams wrote: "For four generations my people were cut off from all intercourse with the rest of the world. During that time they were wrestling with the wilderness. Schools were few and far between. And the art of reading and writing was almost lost. But they had a literature. A beautiful literature, and they preserved it the only way they knew; in the songs they sung [*sic*] and the tales they told their children."[46] Adams, like Kincaid and Frost, transforms rural isolation from a handicap into a virtue. For all of them, folk song becomes a vehicle for the transmission of a racialized ancestral culture.

In another piece in the same issue of the journal, entitled "Bradley Kincaid and His Houn' Dog Guitar," Adams tells the story of Kincaid's musical education:

> Bradley Kincaid was born in the Point Leavell community of Garrard County, Kentucky, thirty-six years ago. Garrard County is in the Cumberland foothills, and Bradley fell into his first sleep, influenced by the crooning of mountain lullabies. Both his father and mother were gifted with good singing voices and for several months following his advent into the world of men and things, anyone passing their humble home could have heard the "rock, rock" of the cradle, keeping time to a mountain tune. . . .
>
> Musical instruments were scarce in the hill country at that time. . . . But one day something wonderful, almost a miracle happened in the Kincaid home.
>
> Father brought home a guitar.
>
> The elder Kincaid was a great hunter; and he had an ear for music. One night as he was returning home from a fox chase he met up with a negro thrumming a guitar. He bartered the Son of Ham for a trade, and a little later he saw the colored fellow lead away one of his hounds and he was the undisputed owner of the "box," as guitars were called in the hill country at that time.
>
> Because he traded a fox hound for it, Kincaid called the newly acquired musical instrument the "houn' dog guitar," and from that day till this it has been the almost constant companion of Bradley's.[47]

Versions of this story appear in Kincaid's songbooks, in press for his concert performances, in journalistic puff pieces, and in interviews that Kincaid gave almost fifty years after the story first appeared. Almost without exception, such retellings emphasize that the guitar's previous owner was African American. A 1929 article in the *Jackson (Miss.) News*, for example, states:

"Kincaid senior was following two of his hounds on a hunt when he came across a darky with the dilapidated instrument."[48] The *Washington Post* the next year elaborated: "A farmer in Garrard County, Ky., was fond of fox hunting. Often after a hurried supper he would 'blow up' his hounds and ride away for a few hours of sport. On one such expedition he traded a dog to a Negro for an old guitar."[49] According to a 1931 article in the *Berea Alumnus*, "Mr. Kincaid, the father, was an ardent hunter, and it was on one of his nightly jaunts into the hills to pursue the tricky fox that he located the music box. The father's desire to obtain the guitar was ended when he arranged a trade of a fox hound to an old Negro for it."[50]

This story economically combines a narrative of filiation—young Bradley receives both the "houn' dog guitar" and his song repertoire from his parents—with one of cultural affiliation—the guitar materializes during a fox hunt, a sporting practice that links the working-class Kincaids of rural Kentucky with the British upper classes. This linking of the Kentucky mountain folk with British ancestors neatly complements the Child ballads and other English and Scottish songs in Kincaid's repertoire. "Barbara Allen" (Child 84) was one of his signature pieces, for example (see fig. 1.1). Kincaid claimed these songs—some of which he learned from his mother, others from published folk song collections or from informants he encountered on collecting trips—as a cultural inheritance, evidence of an ancestral English heritage that had crossed the ocean and taken root in the Kentucky hills. "[M]y mother," Kincaid told an interviewer, "went farther back. She sang the old English ballads. I learned a lot of ballads from her, like 'Fair Ellender,' 'The Two Sisters' and any number of English ballads. I sang these as a kid. . . . My mother never did show too much musical ability, though she used to—in a very lamentable voice—sing some of the old blood curdlers to me, and my hair would stand straight up on end."[51]

The "houn' dog guitar" would become a crucial element in Kincaid's public persona, receiving equal billing with Kincaid himself (fig. 1.2). Significantly, Kincaid applied the name to whatever instrument he was currently playing. The original was a mid-nineteenth-century parlor guitar that somehow made its way from France to rural Kentucky (fig. 1.3). (Though some accounts erroneously describe the original hound dog guitar as a Martin, when Kincaid's son, Jimmie, took it to George Gruhn's vintage guitar shop in Nashville to have it appraised, he learned that it was in fact a French-made model of mid-nineteenth-century vintage. It is currently on display at the Kentucky Museum Hall of Fame in Renfro Valley.)[52] Publicity photographs show him with fancier steel-string Martins of recent manufacture (fig. 1.2), and Sears-Roebuck (which owned WLS, the station on whose *Radio Barn*

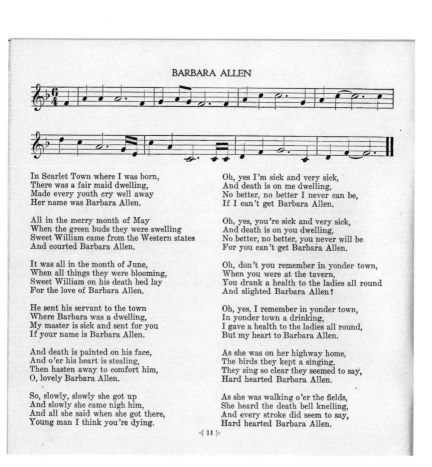

In Scarlet Town where I was born,
There was a fair maid dwelling,
Made every youth cry well away
Her name was Barbara Allen.

All in the merry month of May
When the green buds they were swelling
Sweet William came from the Western states
And courted Barbara Allen.

It was all in the month of June,
When all things they were blooming,
Sweet William on his death bed lay
For the love of Barbara Allen.

He sent his servant to the town
Where Barbara was a dwelling,
My master is sick and sent for you
If your name is Barbara Allen.

And death is painted on his face,
And o'er his heart is stealing,
Then hasten away to comfort him,
O, lovely Barbara Allen.

So, slowly, slowly she got up
And slowly she came nigh him,
And all she said when she got there,
Young man I think you're dying.

Oh, yes I'm sick and very sick,
And death is on me dwelling,
No better, no better I never can be,
If I can't get Barbara Allen.

Oh, yes, you're sick and very sick,
And death is on you dwelling,
No better, no better, you never will be
For you can't get Barbara Allen.

Oh, don't you remember in yonder town,
When you were at the tavern,
You drank a health to the ladies all round
And slighted Barbara Allen?

Oh, yes, I remember in yonder town,
In yonder town a drinking,
I gave a health to the ladies all round,
But my heart to Barbara Allen.

As she was on her highway home,
The birds they kept a singing,
They sing so clear they seemed to say,
Hard hearted Barbara Allen.

As she was walking o'er the fields,
She heard the death bell knelling,
And every stroke did seem to say,
Hard hearted Barbara Allen.

‹ 11 ›

Figure 1.1. "Barbara Allen." From Bradley Kincaid, *Favorite Mountain Ballads and Old Time Songs*, 1928.

Dance Kincaid began his broadcasting career) sold a "Supertone Bradley Kincaid Houn' Dog" guitar mass-produced by Harmony, which was decorated with a depiction of the eponymous canine (fig. 1.4). The term "houn' dog guitar," then, becomes detached from the specific instrument that Bradley receives from his father and instead becomes an abstracted signifier of authenticity and of a racialized musical inheritance.

What, though, are we to make of the guitar's previous owner, who evidently decides (or is persuaded) that a foxhound is more valuable to him than the instrument is? What is this African American man doing in the middle of this story of transplanted musical Englishness? Is the man's race merely incidental, or is this figure's blackness significant? As with Lomax's story about the origin of "Home on the Range," a black man is at once central to

The Breslow Brother's Minstrel

Figure 1.2. Bradley Kincaid and his Hound Dog Guitar. Undated publicity photograph. Photo from the Bradley Kincaid Collection, courtesy of the Southern Appalachian Archives, Hutchins Library, Berea College.

the narrative and yet never fully accounted for. The first article quoted above identifies him within the span of two sentences as "a negro," a "Son of Ham," and a "colored fellow," and such racial designations are echoed in other iterations of the story. More than four decades later, Kincaid would tell an interviewer: "One night my father was on one of these trips with the fox hunters, and there was an old colored feller—they call 'em blacks now, I guess—an old colored feller that had a little ol' guitar, and my father traded one of his foxhounds for that guitar. And he brought it home, and all the kids learned to play chords on it and sing. That was my first introduction to music."[53] In none of these accounts do we learn the man's name, his occupation, or what specific social relationship he might have had with Kincaid's father. The story itself, we might say, takes the form of a ballad or folktale, with "the negro" as a mysterious figure outside the social order around whom the narrative circles.

In other words, his appearance in the story represents an instance of what Toni Morrison calls an "Africanist presence" structuring white American self-understandings. Morrison's explanation of "the self-evident ways in which Americans choose to talk about themselves through and within" this Africanist presence, "sometimes allegorical, sometimes metaphorical, always choked," can perhaps help shed some light on Kincaid's story.[54] This "dark and abiding [Africanist] presence," Morrison explains, is "there for the literary imagination as both a visible and invisible mediating force," a "shadow [that] hovers in implication, in sign, in line of demarcation."[55] At a fundamental level, the presence of the descendant of African slaves in this story reminds us of a

Figure 1.3. The original "Hound Dog Guitar." Photo from the Bradley Kincaid Collection, courtesy of the Southern Appalachian Archives, Hutchins Library, Berea College.

Figure 1.4. 1929 Supertone Bradley Kincaid Houn' Dog Guitar. Photo courtesy of Michael Wright.

transatlantic route—from West Africa to the United States—that complicates the one which connects Kincaid with the British Isles. In other words, this Africanist presence in Kincaid's story is not merely incidental to it. Instead, the racial difference highlighted by the repeated invocation of "the negro" facilitates the transhistorical, transatlantic ethnic identification that undergirds Kincaid's self-presentation. The story of ancestry Kincaid tells proposes a "Scotch" identity that comprises both genealogy and cultural inheritance. His self-identification derives both from the "Scotch" identity he inherits from his great-grandfather and from the English ballads he learns from his mother. The story of the "houn' dog guitar" both contributes to this white ethnic self-identification and complicates it by introducing the nonwhite presence of the guitar's original owner.

At first glance, the story that Kincaid and others tell concerning his guitar suggests a cultural transfer from black to white: Kincaid's father lays claim not only to the material property in question (the guitar) but also, crucially, to the cultural capital it represents. Once it moves from "the negro's" hands to those of the Kincaid family, the guitar serves as a catalyst that eventually enables Kincaid to parlay his English/Scottish/Anglo-Saxon ballad inheritance into commercial success. In this respect, the tale of the "houn' dog guitar" appears to be an iteration in the long history of whites appropriating the property (both literal and figurative) of African Americans for commercial and artistic gain. Lomax's expropriating "Home on the Range" from his "San Antonio Negro saloon-keeper" is an illustrative instance of this phenomenon, but the history of such appropriations extends well into the previous century. Perhaps the paradigmatic instance of this phenomenon is the (likely apocryphal) story of minstrel pioneer T. D. Rice's donning of the clothes of a black man in order to outfit himself for his first blackface performance in Cincinnati in 1830.[56] Or Rice's learning "Jump Jim Crow," as a contemporary account puts it, from "a negro stage-driver, [giving] origin to a school of music designed to excel in popularity all others."[57] Both of these stories, as Eric Lott explains, illustrate "the efficient expropriation of the cultural commodity 'blackness.'"[58] The ways in which Kincaid's story echoes these precedents are not merely fortuitous, as Kincaid, despite his claims to singing "only the typical Folk Songs of the Mountains," in fact performed a number of songs derived from blackface minstrelsy. Significantly, he learned many of these songs from his father. "I used to sing them," he told an interviewer. "My father used to sing them. . . . But when I got into radio, I couldn't use them. They were a reflection on the Negro. In fact, I sang 'Kitty Wells' [a minstrel song that was in print by at least the 1850s] one time. The first line is, 'You ask me [what makes] this darky weep' and this woman called me up and gave me down the road for it. After that I sang, 'You ask me what made the fellow weep.' I've got a big repertory of Negro songs that were written back in the 1800's—minstrel-like songs. I couldn't use them."[59]

Kincaid's cultural inheritance, then, includes the songs—derived from blackface minstrelsy—that he learned from his father, in addition to the English ballads his mother taught him. His story about the irate caller suggests that the emphasis of balladry over blackface was motivated in part by audience concerns. In fact, "Negro songs" were part of Kincaid's public repertoire before ballads were. He first came to WLS with a YMCA quartet in Chicago that included "negro" spirituals in its repertoire, and only later first sang ballads on the air at the request of the station's manager.[60] The legacy of minstrelsy appears elsewhere in Kincaid's repertoire as well. One instance is an undated typescript for a comic monologue entitled "Modern and Up-to-Date History" whose first paragraph ends with this statement: "Assisted by my vocubulary [*sic*] organization to prove to you white folks that a white man am jest [as] good as Nigger, so long as he stays in his place."[61] Beneath its stereotyped mockery of putatively African American dialect, this seemingly atavistic, malapropism-ridden monologue perhaps reveals a racial and class anxiety that links Kincaid with the Irish blackface performers of the previous century.

The narrative of cultural expropriation manifested in the story of the "houn' dog guitar" is a familiar one, structuring not only the nineteenth-century minstrelsy of T. D. Rice and other blackface performers but also a wide range of twentieth-century popular musical forms and performances, from *The Jazz Singer* to Elvis and beyond. Kincaid's story, though, like Lomax's, is different in that it traffics not in expropriated and commodified *blackness* but rather in an ancestral *whiteness*, figured variously as Elizabethan, Anglo-Saxon, or "Scotch," and encapsulated in ballad form. But again, what are we to make of the centrality of "the negro" (both as an individual and as a category) to this process?

The story of the "houn' dog guitar" helps illuminate these questions. Kincaid told Dorothy Gable in a 1967 interview at the Country Music Hall of Fame and Museum in Nashville:

> Well, my father used to go out with some of these fox hunters and they'd take their dogs and they'd get up on top of a ridge, and set the dogs off down in the holler chasing the fox, and build—they'd build a fire and sit around and talk and tell stories. And [on] one of these occasions a negro friend of my father's who used to come and fox hunt with them once in a while had this old—this hound dog guitar here. And my father traded him one of his foxhounds for that guitar. And he brought it home and all of the kids learned to play it.[62]

The key difference between this version of the story and its many antecedents lies in the detail that the source of the guitar is not an anonymous "negro," upon whom the hunting party just chances in the woods, but rather "a negro friend of [Kincaid's] father's who used to come and fox hunt with them." This social relationship is elided in the previous accounts. It is possible that Kincaid's acknowledgment that his father and "the negro" were friends in this account is simply a response to the changed circumstances of the late 1960s during which his interview with Gable took place, a liberal gesture. On the other hand, perhaps this seemingly minor detail provides a key to understanding the complex set of social relationships in which Kincaid's father, his "negro friend," and the prosperous landholding whites who ran the foxhunts were enmeshed.

What is being demarcated by the presence of "the negro" in these accounts is, primarily, the color line between black and white. This imposition of the color line, in turn, facilitates the association of Kincaid's father with the landowners on whose farms he works and whose hunts he and his "negro friend" both join. The presence of "the negro," in other words, allows for what W. J. Cash in *The Mind of the South* called the "vastly ego-warming and ego-expanding distinction between the white man and the black."[63] This distinction enforces a transhistorical association that transcends divisions of class and nation through the shared property of whiteness. Paradoxically, it is the figure of "the negro" that enables Kincaid to claim an English racial inheritance, which manifests itself in "Anglo-Saxon" blood, in fox-hunting, and in balladry.

The class anxiety that underlies this logic of ancestry and cultural inheritance is made even more explicit in later interviews and correspondence. Kincaid wrote to the librarian at Berea College, where he had first become interested in the practice of collecting ballads: "It was at Berea that I first realized that an old country boy like me could be something other than a 'field hand.'"[64] In an elaborate version of the story of the "hound dog guitar," he describes to Loyal Jones, a scholar of Appalachia, the relationship his father had with his neighbors: "These farmers around used to go out—they all had foxhounds—old walker hounds, they called 'em. The walkers used to—they were big fox hunters. They were the landowners. They owned two or three or four hundred acres of land, and you could go by their places any time during the day and you'd see fifteen or twenty foxhounds sleeping out in the field and around the house there. They'd been out all night fox hunting, and they were sleeping during the day. Well my father had two or three foxhounds."[65] Earlier in this same interview, he tells Jones, "I was raised on a farm, of course. My father was a—he wasn't a sharecropper, he just worked by the day . . . on the farm." "He worked on somebody else's farm?" Jones asks. Kincaid replies, "Mmm hmm."

Kincaid's statements in this interview point to an intraracial class difference. Kincaid's father is not a landowner, nor is he a sharecropper, but rather a day laborer on others' farms. Lomax's 1947 autobiography, *Adventures of a Ballad Hunter*, begins with a similar articulation of the liminal class position his family occupied: "My family belonged to the upper crust of the 'po' white trash,' traditionally held in contempt by the aristocracy of the Old South and by their Negro slaves. Father always owned a few acres of land which kept him from being at the bottom of the social scale."[66] Of course, given the presence of "Negro slaves," it is not Lomax's father's land, but rather his whiteness, that insulates him from occupying the bottom rung of Mississippi society. A similar situation obtains for Kincaid's father. He and his "negro friend" occupy similar social roles as agricultural laborers. Loyal Jones, who conducted the aforementioned interview with Kincaid, observes: "[T]he Kincaids were poor, and the father worked as a tenant or farm worker. . . . It may be that they were little better off than the black tenants and farm workers and thus may have had a camaraderie or even friendship with one another. Certainly blacks and whites played music together and felt a commonality in that endeavor, and also blacks and whites worked together pretty well in the eastern Kentucky coal mines."[67]

Viewed from this perspective, the exchange of the foxhound for the guitar is less an act of expropriation from the weak by the powerful than it is an exchange between individuals occupying similar social positions—albeit on opposite sides of the color line. The language of racial difference—the focus on the racial designations of "Negro," "Scotch," and "Anglo-Saxon"—obscures this social relationship. Kincaid Sr.'s "two or three foxhounds" provide him entrée into the social world of the fox hunters; exchanging the guitar for a foxhound likewise suggests an affinity between black and white neighbors of similar economic status.

Both the foxhound that Kincaid's father trades and the guitar he receives facilitate an economic and cultural exchange across the color line. As such, they point to a process of consent through which new affiliations are potentially formed. A similar possibility manifests itself in John Lomax's encounter with the African American singer of "Home on the Range" and registers in Lomax's own accounts—despite his own disavowals of such a possibility. As we trace the routes of American vernacular music, it is important that we not limit our understandings of these routes—as Lomax and Kincaid did—to mapping lines of descent. As the story of Kincaid's "hound dog guitar" and its role in transmitting music from the Old World to the New attests, these routes circulate within the South and across the Atlantic to both Europe and Africa; they are circuitous and surprising. By tracing them carefully, we see not (or at least not only) cultural forms being transmitted via lines of descent from one side of the Atlantic to the other but rather new cultural forms emerging from the crisscrossing and conjoining of such routes, as ballads and songs are sung by new voices in new places.

The idea of white racial or ethnic isolation that undergirds Lomax's and Kincaid's narratives comprises only part of a larger story of segregation, cross-racial musical contact, and interracial masquerade. As Kincaid's early blackface minstrel repertoire and the centrality of African American singers to the preservation and documentation of cowboy song culture suggest, the seeds of musical interracialism had been planted well before the emergence of the ostensibly racially pure folk forms that both men sought and advocated. As I have suggested above, attempts to stake out a musical territory occupied exclusively by white folk are subject to disruption by an Africanist presence that belies sought-for racial purity. A similarly complicating interracialism obtains in contemporary efforts to define "negro" traditions similarly uncorrupted by whiteness, and once again, John Lomax provides an exemplary case.

On November 5, 1940, in an Atlanta hotel room, Lomax interviewed and recorded performances by Blind Willie McTell for the Library of Congress's Archive of American Folk Song.[68] Lomax was nearing the end of his illustrious career as perhaps America's most preeminent collector and scholar of folk songs. McTell, who almost certainly did not conceive of himself as a folk singer, had first recorded commercially in 1927 and was working as an itinerant street performer when Lomax encountered him. A prolific musician, McTell had recorded not only twelve-bar blues (in the so-called "Piedmont" style) but also ballads, spirituals and contemporary gospel tunes, songs from minstrelsy and vaudeville, rags, hillbilly songs, and tunes of indeterminate traditional origin.[69]

These two men bring to this meeting dramatically different understandings of twentieth-century American vernacular music. Lomax, a folklorist and collector, is interested in typologies and aims to collect specimens of "negro" folk song for preservation and analysis. McTell, a consummate professional adept at giving audiences what they want, dutifully complies. Not only does he provide Lomax with examples of spirituals, ballads, and blues, but he also accompanies them with ornate impromptu histories of African American religious and secular songs. The exchange between the two men voices a central tension underlying twentieth-century understandings of the relationships between music, race, and culture. As we saw in his treatment of cowboy songs, Lomax's scholarly, archival approach is based on a logic that understands musical forms as products of racially defined traditions. McTell's performances, on the other hand, complicate the homology between race and musical form that Lomax seeks. In the 1940 Library of Congress sessions, McTell and Lomax negotiate the fault line between folkloristic conceptions of "negro" music and the performance practices of working African American musicians. Their interaction reveals critical insights into the dynamics of this negotiation, in particular the ways in which musical authenticity is inscribed as racial difference. One such example appears on record under the title "Monologue on Accidents":

Figure 1.5. Blind Willie McTell with twelve-string guitar, Atlanta, Georgia, November 1940. Original in the John Lomax Collection, Library of Congress.

LOMAX: I wonder . . . I wonder if you know any songs about colored people having hard times here in the South.

MCTELL: Well, that . . . all songs that have reference to our old people here . . . they hasn't very much stuff of the people nowadays because . . .

LOMAX: Any complaining songs, complaining about the hard times, and sometimes mistreatment of the whites. Have you got any songs that talk about that?

MCTELL: No, sir, I haven't. Not at the present time because the white people's mighty good to the southern people, as far as I know.

LOMAX: You don't know any complaining songs at all?

MCTELL: Well . . .

LOMAX: "Ain't It Hard to Be a Nigger, Nigger," do you know that one?

MCTELL: Well . . . that's not in our time. And . . . now, there's a spiritual down here called "It's a Mean World to Live In," but that don't have . . . still don't have reference to the hard times.

LOMAX: It's just because of the . . . Why is it a mean world to live in?

MCTELL: Well, no, it's not altogether. It has reference to everybody.

LOMAX: It's as . . . It's as mean for the whites as it is for the blacks, is that it?

MCTELL: That's the idea.

McTell's proffering a spiritual instead of the "complaining song" Lomax asks for speaks volumes about the uncomfortable relationship between white collector and black informant. So too does his insistence on the spiritual's universality in the face of Lomax's somewhat abrupt demand for a racially specific song of social protest. McTell—normally precise, articulate, and self-assured—first responds incoherently to Lomax's question before pulling himself together to deliver what both he and Lomax must have understood was a deliberate lie: "No, sir, I haven't. Not at the present time because the white people's mighty good to the southern people, as far as I know." McTell's contrasting "the white people" with "the southern people" is at first puzzling, although it ultimately seems to signify McTell's unwillingness to accommodate the black-and-white racial logic inherent in Lomax's line of questioning. It also anticipates McTell's equating southern whites and blacks in order to change the subject of his exchange with Lomax from the decidedly uncomfortable topic of African Americans' responses to white racism.

Of course, both Mississippi-born, Texas-raised Lomax and Georgia native McTell are themselves "southern people," and their interaction is itself but one instance in a long history of musical exchanges across the color line that have helped define the music of the region. Despite Lomax's attempt to unearth a racial genealogy of negro folk song and McTell's game efforts to provide what Lomax asks for, their disparate racial and class positions make this endeavor nearly impossible. I think we should understand as genuine Lomax's desire to record and give voice to southern African Americans like McTell, in the process producing an archive of recordings unparalleled in its importance to the story of vernacular musical traditions in the United States. What the Lomax/McTell exchange illustrates, though, is that the parameters of this story are determined in large part by the social strictures that separated black and white in the Jim Crow South. McTell knows this, and we can hear in his nervous declaration that racial oppression is "not in our time" a refusal to discuss the musical effects of contemporary racism with a southern white man. At the same time, despite the cultural imperative that manifests in a musical color line (a phenomenon that historian Karl Hagstrom Miller terms "segregating sound"), this musical segregation is far from absolute. In fact the very song that Lomax seeks from McTell, which he understands as a documentary artifact of racial difference under Jim Crow, tells a more complicated story.

The particular song Lomax has in mind, which here he calls "Ain't It Hard to Be a Nigger, Nigger," was apparently of keen interest for him. More than a quarter-century earlier, in a 1913 letter to a folksong-collecting correspondent, Mrs. C. S. Prosser, Lomax includes lyrics to one variant of the song, together with a suggestion regarding their interpretation: "I enclose . . . a copy of the negro song you request. . . . At the risk of being misunderstood I feel that I should caution you to remember that the class of negroes from which this song came are inclined to indulge in moods of self-pity. In one moment they sing as though they were in the depths of despair and in another some . . . lively ditty that breathes anything else than sadness. Please, however, do not understand me to say that I do not believe that 'it is hard to be a niggah.'"[70] The lyrics of the song that Lomax provides, in other words, should not be taken at face value. A guiding principle in their interpretation is the understanding that the lyrics of "negro" folk songs represent less the specific feelings of individuals than they do evidence of a generalized negro character.

Lomax would develop this premise as the thesis of an article, "Self-Pity in Negro Folk-Songs," that he published in the *Nation* four years later, in which he explains that "[g]enuine negro folk-songs . . . will afford an insight into the negro mind that will prove interesting to the psychologist, the sociologist, and, perhaps, even the historian."[71] As his letter to Mrs. Prosser suggests, the racial knowledge that Lomax seeks in negro folk songs takes the form of a tautology: while the lyrics he collects provide an insight into the negro mind and character, so too must these lyrics be interpreted through the lens that a knowledge of negro psychology provides. "There surely exists no merrier-hearted race than the negro," Lomax explains, "especially in his natural home, the warm climate of the South."[72] At the same time that he explains the presence of the descendants of African slaves in the South as "natural," Lomax dismisses the legacy of slavery on African Americans' understandings of themselves and their relations with whites: "Slavery [is] a thing of the past . . . and, after all, as part of the race history, formed but a brief interlude . . . between many generations of barbaric freedom and the present status of liberty in a civilized land."[73] The "complaining songs" he seeks, then, attest not to African Americans' responses to the lingering effects of slavery or to the immediate insults of Jim Crow, but rather to their inherent racial tendency toward self-pity, attributable to their understandable "feeling of race inferiority."

Lomax's article ends by quoting two verses and a refrain from the song, the first of which begins with a couplet bemoaning the structural inequality that Jim Crow enforced: "White folks go to college, niggers to de fiel' / White folks learn to read an' write, niggers learn to steal." The final verse—ironically, given Lomax's editorial comment—clearly addresses the economic exploitation and intimidation of African Americans by whites:

> If a nigger git arrested an' can't pay his fine,
> Dey sho' sen' him out on de county line.
> Nigger an' white man playin' seben-up,
> Nigger win de money, 'fraid to pick it up.
> If you work all de week an' work all de time,
> White man sho' to bring nigger out behin'.

The song's chorus echoes this sentiment:

> Ain't it hard, ain't it hard,
> Ain't it hard to be a nigger, nigger, nigger?
> Ain't it hard, ain't it hard,
> Caze you can't git yo' money when it's due?[74]

Lomax quotes these same lyrics in a 1915 letter to folklorist Frank C. Brown at Trinity College (later Duke University) and publishes an abbreviated version of the song in his *American Ballads and Folk Songs* in 1934.[75] Newman Ivey White cites essentially the same verse ("Nigger and white man playin' seven-up / Nigger won the money an' skeered to pick it up") and likewise glosses it not as a sardonic comment on economic exploitation and the pervasive threat of white-on-black violence but rather as evidence of the "negro's" willingness "to laugh at himself," much like the "conventionally humorous touches concerning chicken-stealing" that White also notes.[76]

It is fairly likely that McTell did in fact know a version of the song that Lomax asks for, given his encyclopedic knowledge of the folk and popular music of the South. Not only do variations of the lyrics Lomax quotes in his correspondence and in print appear among his African American folk song informants, but they show up on commercial recordings as well. As Paul Oliver observes, "Overt comments on relations between the races [like the ones Lomax seeks] were rare, and if there were many such songs they scarcely got on record. Few songsters would have performed them to a white or mixed

Southern audience, except under the cover of a heavy screen of other associations."[77] McTell's refusal to sing Lomax a "complaining song," in other words, is typical and wise. As a noteworthy exception to this rule against singing such songs, Oliver cites Mississippi guitarist Bo Chatmon's "Good Ol' Turnip Greens," recorded in New Orleans in 1928.[78] That recording's final verse begins nearly identically to one Lomax cites in his "Self-Pity in Negro Folk-Songs":

> White man goes to the college
> And the negro to the fields
> The white man will learn to read and write
> And the nigger will learn to steal.

Chatmon's rendition continues, deviating from the versions of the tune Lomax collects:

> Oh, the white folks in their parlor, just eatin' their cake and cream
> But the darky's back in the kitchen, just a-scrappin' over the turnip greens.[79]

As Tony Russell aptly observes, Chatmon's performance "reads like a minstrel song with teeth," offering trenchant social critique under a veneer of coon song stereotype.[80] The song's meaning is unstable: what sounds like a criticism of Jim Crow segregation and racial oppression to one set of ears may sound to others as confirming stereotypes of African Americans as feckless and self-pitying. Chatmon's "burly coons, just a-scrappin' over their turnip greens" could hardly cater more directly to stereotyped white fantasies of blackness—stereotypes that had originated in the blackface minstrelsy of the nineteenth century and then mutated into the myriad forms of folk and popular culture captured in print and on record both by Lomax and his folklorist contemporaries and by the twentieth century's emerging culture industry. Trafficking in the stereotyped imagery of minstrelized "coons," though, provides Chatmon the ideological cover that he needs to voice a powerful and poignant critique of Jim Crow racism.

As it turns out, "Ain't It Hard to Be a Nigger, Nigger" provides a direct link from the commercial and popular tradition Chatmon represents back through Lomax's African American informants to blackface minstrelsy. In 1883 the Ludden and Bates Southern Music House, a Savannah, Georgia, piano and organ dealer, published sheet music for "It's Hard to Be a Nigger," credited to composer J. Haygood Armstrong; the sheet music's cover sheet promises that the song had been "[s]ung with great success by the Armstrong Minstrels."[81] Written in conventional "negro" dialect, Armstrong's song is clearly related to the one Lomax quotes three decades later. Its first verse, for example, reads:

> You can work for dis an, You can work for dat,
> You can work for wages or part ob de crap
> Faw it makes no dif'rence you'll find in time,
> White man's boun to bring you out behime,

and is followed by the chorus:

> Oh it's hard, it's hard, it's hard to be a nigger,
> Oh it's hard! it's hard! It's hard to be a nigger
> if you can't get yer wages when dey's jue.

As far as I have been able to tell, the trail of documentary evidence ends with Armstrong's 1883 copyright filing for this song's sheet music. What are we dealing with, then? In attempting to trace a genealogy of this song from Armstrong's "It's Hard to Be a Nigger" to Chatmon's "Good Ol' Turnip Greens," we encounter a history of cross-racial mimicry and musical appropriation across the color line. Armstrong's original composition appears to be a white-authored fantasy of black discontent (what Lomax terms "self-pity"). On stage, the Armstrong minstrels would have performed the song in blackface, embodying in their artificial blackness post-Reconstruction stereotypes of actual African Americans. Of course, as Eric Lott and others have made clear, minstrelsy's stereotyped depictions of blackness are critical not only to the ways that whites have perceived black people but also to the self-conceptions of white people.[82] During the antebellum period, minstrelsy, a product primarily of the urban North, trafficked in images of an imagined South. Armstrong's song, though, is a product of the actual South, albeit one that has incorporated the simulacra of minstrelsy into the fabric of its own self-conception.

We might understand "It's Hard to Be a Nigger," then, as a white-authored fantasy that serves as a screen through which white listeners view their relationships with their black neighbors, and through which they imagine themselves being perceived. To be sure, racial mockery is key to the song's appeal to the racist tastes of nineteenth-century white listeners. By the same token, though, this manifest racism is tempered by an accurate diagnosis and implied critique of the exploitative economic relations of Jim Crow that were emerging in the aftermath of Reconstruction. As the promise of legal freedom and social equality gave way to segregation and new forms of economic oppression at the end of the nineteenth century, the deck was actually stacked,

Figure 1.6. J. Haygood Armstrong, "It's Hard to Be a Nigger," 1883. Original in the Music Division, Library of Congress.

as the song declares, against former slaves and their descendants. The racialized system of economic and social oppression that emerged around the time Armstrong was composing his song and persisted to the time of Lomax's interview with McTell assured that for the majority of African Americans, particularly in the South, it "[m]akes no difference, you're comin' out [behind]."

That, beneath its conventional stage negro dialect, "It's Hard to Be a Nigger" conveys such a clear critique of the exploitation of blacks under Jim Crow suggests that perhaps Armstrong's song derives in whole or in part from songs that he heard from African American singers, much as fellow Georgian Joel Chandler Harris claimed to have adapted his Uncle Remus stories from those told by slaves on Turnwold Plantation in Putnam County, Georgia. In any case, what Lomax's evidence makes clear is that—whatever their ultimate origin—both the sentiments and the specific lyrics of Armstrong's song appear to have escaped both the page and the stage and taken on new life in the repertoires of African American singers throughout the South.[83] By the time Bo Chatmon records "Good Ol' Turnip Greens" in 1928, the question of whether the song ultimately originated on the minstrel stage or in the work songs of African American laborers is almost entirely moot. Much as fantasies about the plantation South that originated in the urban North had been absorbed into white southerners' conceptions of themselves and their relationships with their African American neighbors, so too had African American musicians incorporated the stereotypes of minstrelsy into their own performances, subtly and ironically transforming these stereotypes through parody and misdirection.

McTell's conversation with Lomax is by now a fairly well-known event in the history of interactions between white folklorists and collectors and black musicians, although as we have seen, there is more to their exchange than is immediately apparent. Where Lomax sees a discrete African American tradition that speaks to the distinctive racial psychology of "the negro," we can, with some digging, unearth a history of cross-racial mimicry, racial masquerade, and imaginative projections across the color line. As much as Lomax's approach can seem at times to be blinkered and overly circumscribed by the racial prejudices of his background as a white southerner, his efforts at times evince a sincere desire to pull back the veil between white and black, to breach the color line through dialogue and musical exchange. At the same time, we can understand McTell's wariness. Forty-two years old at the time of his meeting with Lomax, he had lived his whole life under the sign of W. E. B. Du Bois's famous admonition that "[t]he problem of the Twentieth Century is the problem of the color line."[84] If Lomax's interrogation aimed to produce insight into the souls of black folk, McTell seems to have understood the importance of parrying those questions. While he shares with Lomax (and with us) a number of priceless performances, only he knows how he might have answered Lomax's queries in another time and place, in a situation where the color line did not loom so heavily.

CHAPTER TWO

Country Music and the Souls of White Folk

In the opening paragraph of "The Souls of White Folk" (1910), a prescient rumination on the problem of whiteness in the twentieth century, W. E. B. Du Bois observes: "I know many souls that toss and whirl and pass, but none there are that puzzle me more than the Souls of White Folk. Not, mind you, the souls of them that are white, but souls of them that have become painfully conscious of their whiteness."[1] Du Bois continues, "Forgetting (as I can at times forget) the meaning of this singular obsession to me and my folk, I become the more acutely sensitive to the marvelous part this thought is playing today and to the way it is developing the Souls of White Folk, and I wonder what the end will be."[2] Du Bois's description of this newfound obsession with whiteness provides a key to understanding the racialized discourses of musical authenticity that took shape in the early decades of the twentieth century, which continue to inform both critical and popular notions concerning the relationships between racial identities and musical forms. Of course, Du Bois had himself articulated an influential conception of African American racial identity grounded in the musical traditions of a racially defined "folk" in his "Of the Sorrow Songs" (1903).[3] In an important sense, the idea of a musical tradition produced by a racially circumscribed white folk is a corollary of this earlier idea. Underscoring this symmetry, though, is the line demarcating the boundary between these putatively separate traditions: a musical color line, to borrow Du Bois's famous term.

The music listed as "hillbilly" in record company catalogs was in fact steeped in African American traditions and shared by whites and blacks, yet in the 1920s it was distilled into a form that came to be identifiably—indeed quintessentially—white in the public mind. The recordings that Jimmie Rodgers, the "Father of Country Music," made for the Victor Recording

Company between 1927 and his death in 1933 serve as a flashpoint for the emerging commercial genre of country music.[4] Rodgers's music is located at the crosscurrents of folk traditions and commercial forms, black- and white-identified styles, reactionary plantation nostalgia and forward-looking jazz-inflected pop. His music became "white" through the combined and at times contradictory workings of academic folklorists on the one hand, and the culture industry on the other. In this chapter, I argue that the investment of this new music with whiteness in the 1920s should be understood as a response to the threat that the potential permeability of this racial sound barrier poses to the cultural logic of segregation. In response to this threat, a range of discourses—academic, literary, commercial—work to police this border in order to keep different musical forms on either side of the line. As Du Bois recognized, the significance of "this singular obsession" with whiteness extends to both sides of the color line.

Yodels, Blues, and the Sound of Racial Difference

As we saw in the previous chapter, the exchange between folklorist John Lomax and musician Blind Willie McTell preserved on the 1940 Library of Congress recordings exemplifies this dynamic, and another moment in their conversation further reveals its effects on the story of popular music in the twentieth-century U.S. South. In a recording entitled "Monologue on the History of the Blues," McTell demonstrates the difference between what he identifies as "white" and "colored" musical styles:

> Now we take our white race of the southern states. They play a little bit different from we colored people. Now here's some of their pieces. . . . That's the idea of the white people. Now you come back to the colored, they have a different type of playing. Now we have some pieces goes like this. . . . Now that's a colored. Here's our colored again. . . . And still, we have down in the alley of blues, just like the whites when they play they yodelin' songs. But we have our blues, a little bit different . . . I thinks.

Several elements of McTell's playing and commentary illuminate his and Lomax's negotiation of the rocky terrain of racial identity and musical authenticity. One is his seeming facility with the range of musical styles he demonstrates—both those he identifies as "colored" and those of "the white race of the southern states."[5] This flexibility is a professional proficiency; McTell would have played in these styles and many others, though his recorded output tended toward blues and religious songs, answering to the demands of record producers. According to McTell's widow, Kate, he learned "white" songs and styles not only from records but from playing with white musicians as well. She describes a jam session with white musicians in Chicago in 1935: "The white musician would say, 'Play it for me: I want to see if I can play it,' and Willie would play it for him and he'd catch it and learn it, and Willie would say 'OK, give me that hillbilly,' and he'd get on the hillybilly [sic] and give it right back."[6]

By "yodelin' songs," McTell is referring to the blue yodel, a hugely popular and influential musical style popularized by the singer Jimmie Rodgers and performed by both white and black musicians. The blue yodel was a chief component of the emerging commercial genre of country music, then as now primarily identified with white performers and audiences. Rodgers recorded a dozen numbered blue yodels and a number of other "yodelin' songs," beginning with "Blue Yodel (T for Texas)" in 1927 and ending, appropriately enough, with "Jimmie Rodger's [sic] Last Blue Yodel" in 1933. Rodgers's blue yodels are based on a twelve-bar blues pattern, comprising three four-bar phrases following a tonic–subdominant–dominant (I–IV–V) chord progression and an *aab* form. By the time of McTell's Library of Congress session, the twelve-bar blues had come to be held as a marker of black musical difference in both popular and academic conceptions of African American secular music. A 1923 OKeh catalog informed its readers: "No one knows, exactly, what makes a 'blues.' But, it is conceded that no other people have sung or played these soothing, pleasing, musical concoctions more fascinatingly than the colored race."[7] Though the blues has come to connote a twelve-bar *aab* form, the term had long been applied somewhat haphazardly to a wide array of song forms. The OKeh catalog suggests that the blackness of their performers provided a common denominator, though whites recorded many "blues" songs as well. McTell's explanation, though, suggests ambivalence about this difference: "down in the alley" blues, a "colored" style, is "just like" the whites' yodelin' songs, but "a little bit different." McTell punctuates this already ambivalent assertion of racialized musical difference with a final qualification: "I thinks."

To stress what I hope is not too obvious a point, McTell was blind. Consequently, the logic of race he proposes is not ocular—a logic of sight—but rather aural, a logic of sound. In McTell's formulation (to be taken with a grain of salt, to be sure, given the palpable discomfort we hear as he works to divine and speak to Lomax's expectations and prejudices), music expresses a racial identity: "That's the idea of the white people." As "Monologue on Accidents" demonstrates, for both McTell and Lomax, race is an undeniable and unavoidable social fact. Yet McTell's facility with both black- and white-identified styles suggests that the aural component of racial identity as figured in music is at least in part performed. This element of performance allows for a range of possibilities: cross-racial identification, "passing," and cases of mistaken identity among them. Folkloristic practice has often served to obfuscate this crossing of racial sonic borders.

Such an effort is at work in the exchange between Lomax and McTell. The categories that Lomax proposes and that McTell struggles to corroborate are those of a folk authenticity grounded in racial difference. These forms of authenticity are produced by folkloristic projects such as Lomax's, and are reflected too in the commercial products of the culture industry with which McTell had been involved for over a decade. At the same time, both the formal heterogeneity of McTell's repertoire and the difficulty he seems to evince in maintaining strict racial categories as he discusses and plays examples from it point to the ways in which distinctions between the categories of black and white prove chimerical, as folk forms are mediated and creolized even as they are pressed into the service of racialist ideologies. This process of generic and formal admixture was catalyzed by the recording industry, despite its segregationist policies—separate series for records by black and white artists, for example—not to mention the long-standing exploitative appropriation by whites of the compositions and performances of black musicians. Alongside attempts by folklorists and collectors to assign musical categories to racially defined folk, the culture industry worked both to subvert and to reproduce racial hierarchies, simultaneously effacing and reinscribing the color line.

In the schema that McTell proposes in response to Lomax's prompting, yodeling serves as a marker of racial difference, a defining characteristic that distinguishes the "yodelin' songs" of the whites from the "colored" blues. That McTell would posit the yodel as key to this distinction suggests that by 1940, when Lomax interviewed him, both the yodel and the commercial genre with which it was most commonly associated were understood to be decidedly white. This association of yodeling with whiteness is largely a product of the enormous popularity of Rodgers's music and of the subsequent identification of this music as white. It has long been a commonplace that Rodgers invented the blue yodel by appending a yodeled refrain derived from Swiss or alpine yodeling to a blues song form. Robert Coltman, for example, asserts that Rodgers "was the first singer clearly to establish the yodel as an echo and comment on the blues"; David Evans advances a similar claim.[8]

The actual history of this innovation, however, is a great deal more complicated. While Swiss yodeling was popular in traveling shows during the late nineteenth and early twentieth centuries, and Rodgers was almost certainly aware of and influenced by such popular traditions, it is not necessary to look so far afield for antecedents to Rodgers's blue yodel. Rodgers was raised

Figure 2.1. Vocal line from Jimmie Rodgers's "Blue Yodel."

in Meridian, Mississippi; this state is, significantly, the epicenter of yodeling blues.[9] Viewed from this local perspective, Rodgers's incorporating yodels into blues song forms does not seem particularly unusual, as falsetto breaks and outright yodels are common among recordings by African American singers active in Mississippi in the 1920s. Tommy Johnson's "Cool Drink of Water Blues" is a key example. Like Rodgers, Johnson deploys a number of jumps from chest voice to falsetto, usually an interval of a sixth, and punctuates each verse with a yodeled refrain (see fig. 2.2). Folklorist David Evans points out these similarities but then takes pains to disavow them. According to Evans, "Johnson's refrain derives mainly from the Afro-American field holler tradition, while Rodgers's refrain displays an obvious debt to Swiss yodeling style. The melodic similarities between the two singers are probably purely coincidental."[10]

Figure 2.1 shows the vocal melody of "Blue Yodel," Rodgers's breakthrough hit, recorded in November 1927. The song is a twelve-bar blues in G major (though the verse itself comprises more than twelve actual bars; characteristically, Rodgers is not particularly concerned with formal structure) with a yodeled refrain. The yodel is anticipated by the falsetto break at the end of the verse, where Rodgers divides the final word, "me," into two syllables, spanning an octave leap.

Figure 2.2 shows the vocal melody of the first verse of Tommy Johnson's "Cool Drink of Water Blues," recorded in Memphis in February 1928. This piece is also a twelve-bar blues. Though it is in a different key (E major), its harmonic structure is fundamentally the same as that of Rodgers's "Blue Yodel." Rodgers uses a conventional *aab* line structure—the first line is repeated, followed by a new third line. Johnson uses the more unusual, though not uncommon, *aaa* structure, in which the same line is repeated three times. In this, Rodgers hews closer to the conventional blues form than Johnson does. This modification aside, however, the harmonic structure of both pieces is essentially the same. The yodeled turnaround in Johnson's piece ("Lord,

Figure 2.2. Vocal line from Tommy Johnson's "Cool Drink of Water Blues."

Lordy, Lord") follows the same pattern as does the one in "Blue Yodel," with the vocal line jumping a sixth (from D to B, C to A, and B to G in Rodgers's song; from B to G and G to E in Johnson's). Johnson is less sparing with these falsetto embellishments than Rodgers is, deploying them up to three times in each line. Nonetheless, Rodgers's falsetto leaps of a sixth and an octave, and Johnson's of an interval of a sixth or a fifth, are remarkably similar. These parallels, then, mark the "melodic similarities" that Evans dismisses as coincidental. Evans's insistence on the separateness of Johnson's and Rodgers's musical influences is undermined somewhat by his assertion that the two men actually knew each other and played music together.[11] He provides no real evidence for this claim, however, though Charles K. Wolfe speculates in a similar vein.[12] Evans takes this racialist logic one step further, asserting that the falsetto break on a single word discussed above is borrowed from "black folksingers and . . . is undoubtedly indigenous to their music, since it can also be heard in some recordings of African tribal music."[13] A recently unearthed recording Johnson made in 1929, "I Want Someone to Love Me," provides even more direct evidence of the fundamental similarity between Rodgers's music and Johnson's.[14] As Barry Mazor describes it, the song "proves to be an outright Jimmie Rodgers–style ballad with 1890s sentimental overtones— and Johnson's moan, in this case, does turn into an outright yodel."[15]

The argument that Johnson's and Rodgers's influences can be effectively segregated recapitulates the racialist logic that informs earlier folkloristic endeavors at musical classification. That said, my intention is not simply to equate the racialist logic evident in Evans's analysis with that of his predecessors. Instead, I want to emphasize the persistence of such racialist logics across differing ideological and political conceptions of vernacular music. Despite the relatively liberal and benign racial attitudes evident in Evans's argument, it nonetheless insinuates that Johnson was hollering in the fields while Rodgers was listening to Swiss yodelers. Such an assertion does not bear scrutiny. For one, by Rodgers's own account and by that of his widow (whose biography of her late husband, despite its unreliability and its own problematic romantic racialism, provides the basis for all subsequent biographical work about him and his music), the work songs of African Americans provided him with his formative musical education.[16] As Rodgers never traveled to Switzerland, any knowledge of "Swiss yodeling style" he might have obtained would have come from traveling vaudeville-style revues. So-called "Swiss yodeling" achieved its initial popularity in the United States in 1840 following the success of the Tyrolese Rainer Family.[17] Far from an unadulterated folk tradition, Tyrolese yodeling was disseminated largely through the performances of blackface minstrels, who incorporated burlesques of Swiss yodeling into their performances. Dan Emmett, the famous blackface minstrel composer, wrote a number of Swiss-flavored yodeling songs that were recorded at the turn of the century, and the very name of his Virginia Minstrels burlesques that of the Tyrolese Minstrels whose popularity preceded the debut of Emmett's group.

The "obvious debt to Swiss yodeling" evident in Rodgers's recordings is directly traceable through vaudeville and minstrelsy. "Sleep, Baby, Sleep," (the "most enduring vehicle for American yodelers") was written in 1869 and maintained its popularity into the 1920s.[18] It was also the first song that Rodgers recorded. Although Carrie Rodgers later reported disappointment that Rodgers chose this "thousand-year-old lullaby" as his first recording, it served as a convincing vehicle both for his voice and for his distinctive yodel.[19] It is also indicative of Rodgers's familiarity with the long-standing commercial tradition of which "Sleep, Baby, Sleep" was a product. The guitarist and singer Riley Puckett—a contemporary of Willie McTell's who attended the same school for the blind in Macon, Georgia—recorded a version of the song, complete with yodeled refrain, in 1925.[20] His version is generally considered a model for Rodgers's; this linkage upsets no racialist assumptions, since Puckett too was a white "hillbilly" singer, though like Rodgers he demonstrates a strong affinity for musical styles associated with African Americans. A mere two years earlier, a similar arrangement of the same song—again, complete with yodeled refrain—was recorded by Charles Anderson, a black vaudevillian who recorded on eight records "a near even mixture of yodels and blues songs."[21] Anderson's example suggests that the synthesis between yodels and the blues that appears so distinctive in Rodgers's music—and that, as McTell suggests, differentiates it from "colored" styles—was already taking place earlier in the decade and even before and was a product of the combined efforts of white and black musicians.

"The hillbilly and the nigger stuff"

Most accounts credit the inception of country music as a commercial genre to record producer and talent scout Ralph Peer. In June 1923 Peer traveled to Atlanta to record local black musicians for the race market (i.e., recordings by black musicians aimed primarily though not exclusively at African American audiences). While there, he also recorded two tunes by Fiddlin' John Carson, a local white musician, at the request of a local furniture store owner, who agreed to purchase five hundred copies of the resulting record. A skeptical Peer agreed, and to his surprise the initial pressing of "The Little Old Log Cabin in the Lane" backed with "The Old Hen Cackled and the Rooster's Going to Crow" sold out immediately. More records were pressed, as Peer and his label (OKeh) recognized that the rural whites who bought Carson's record represented a potentially untapped market—one that was an analog of the race market to which OKeh and other labels sold recordings by black artists. In 1958 Peer told an interviewer about his time at OKeh in the 1920s: "I went to New York and worked for OKeh Records. That's where I invented the hillbilly and the nigger stuff."[22] Peer means to differentiate between the two, though a song like "The Little Old Log Cabin in the Lane" proves to be embedded deeply in "nigger minstrelsy," African American popular music, and the commercial hillbilly tradition that draws from both. The history of this song demonstrates that "the hillbilly and the nigger stuff" are in fact cleaved inseparably together.

"The Little Old Log Cabin in the Lane" is neither the product of an autochthonous folk tradition nor a recent composition; rather, it is a minstrel song gone feral. The tune was copyrighted in 1871 by William Shakespeare Hays—author of such sentimental tunes as "I Am Dying, Mother, Dying" (1865) and "Out in the Snow; or, the Drunkard's Child" (1874), *faux* Irish numbers like "Seamus O'Brien" (1870) and "Molly McGuire" (1874), and racist caricatures like "Nigger Will Be Nigger" (1864) (whose chorus, "Oh! a Nigga will be Nigga, dey kin nebber make him white!," expresses a particularly acute racial anxiety). "The Little Old Log Cabin in the Lane" was popularized by Manning's Minstrels, a blackface minstrel troupe. The piece remained popular into the twentieth century, and versions of it appear on a number of cylinder recordings from the turn of the century.

An illustrative example is a 1909 Columbia Records recording by baritone Carroll C. Clark accompanied by banjo virtuoso Vess Ossman. In this rendition, the piano from the sheet music is replaced by Ossman's banjo, but Clark sings the vocal part straight, maintaining both the strict eighth-note rhythm and the blackface dialect of the original. Clark was a prolific African American singer; in 1921 the *Crisis* would hail him as "Premier Baritone Soloist of the race."[23] He began recording for Columbia in 1908, and these early recordings evince a smooth, trained baritone. The label put him to work singing sentimental dialect songs, "mostly plantation songs portraying life in the Old South in a positive, nostalgic light."[24] The initial release of his rendition of "De Little Old Log Cabin in de Lane" was paired with another artist's recording of "Dixie," and remained in the Columbia catalog until 1925.[25] Columbia made no reference to Clark's race in promotional materials, published no biographical information, and "never included his picture in any of its literature."[26] Clark's recording is essentially a domesticated minstrel performance. If we assume that its consumers were unaware that Clark was black, we then understand it to entail a multilevel racial masquerade: a genteel, trained African American singer imitating a white man imitating a plantation "darky." Another recording, also on Columbia, featuring the same banjoist with a different singer, Bob Roberts, from sometime between 1904 and 1909, points away from the minstrel stage.[27] This version, though its instrumentalist (banjoist Vess Ossman) is the same as in the first example, demonstrates a much more elastic sense of time, and while the singer maintains the blackface dialect of Hays's composition ("ole massa an' ole miss's am dead," etc.), his desultory delivery suggests an inability or a reluctance to don fully the blackface mask; in this, Roberts points the way to Fiddlin' John Carson's later rendition. But while Roberts's reading emphasizes the stilted artificiality of the piece's dialect lyrics, Carson takes a rather different tack.

While composed pieces are often simplified melodically and harmonically when appropriated by untutored musicians, quite opposite effects can also be discerned in Carson's rendition of "The Little Old Log Cabin in the Lane." Hays's 1871 sheet music arrangement is for piano and voice (though this instrumentation certainly differs from that used on the minstrel stage), the key is G major, and the piece's rhythm, melody, and harmony are relentlessly regular (see fig. 2.3). The melody, for example, consists primarily of uniform eighth notes. The piece undergoes significant formal transformation in Carson's hands. He elongates some notes, truncates others, and at times collapses

Figure 2.3. William Shakespeare Hays, "The Little Old Log Cabin in the Lane," 1871. Original in the Music Division, Library of Congress.

space between adjacent notes. Similar effects are apparent in his rendering of the melody, for example, double stops on the fiddle, melisma (extending a single syllable over multiple notes) in the vocals, and glissandi (slides between tones) in both fiddle and vocal lines. These formal changes accompany textual changes as well, and these changes—formal and textual—mark the generic shift from published minstrel song to vernacular fiddle tune that Carson's recording represents.

Carson abandons Hays's ersatz plantation "darky" dialect entirely, regularizing not only grammar and pronunciation but also phrasing. The first lines of Hays's first stanza read as follows: "I am getting old and feeble now, I cannot work no more / I've laid de rusty bladed hoe to rest. / Ole massa an' ole miss's am dead, dey're sleepin' side by side / Deir spirits now are roaming wid de blest." Carson amends them to "Now, I'm getting old and feeble, and I cannot work no more / That rusty bladed hoe I've laid to rest / Ole master and ole misses, they are sleeping side by side / Their spirits now are roaming with the blest." The transposition of "now" from the end of the first phrase to the beginning and the addition of "and" between the two phrases of the first line indicate that Carson has reworked the lyrics to fit into a more natural, less conventionally dialectal diction than that of Hays's text. Likewise, he corrects the egregiously ungrammatical ersatz "Negro" "Ole massa an' old miss's am dead," while maintaining the line's rhythm. Carson's editing continues with the next lines, as "De scene am changed about de place, de darkies am all gone" becomes "Things have changed around the place, now, and the darkies they have gone," and so on. It is unlikely, of course, that Carson was particularly concerned with grammatical correctness, but at the same time, he quite thoroughly expunges conventional blackface dialect from the song's text.

These textual emendations work in concert with the musical adaptation the song undergoes in Carson's hands. Bill C. Malone has argued that through the cumulative effect of these transformations, the song, "once intended as a lament of an ex-slave, became metamorphosed through time into a piece of nostalgia for the rural past."[28] While I take Malone's point that Carson repurposes a post–Civil War fantasy about an ex-slave's nostalgia for his bondage as an account of white rural southerners' urban displacement, I am reluctant to accept the implication that the racial significance of the piece is evacuated in the process. I think it unlikely that the piece, a lament for the days of slavery written by a white Kentuckian in the midst of Reconstruction, could be so thoroughly dehistoricized a mere fifty years after its composition. "The Little Old Log Cabin in the Lane" is but one example of the plantation nostalgia that became prevalent in minstrelsy after the end of the Civil War, and such nostalgia occupies a prominent place in commercial country music in the 1920s and 1930s. In addition to the development of country music, the 1920s also saw the resurgence of the Ku Klux Klan—another fixture of Reconstruction; Carson "regularly played for Klan functions."[29] The plantation nostalgia present in country music of the 1920s and 1930s may obscure and displace contemporary racial concerns, but it does not erase them. This new music sublimates the racial mimicry inherited from its predecessors into new formulations of musical whiteness. This inaugural hillbilly recording demonstrates clearly the blackface blood that runs in country music's veins.

A particularly illuminating case of the intersection of blackface impersonation and the emergence of commercial hillbilly music is that of Vernon Dalhart, whose career as the first nationally successful hillbilly singer was launched with the release of the "Wreck of the Old 97" backed with "The Prisoner's Song" in 1924. Dalhart (a one-time cowboy born Marion Try Slaughter in east Texas) found success as a hillbilly singer after seven years spent as a singer of "coon" songs. The first of these releases (reportedly the song with which Dalhart auditioned for Thomas Edison) was "Can't Yo' Heah Me Callin', Caroline," released in 1917. Walter Darrell Haden attributes the record's success to Dalhart's "convincing black dialect coupled with the singer's obvious flair for histrionics."[30] Of course, Dalhart's "convincing black dialect" was highly affected, and recalled the similar affectations of minstrels and other singers of coon songs. Dalhart, like others purporting special skill in imitating "Negro" dialect, denied this affectation. Significantly, Dalhart claimed not that he had spent time studying "Negro" dialect but that he "never had to learn it. When you are born and brought up in the South your only trouble is to talk any other way." In fact, he explains, "the sure 'nough Southerner talks almost like a Negro, even when he's white."[31]

Following the early success of Fiddlin' John Carson's early records, hillbilly recordings became increasingly popular, and in the summer of 1927 Peer traveled to Bristol, on the Tennessee/Virginia border, to audition and record another batch of rural performers, this time for the Victor Talking Machine Company. This trip resulted in the discovery of Jimmie Rodgers, who would quickly become hillbilly music's first superstar, earning him the title "The Father of Country Music." The Bristol sessions, as they have come to be known, with their cast of characters trekking in from the surrounding hills to audition for the enterprising record company scout, serve as a convenient and appealing point of origin for commercial country music—what Nolan Porterfield in an evocative metaphor calls "the Big Bang of country music evolution."[32] Like his predecessors and contemporaries, Rodgers trafficked in musical styles drawn from both black and white sources. His recording career, which lasted from 1927 to 1933, serves in an important sense as a microcosm of the initial stages of country music's development as a commercial and artistic genre. Country music in Rodgers's recordings is a synthetic form, distinctly modern, crafted from a heterogeneous and eclectic amalgam of nineteenth- and early-twentieth-century folk and popular sources. As such, it contains within it a wealth of intermingling and sometimes contradictory elements: rural and urban, black and white, southern and nonsouthern, "folk" and commercial, traditional and modern.

"White man gone black"

In 1928, a year after both Willie McTell and Jimmie Rodgers made their first records, Newman Ivey White, a professor of English at Duke University whose interests extended from Shelley to African American folk songs and poetry (he compiled an anthology of the latter in 1924), published *American Negro Folk-Songs*, an exhaustive collection of hundreds of songs that he had collected, not primarily from African American singers, but "from students who had learned them from the Negroes" and from manuscripts of diverse provenance.[33] White's book was very much in the mainstream of American folklore studies. It was published by Harvard University Press, and White concludes his acknowledgments by thanking Professor George Lyman Kittredge, the Harvard professor largely responsible for folklore study's respectable status in the academy.[34] The tenor of this project, which generalizes at length about "the character of the folk Negro," is summed up accurately if ironically by its epigraph, credited as an "Old Minstrel Song": "SING, SING! DARKIES, SING— / DON'T YOU HEAR DE BANJO RING, RING, RING! / SING, SING! DARKIES, SING / SING FOR DE WHITE FOLKS, SING."[35] This epigraph's exhortation to minstrel "darkies" to "sing for de white folks" serves as an uncomfortable reminder of the wildly unbalanced power dynamic underlying African American performers' relationships to their white auditors. At the same time, that White without any apparent self-consciousness or embarrassment begins a book that purports to detail the character of the "folk Negro" with an invocation of blackface minstrelsy attests to the pervasiveness of white fantasy in constructing this character. White at one point addresses his imagined critics:

> I am cheerfully suspicious that my own attempt [to characterize the Negro] will seem in some quarters to be tinged with the racial prejudice of the white man; nothing more could be expected in the state of acute race-sensitiveness that involves the discussion of anything pertaining to the Negro. I am fully aware that the white man has certain inescapable prejudices and that I am writing as

a white man; but I also know that I greatly respect the Negro race for its character and accomplishments, and have had from childhood a positive affection for many individual Negroes.[36]

Some of White's best friends, in other words, were black.

Central to White's claims are the transparency of African American folk culture and a confidence in his ability to access it. Such claims highlight White's position as an exemplar of a generation of "pioneer analysts and collectors" whose efforts have provided an invaluable archive of African American folk materials at the same time that their "selective myopia" concerning the potential meanings of such materials distorted the very culture they aimed to document and analyze.[37] White's insistence on the naïveté of singing "darkies" is paired with the claim that these simple black folk derived their musical culture wholesale from "variational imitation of the . . . songs of the white man."[38] White's position is in line with that of George Pullen Jackson and others who argued that Negro spirituals were largely or wholly derived from the camp meeting songs of southern whites in the first half of the nineteenth century.

White goes a step further, however, in insisting not only that African American religious song is derived from white sources but that secular and popular music were likewise adapted by blacks from white antecedents, specifically minstrelsy and "coon songs."[39] That both these genres are centered expressly on whites imitating blacks does not register in White's analysis. Where the musical practices of whites and that of blacks differ, he argues, we see the effect of the "folk Negro's" nature on his white sources. Foremost among these characteristics are the Negro's "improvising tendency and the imitative tendency."[40] In a short essay, "Racial Traits in the Negro Song," published in 1920, White states his claim bluntly. "Many of the work-songs," he writes, "reflect no significant ideas at all, and thus attest the negro's indifference to ideas, his careless unconcern."[41] Likewise, the negro's "genuine naïveté" is "accompanied by a lack of logical sequence of thought, by frequent interposition of the trivial, and by startling and ludicrous transitions and juxtapositions," all of which are ultimately evidence of his "inability to discriminate between what is worth expression and what is not."[42]

Looking past the unsavory racial politics of much of White's argument and its internal contradictions, some significant points emerge. One is his claim that African American secular music is derived from the songs of whites, particularly those derived from minstrelsy and vaudeville. Though in "Racial Traits" he had argued that such songs are "corrupting influences . . . affecting the genuineness of many negro songs," by 1928 the commercial derivation of black folk songs has become "the least significant" element of their racial meaning.[43] Despite the importance to White's argument of establishing white musical priority, embedded in the racist generalizations of *American Negro Folk-Songs* is the implicit suggestion that the cultural meaning of musical forms is less a function of origins than of the myriad ways in which materials of diverse provenance are appropriated and used by musicians and their audiences. The racial purity of folk expression that White claimed to find in negro folk songs proves more idealized than actual. To the contrary, his subjects had long been creating new forms of musical expression from the manifestly impure flotsam of nineteenth-century commercial culture, including minstrelsy, parlor songs, and vaudeville as well as from noncommercial (i.e., "folk") sources, such as dance music, fiddle tunes, work songs, and the like. White acknowledges as much in a 1929 essay, "The White Man in the Woodpile," where he observes that "the assimilation of factory-made 'blues' into Negro folk-song taking place at the present time" mirrors the earlier adoption of manifestly inauthentic songs of the minstrel stage into African American vernacular culture in the rural South.[44] As is the case elsewhere in his work, White's analysis of this process of adaptation is colored by his zeal to document the hand of "the white man" in facilitating the transmission of songs to the black folk.

Despite his effort to establish the priority of white sources for black songs, White nevertheless steadfastly maintains that the texts of such songs (he pays little attention to musical style or technique) reveal the negro's essential character: he is "a most naïve and unanalytical-minded person, with a sensuous joy in his religion; thoughtless, careless, unidealistic, rather fond of boasting, predominantly cheerful, . . . charitably inclined toward the white man," etc.[45] White purports to draw these conclusions regarding "the Negro's" character from the texts of the songs in his collection; their formal characteristics reflect the nature of "the Negro." The recurrence of floating or maverick stanzas (which folklorist John Greenway defines as "the fragmentary, ephemeral phrases of the Negro folksinger"), for example, attest to a racial inability to string together a coherent song. Due to this deficiency, according to White, the stanza, not the song, is the fundamental unit of Negro folk music.[46]

Rodgers's unself-conscious appropriation of African American–identified musical styles, lyric fragments, and songs represents a substantial challenge to this conception of African American folk song as evidence of "the Negro's" racial distinctiveness and inferiority. Literary critic Abbe Niles's early reviews of Rodgers's early records illustrate this challenge. Niles's reviews in his "Ballads, Songs, and Snatches" column in *The Bookman: A Review of Books and Life* are a cornerstone of critical appraisal of Rodgers's music, as they are probably the first reviews of Rodgers's records to see print.[47] Nolan Porterfield—Rodgers's biographer—and, more recently, J. Lester Feder have noted the paradox that these reviews illustrate: to Niles, the inaugural recordings of the man who would come to be seen as the father of a musical genre commonly held to be quintessentially white sounded fundamentally *black*.[48]

Niles's first review, from July 1928, is succinct: "Meet also, Jimmy [*sic*] Rodgers singing 'Down on the Mountain' [*sic*; Niles is referring to 'Away Out on the Mountain'] and his engaging, melodious and bloodthirsty 'Blue Yodel.'"[49] He then cites what is presumably a particularly bloodthirsty passage:

> If you don't want me, mama, you sho' don't have to stall,
> 'Cause I can git mo' women than a passenger train can haul.
> I'm gonna buy me a pistol just as long as I'm tall, Lawd, Lawd.
> I'm gonna shoot po' Thelma, just to see her jump an' fall.[50]

In retrospect, it seems significant that Niles includes no indication of Rodgers's race. Porterfield sees this as evidence that Niles assumed Rodgers was black, and supports this claim by associating Niles's description of "Blue Yodel" as "bloodthirsty" with coon-song stereotypes of violent, razor-toting Negroes.[51] Feder argues otherwise, and points out that Niles is generally careful to indicate the racial status of the records he reviews, either by appending the label "colored" to an artist's name (as he does with Rabbit Brown at the beginning of the column in which he first reviews Rodgers) or through such headings as "White singers" and "The singing Negro."[52] Niles's July 1928 review of Rodgers's record, however, includes no such racial markers.

Whatever Niles's potential status concerning Rodgers's racial identity, his transcription of "Blue Yodel" seems to mark the *song*, at least, if not the singer, as black. Though it sounds to me that Rodgers enunciates the "r" sound at the end of "sure," "more," and "poor," Niles renders these words as "sho'," "mo'," and "po'," respectively. Porterfield suggests that "the cultural chasm separating [Niles's] life from the raucous country blues and hillbilly wails was often simply too great to bridge," and it may well be that to Niles's ear, Rodgers's drawn-out vowels eclipse these words' final consonants.[53] Other orthographic choices, though, like "git" for "get" and "an'" for "and" are clearly less attempts at phonetic accuracy than they are eye dialect, serving to mark Rodgers's speech as nonstandard, rural, and black.

Whatever ambiguity concerning Rodgers's race that remained from this first mention was promptly addressed by the title of the next one, in Niles's September column: "*White man singing black songs.*"[54] Though here Niles acknowledges that Rodgers's "Blue Yodel" "started the whole epidemic of yodelling blues that now rages," he devotes a quarter of the very brief column space he devotes to Rodgers's second blue yodel to the fact that Clarence Williams, an African American singer, had written "a good one five years ago."[55] Though Niles does not mention it by name, Williams recorded his "Yodeling Blues" in 1923, complete with what Lynn Abbot and Doug Seroff describe as "a distinct, if slightly inane, 'yodel-odel-odel, de-yodel-odel-odel,'" and no less a figure than Bessie Smith recorded a version of it (*sans* yodel, oddly) the next year.[56] In this forty-word blurb, Niles embeds Rodgers's blue yodel in the context of a largely urban, sophisticated, African American vaudeville–derived blues tradition, though subsequent decades of record company publicity, romantic mythologizing, and racially blinkered folk song scholarship have largely obscured this relationship.

Niles takes the identification of Rodgers as black one step further in his November 1928 column, as Rodgers is no longer merely a "*White man singing black songs*" but a "*White man gone black.*"[57] Niles deflates this rather startling transformation by faintly praising Rodgers's singing and "guitaring" as "as easy and lazy as ever," but complains that "he needs a gag-writer, for he's running short of verses." By December, Niles appears to have lost interest in Rodgers's blues records, as he instead reviews two of his sentimental ballads, one of whose labels credits Rodgers as composer but was in fact, Niles points out, copyrighted in 1896.[58] In the five-month span of Niles's reviews, Jimmie Rodgers goes from a racially ambiguous figure marked by signifiers of black speech and song to an imitative vaudevillian. Judging from Niles's assessment, it seems that the uncertain racial identity suggested by Rodgers's blue yodels is resolved by retreating into the relative safety of blackface imitation.

A somewhat different relationship between Rodgers's music and black-identified blues traditions is suggested by the frequent appearance of fragments of his lyrics and of whole songs in folk song collections in the years after his death. Folklorist John Greenway in 1957 noted that Rodgers's records were "bought by country folk who turned up for the next twenty years as folk informants, even in the Archive of American Folk Song."[59] "Blue Yodel (T for Texas)," for example, was "collected and published as genuine folksong by [Mellinger Edward] Henry as well as by [Frank C.] Brown and his editors; his 'Blue Yodel Number Four ('California Blues')' and 'Blue Yodel Number Five' by Brown; his 'Blue Yodel Number Eight ('Mule Skinner Blues')' by [MacEdward] Leach and [Horace P.] Beck," etc.[60] Much like Newman Ivey White in his *American Negro Folk Songs*, the editors of the 1952 collection, *Folk Songs from North Carolina*, express confidence in exactly what they are dealing with, writing of "Blue Yodel Number Five": "As we have it here it is clearly a Negro blues song."[61] As Greenway points out, the song text in this volume is actually a word-for-word transcription of Victor 22072, written and performed by Jimmie Rodgers.[62] The same volume includes two versions of Rodgers's "Blue Yodel (T for Texas)." One ("Obtained from Mrs. Minnie Church, Heaton, Avery county, in 1930") mangles the lyrics a bit, so "T for Texas, T for Tennessee" becomes "Leave for Texas, leave for Tennessee" and "Thelma" is renamed "Thalma" (this may indicate an orthographical eccentricity of the song's transcriber, or an attempt at representing the singer's pronunciation); the first two verses of this transcription are followed by the instruction, "(yodel)."[63] The second version omits the yodel but is otherwise nearly identical to Victor 21142.[64] "Blue Yodel #4" (Victor 40014) appears as "The California Blues"; an editorial note identifies it as "a blues song that I have not found recorded elsewhere, though the feeling it expresses is common in Negro song."[65] "Away Out on the Mountain" (Victor 21142) appears, prefaced by the peculiar question, "Is it a relic of Davy Crockett?"[66] (It was not, having been written for Rodgers by the well-known songwriter Kelly Harrell and released as the B-side of "Blue Yodel.") "Waiting for a Train" (Victor 40014) is described in a headnote as "[o]ne of many nondescript hobo songs," and it is further noted that "the Archive of American Folk Song has a recording of it made in Kentucky."[67]

The presence of Rodgers's compositions in such collections of folk songs confounds the segregationist racial logic that would erect barriers between the products of black and white folk; it also calls into question the boundary between the folk and the popular, the vernacular and the commercial. The African American singers whose performances are recorded in these volumes apparently accepted Rodgers's music as their own, in which case they must have been either unaware of or indifferent to Rodgers's racial status. The collectors of these songs were also apparently unaware that the source of these "Negro blues songs" was white, insisting as they do on the representative blackness of Rodgers's music. Rodgers's contribution to the musical traditions that such collectors sought to document undermines the racialist logic that undergirds the identification of these traditions as racially homogeneous, or as expressive (as White would have it) of "the Negro's" essential racial characteristics. While academic folklorists like White and his followers were documenting folk music traditions defined along racial lines, the products of the recording industry both confirmed and subverted these racial boundaries. Despite the early record industry's longstanding traffic in racist representations, it actually allowed for cross-racial identification in ways that often confounded the racialist strictures of academic folklore. This is not to say that its practices should be understood as nonracist. Instead, as Rodgers's example illustrates, popular vernacular music during this period both crossed racial lines and reinforced them, simultaneously effacing and reinscribing the color line.

Imagined Irishness and the Anxiety of Whiteness

Cliff Carlisle, one of many musicians who developed a musical style based on Rodgers's, described him in an interview: "He crossed that leg—well, his leg didn't do like mine does; *my* leg won't hang down . . . he put one leg over the other, and it was hangin' right down. . . . And he opened that mouth—he had a long face, you know, long jaw, like; anyhow, it just flopped! Jimmie, he reminded me more of a colored person, or a negro, or whatever you want to call 'em . . . than anybody I ever saw."[68] Carlisle's comment suggests that, in his view at least, the racial instability of Rodgers's music extended to his person; he implies that Rodgers himself had to some extent become "a negro." Rodgers's cross-racial musical affiliations, in this account, are inscribed in his physiognomy. Carlisle echoes Abbe Niles's description of Rodgers as a "white man gone black," but in a different, more personal, register. While Carlisle's description is somewhat inscrutable, it suggests that he perceived Rodgers as racially other, and that part of his appeal was his nonwhiteness, whether performed or natural. Carlisle's description of Rodgers illustrates Joel Williamson's claim that "by about 1900 it was possible in the South for one who was biologically pure white to become black by behavior. . . . Blackness and Whiteness became a matter not just of color or even blood, but of inner morality reflected by outward performance."[69] The blackness of Rodgers's music, in other words, complicates his personal whiteness. Such a complication was not to be taken lightly in the 1930s among those, in Du Bois's formulation, "in whose minds the paleness of their bodily skins [had become] fraught with tremendous and eternal significance."[70]

In Rodgers's case, an imagined ethnic Irishness serves as a solution to this problem, though this solution brings its own complications. Scholars in a number of disciplines have called attention to the ways in which whiteness is negotiated by successive waves of immigrants and U.S.-born people of Irish descent, beginning with the first significant Irish migrations in the eighteenth century and continuing at least until the early twentieth. Noel Ignatiev, Theodore Allen, and David Roediger, for example, have all examined the ways in which members of an oppressed Irish peasantry were able, after immigrating to America, to leverage their status as free labor to assume the social benefits of whiteness.[71] Robert Cantwell and Eric Lott, meanwhile, have argued that participation in the symbolic economy of blackface minstrelsy allowed Irish performers, paradoxically, to solidify their at times tenuous claims to whiteness through "acting black."[72] Both these threads help illuminate Rodgers's own peculiar relationship to Irishness.

In *My Husband, Jimmie Rodgers*, a biography of her late husband published in 1935, Carrie Williamson ("Mrs. Jimmie") Rodgers presents Jimmie as a crucible in which the "darkey songs" he learned as a boy are transmuted by "the natural music in his Irish soul" into something distinctive and new.[73] Of the early influence of the African American railroad laborers with whom Jimmie had extensive contact as a water boy, she writes: "The grinning, hard-working blacks who took Aaron Rodgers's orders made his small son laugh—often. Though small he was white. So, even when they bade him 'bring that water 'round' they were deferential. During the noon dinner-rests, they taught him to plunk melody from banjo and guitar. They taught him darkey songs: moaning chants and crooning lullabies."[74]

Carrie Rodgers's understanding of Jimmie's relationship to the blacks from whom he learned exhibits quite vividly what W. J. Cash, six years later in *The Mind of the South*, calls the "vastly ego-warming and ego-expanding distinction between the white man and the black."[75] Cash identifies this distinction as key to the notion of a southern white identity that transcends class, as the justification for poor whites' and small farmers' identification with the planter class. Of course Cash also asserts, famously, that through the mechanisms of plantation life, "Negro entered into white man as profoundly as white man entered into Negro—subtly influencing every gesture, every word, every emotion and idea, every attitude."[76] This tension—between very real social distinctions between blacks and whites and the multifarious ways in which these distinctions were troubled on a cultural level—animates Rodgers's music.

While it's likely that by "darkey songs," Mrs. Rodgers means simply songs sung by black people, her choice of phrase, unconsciously or not, again points back to the tradition of blackface minstrelsy, whose stereotyped representations of antebellum plantation life were the most popular and important entertainment form of the nineteenth century throughout the country. The minstrel show constituted a series of stylized public engagements with Cash's "vast and capacious distinction" between blacks and whites.[77] The representational forms and characters of blackface minstrelsy persisted well into Rodgers's time, and Rodgers himself had worked as a blackface performer.[78] In Mrs. Rodgers's account, Jimmie Rodgers's mimicry of the songs of his black fellow laborers and their tutelage of the young water boy are sublimated into a romantic notion of musical expression that is racial above all. The racial identity of Rodgers's music, though, is not merely white but specifically Irish: "Well, Jimmie knew he was no genius, then or ever. All he knew was that he had done his best to make good with what humble gifts he possessed; although he was confident that he had 'just sort of happened' on an unusual method of expressing the music that was in his Irish heart, and he was shrewd enough to gauge its potential value."[79]

The idea that Rodgers's music came not from a synthesis of current popular styles but rather from the racial wellspring of Rodgers's "Irish heart" is a persistent theme of *My Husband, Jimmie Rodgers*. His songs, "simply because they were there in that Irish soul of his[,] . . . would give him no rest until he could give them to God's whole world in song."[80] He becomes frustrated with his bandmates "because he couldn't seem to communicate to his boys his wish for 'feeling' their music; couldn't seem to get them to put their hearts into it. But they had not his Irish gift for whimsical gaiety, his Irish soul with its instant response to any emotion."[81] Finally, Mrs. Rodgers asks rhetorically, "Was Jimmie Rodgers always sunny-natured? Could he . . . take just everything, the good and the bad, with the same sweet, patient smile? Didn't he have even one tiny little spark of fire—of temper? . . . Well, Jimmie Rodgers was Irish. What do you think?"[82] The stereotyped romantic racialism that informs these statements is perhaps unsurprising. They are rendered somewhat perplexing, on the other hand, by the fact that Jimmie Rodgers was not Irish, at least not in the straightforward way that Carrie Rodgers claims.

In their 1977 biography of Rodgers, Mike Paris and Chris Comber state matter-of-factly and without evidence of any kind that "the Rodgerses were of Scots-Irish origin and may have descended from the trappers and hunters who had settled the Mississippi Valley in the early 19th century."[83] This genealogical claim is pure speculation; it also deploys a racial/ethnic term—"Scots-Irish"—that differs subtly but significantly from the one Mrs. Rodgers uses. In his 1979 biography of Rodgers (well-researched and published by a university press), Nolan Porterfield cites Paris and Comber's description of Rodgers as "Scots-Irish."[84] Porterfield correctly identifies this genealogical claim as speculation, offers no additional evidence, and then goes on to claim that Rodgers's "paternal ancestors . . . were obviously of Irish origin."[85] The slippage in these descriptions between two overlapping but not synonymous terms—"Irish" and "Scots-Irish"—suggests the instability (as well as the invention and redefinition) of these terms in a twentieth-century American context. In the liner notes to Bear Family Records' 1992 reissue set of Rodgers's recordings, Porterfield reverts to the more general term, echoing Carrie Rodgers's racialist descriptions, describing "Jimmie's lively yet brooding Irish temperament," offset by "a certain wistful Irish charm," perhaps inherited from "[h]is father, Aaron Woodberry Rodgers, . . . a wiry, quick-fisted Irishman from Alabama."[86]

In contrast to the speculative nature of Rodgers's "obviously" Irish paternal line, Porterfield documents his maternal line as descending from Dutch immigrants (originally Boschman or Bosman, later anglicized to Bozeman).[87] Presumably Mrs. Rodgers would have been aware of this genealogy as well. Why then do all these accounts insist that Rodgers was Irish (or Scots-Irish), rather than, say, Dutch? Part of the answer may be an unconscious deference to a patrilineal idea of ancestry, but I don't think that's a sufficient explanation. It is clear that Rodgers's putative Irish patrimony trumps his matrilineal Dutchness. This situation obtains at least in part because of the ways a romanticized understanding of Rodgers and his music as racially Irish or Scots-Irish—which term we choose doesn't really seem to matter, history notwithstanding—squares with long-standing notions of "Celtic" peoples as inherently musical. By the 1930s, it seems, the Irish are safely white, but at the same time they possess a "racial" gift for music that countervails the influence of the musical blacks from whom Rodgers first learned. Ascribing an Irish provenance to Rodgers's music in the face of much of the music's manifest "blackness" helps lay claim to it as a product of white folk, rather than an imitation of the music of African Americans or a product of interracial cultural exchange.

Nineteenth-century listeners had noted resemblances between Scottish and Irish folk music with some African American music. An 1892 article, for example, inaccurately but suggestively observes: "Genuine Negro music is invariably in a peculiar minor, which differs from the civilized scale in two particulars; the sixth note . . . is omitted and the seventh is a half a tone lower," and then notes that "[t]here is the same omission of the seventh in Scotch music."[88] Likewise, syncopation—another hallmark of African American music—a 1901 piece notes, "has been observed in the songs of Scotland[,] and English writers call it the 'Scotch snap.'"[89] Such formal correspondences between African American music on the one hand and Scottish and Irish folk music on the other led to a line of argument that held that much of the music which had been erroneously credited to African Americans was in fact derived from the folk music of Ireland and Scotland and that its exotic provenance accounted for its unfamiliar and strange-seeming rhythmic and harmonic elements. The author of a 1906 article entitled "Negro Melodies of Scotch Origin," for example, claims that "the Negro assimilated much of the music of his superiors in education during his earlier days of slavery. Especially may this be said of the Southern districts inhabited by the Scotch settlers."[90] As evidence, the author cites the use of pentatonic scales and flatted sevenths in "Negro music"; it is obvious "that the Negro was impressed by this Scotch music," since such scales and intervals are also present there. This argument is fairly representative of mainstream musicology in the first decades of the twentieth century.

Considerations of the relationships between black and white musical forms generally operated according to a transparently white-supremacist logic: if a song, tune, text, scale, or technique appears in both collections of white and black performances, its direction of cultural transmission must be from white to black, not the other way around. Dissenters from this view, like Henry Edward Krehbiel, whose 1914 *Afro-American Folksongs* argued for an African origin for African American music, likewise noted that it bore a strong tonal and rhythmic resemblance to "the one body of specifically national song with which the slave could by any possibility have become familiar—the Scottish, with its characteristic pentatonic scale and rhythmical snap; but the singing of Scottish ballads was not so general in the South that their peculiarities could become the common property of the field-hands on the plantations."[91] Irish (or Scottish or Scotch-Irish) music, then, serves as an ethnic wellspring *within* whiteness, and helps account for the exotic modal and rhythmic elements not only of the folk music of whites but of blacks as well, at the same time as it denies the possibility that whites could have adopted musical practices originated by African Americans. While champions of the white-origins-for-Negro-music hypothesis at times acknowledge that whites might have learned from blacks, these acknowledgments tend to involve only specific songs, rather than general musical styles or modes of performance.[92]

These discussions of the racial provenance of the spirituals and ragtime highlight a problem of racial and musical identity in which Rodgers and the genre he inaugurated are thoroughly enmeshed. Carlisle's comment about Rodgers's "negro" characteristics, as Robert Cantwell points out, likens Jimmie Rodgers to earlier Irish American performers, who occupied "a socially marginal position from which minstrelsy offered an escape."[93] But while donning the blackface mask provided Dan Emmett and other nineteenth-century minstrels a way to transcend their racially marginal status as Irishmen and fully adopt the mantle of whiteness, the situation for Rodgers is significantly different. In the face of the indeterminate racial status of Rodgers's music, an identification as Irish shores up Rodgers's claim to personal whiteness. His music may have led him to the margins of whiteness, but Irishness, it would seem, offers a way back to its center.

It is important to recognize—as Rodgers apparently did—that the romanticism and sometimes maudlin sentimentality of the "darkey songs" that keenly influenced his repertoire were quite dated and reactionary by the late 1920s. Mrs. Rodgers quotes Jimmie as giving the following rationale for trying to get his music on the radio: "[H]ere's what I figure. Folks everywhere are gettin' kind of tired of all this Black Bottom—Charleston—jazz music junk. . . . They tell me the radio stations keep gettin [*sic*] more and more calls for old-fashioned songs: 'Yearning,' 'Forgotten'—things like that, and even the old plantation melodies. Well, I'm ready with 'em."[94]

Rodgers would indeed record such material throughout his six-year recording career. At his last session, in New York in May 1933, he recorded "Mississippi Delta Blues," a sprightly, banjo-led bit of plantation nostalgia whose evocations of an idyllic southern home replete with whippoorwills, steamboats, and moonlit levees are accompanied by such seemingly anachronistic lines as: "I long to hear them darkies sing those old melodies / 'Swanee River' and 'Old Black Joe.'"[95] As the titles of the "old melodies" Rodgers's imaginary "darkies" sing attest, the South of this and many of Rodgers's other songs had more to do with Stephen Foster's deeply romanticized minstrel songs than with any actually existing place or people. That such imagery occupied such a prominent place in Rodgers's repertoire in the 1930s suggests that the aesthetic and political content of country music was out of sync with the contemporary zeitgeist. In his introduction to *The New Negro* in 1925, Alain Locke describes "The Old Negro" as "a stock figure perpetuated as an historical fiction partly in innocent sentimentalism, partly in deliberate reactionism."[96] "The day of 'aunties,' 'uncles,' and 'mammies' is . . . gone," Locke proclaims hopefully. "The popular melodrama has about played itself out, and it is time to scrap the fictions."[97] As it turns out, the popular melodrama had not nearly played itself out, at least not in cultural realms such as Rodgers's music that were in important ways far removed from Locke's purview. As Rodgers's "Mississippi Delta Blues" attests, in country music well into the following decade, "You can hear old mammy shout / 'Come on in here you all.'"

In Mrs. Rodgers's account, Jimmie's parlor-song-and-minstrel-show-tune-influenced repertoire was a calculated commercial response to the popular jazz of the time. While this would seem to suggest an antipathy to the African American popular music of the day, a more likely object of Rodgers's comment is likely the "Hebrew Broadway jazz" excoriated by contemporary folk purists as a modernist, urban, Jewish threat to traditional Anglo-American rural traditions.[98] Such sentiments are of course replete with racism and anti-Semitism; significantly, they also represent the antimodernism that helped fuel the folk revival of the 1920s and 1930s. Jeffrey Melnick argues that "Jewish blackface represented a victory for the (northern) city, for the urban entertainment complex which consistently proposed that the South had no current identity but only a history."[99] Ralph Peer's commercial coup in discovering Rodgers represents a continuation of this victory, as the northern entertainment complex enlisted southern performers to record nostalgic reminiscences of an idealized, vanished South. Ironically and significantly, these nostalgic early styles would soon engage vigorously with the urban, black-originated styles that the Rodgers quotation above posits—somewhat disingenuously, it would seem, given his own predilection for such styles—as standing in antipathy to them. This very engagement would allow for the creation of vibrant, hybrid styles like that of Rodgers himself. As Rodgers's career progressed, the distinction in his music between antediluvian folk- and minstrel-derived tunes and thoroughly modern commercial jazz would be continually undermined, as the Father of Country Music would record with old-time string bands, black jug bands, small concert orchestras, blues guitarists, Hawaiian groups, a musical saw player, white jazz bands, and Louis Armstrong. The music that Rodgers brought to his first recording session was already thoroughly heterogeneous, and his collaborators contributed even more wide-ranging elements to his recordings. This musical admixture marked his transition from itinerant local entertainer to the progenitor of a hugely popular commercial genre.

Still, despite this remarkable generic heterogeneity and despite the amusing, deferential "darkies" Mrs. Rodgers identifies as the formal sources of her famous husband's music, she also insists that Rodgers's music was both sui generis and racially bound. He simply expressed "the natural music in his Irish soul."[100] In his wife's account, Rodgers's music is an expression of a specifically white racial heritage. Mrs. Rodgers's invocations of Jimmie's "Irish soul" serve to dissociate the music of white folk from that of their nonwhite neighbors. Instead, these invocations assign it a place in an unbroken white musical tradition extending back to the British Isles and Ireland, much like Lomax's claims concerning the Anglo-Saxon provenance of his cowboy subjects' songs, or Cecil Sharp's or Bradley Kincaid's similar claims concerning mountain songs. In each case, it matters little whether the presumed tradition is Anglo-Saxon, Elizabethan, or Irish. In fact, Bill C. Malone notes that the first two terms were often used interchangeably by advocates of a British folk culture in the South; evidently, however, those advocates did not realize "that the two terms were not synonymous."[101]

Mrs. Rodgers's description of Jimmie's music as a product of his Irish soul, rather than Anglo-Saxon blood, is more in line with the claims of later proponents of a Celtic South than with the Anglo-Saxon–oriented view common when she was writing in the mid-1930s. This view of a Celtic South, best articulated in Cash's *The Mind of the South*, holds that the culture of the North was predominantly English while the South was instead settled predominantly by "Celts" (Irish or Scotch-Irish), and that long-standing differences in the cultures of the differing populations of settlers largely determined the differences in the cultures of the American North and South. Whether malignant or benign, the notion of southern culture as a product of a "Celtic" racial heritage—like similar notions that identify it as Elizabethan or Anglo-Saxon—ultimately serve to obscure actual social relations "under a murky veil of romanticism."[102] Mrs. Rodgers's insistence on Jimmie's Irishness illustrates the effects of the anxiety that Du Bois observes in "The Souls of White Folk"—the "[painful] conscious[ness] of their whiteness" that her repeated assertions of Irishness evince. This racial anxiety sets the stage for the invention of country music and contributes to the racially circumscribed accounts of its history as a product of the souls of white folk.

Jimmie Rodgers in Africa

In the late 1920s, Jimmie Rodgers's records—distributed on the English Zonophone label—were widely available in Durban, South Africa's second-largest city, with a large Zulu majority, and they quickly gained widespread popularity. In 1930 South Africans Griffiths Motsieloa and Ignatius Monare had recorded a blue yodel, titled "Aubuti Nkikho," in London.[103] Two years later, William Mseleku, a popular black South African singer and bandleader, recorded two sides—"Eku Hambeni" and "Sifikile Tina"—that were "directly modeled on Rodgers's 'Blue Yodel' series."[104] Mseleku's recordings resemble not only Rodgers's blues recordings but also his sentimental ballads. "Eku Hambeni," for example, begins with a Jimmie Rodgers–signature run on the guitar's bass strings before settling into a tenor melody line with strummed accompaniment. Harmonically, the tune clearly derives from a different tradition than Rodgers's twelve-bar-blues–based blue yodels, although both its bass runs and yodels make Rodgers's influence clear. "Sifikile Tina" shares its 3/4 waltz time and guitar instrumentation with early Jimmie Rodgers recordings like "The Soldier's Sweetheart" and "Sleep Baby Sleep" and, apart from its Zulu-language lyrics, would not sound out of place on a Rodgers record.

South African writer Es'kia Mphahlele recounts in *Down Second Avenue*, his 1959 autobiography, that when he was twelve years old (i.e., in 1931), young men from his village would travel to Pretoria—South Africa's administrative capital—for work: "They brought gramophones which they said they had played all the way in the train. . . . For a long time they made us believe that there were very small people singing inside the gramophone. They probably believed it themselves. At Christmas time Jeemee Roe-Jars (Jimmy [*sic*] Rodgers), then in fashion, yodeled plaintively from various parts of the village."[105]

Likewise, in Dugmore Boetie's autobiographical novel, *Familiarity Is the Kingdom of the Lost*, a young boy in 1930s South Africa is entranced when he hears a gramophone record of Rodgers's "Waiting for a Train." American folklorists Henry Belden and Arthur Hudson, editors of *Folk Songs from North Carolina* (1952), describe "Waiting for a Train" as "[o]ne of many nondescript hobo songs,"[106] though Boetie's narrator perceives Rodgers's recording quite differently: "The voice in the record belonged to Jimmy [*sic*] Rodgers. He was singing a song called 'Waiting for the Train' [*sic*] with guitar accompaniment. The first time I heard that record, I took to it like a drunkard takes to drink. . . . I didn't want anything to go wrong. Not while I was listening to that record."[107]

Unfortunately, the narrator's father accidentally breaks his prize possession, at which point "a nightmare search for the record started. Every time I stole a record, it would turn out to be the wrong one. You see, I couldn't read. If I could, I would have saved myself a lot of trouble."[108] Boetie finally obtains a replacement copy, but at a price: "At last I got the record and six months in the reformatory."[109] Upon his release, he discovers that his father had sold his gramophone, so he packs his guitar and goes to Cape Town to find work. There he plays "with a Coon Carnival group known as The Jesters. There was a guitar player that I greatly admired. He played almost like my Jimmy [*sic*] Rodgers."[110] Boetie's narrator evinces a powerful identification with Rodgers. That the guitar player in "a Coon Carnival group" would play in a style "almost like" Rodgers's suggests that Rodgers's music was understood by black South African musicians not as "hillbilly" or "country" music (i.e., as "white") but rather as an element of an African American minstrel inheritance that, despite its stereotypically racist trappings, nonetheless provided an opportunity for the creation of new musical performances and for affective identification on the part of black South African musicians and listeners.

It is difficult to determine what precisely about Rodgers's records South African listeners found so appealing, though both Mphahlele's and Boetie's narratives point to an affective identification with the voice on Rodgers's records as a key component of their appeal. For the people in Mphahlele's village, Rodgers's plaintive yodel—the very marker of white racial difference in the American racial imagination—provides the sonic key to this cross-racial, cross-national appeal. As Christopher Ballantine has argued, black South African popular music was undergoing rapid development and change during the late 1920s and 1930s, and Rodgers was likely appropriated as part of the influx of American (predominantly African American) music that

South African musicians were adapting to their own uses.[111] The adoption of Rodgers's blue yodel also suggests a fortuitous syncretism; it is possible that Mseleku, Motsieloa, and Monare heard in Rodgers's yodel an echo of black South African traditions of falsetto singing. On the other hand, as discussed above, Lynn Abbott and Doug Seroff suggest that Rodgers's yodel was derived largely from vaudeville traditions, and they subsequently trace the commercial history of the yodel in American minstrelsy and vaudeville to the Civil War era. Blackface minstrelsy had arrived in South Africa in 1862, and South African vaudeville had largely developed parallel to and in sync with its American counterpart.[112] Mseleku was himself a key figure in early South African vaudeville; Boetie's protagonist's stint with a "Coon Carnival" group provides another example and illustrates the pervasiveness of minstrel-derived stereotypes, terms, and musical configurations in South Africa. Viewed from this perspective, Rodgers's music became accessible to Mseleku and other black South African musicians due to shared (or at least overlapping) popular musical cultures. The seeming acceptance of Rodgers's music as "black" by black South Africans points to ways in which intercultural musical exchanges can destabilize and transform the racial significances ascribed to musical performances, artifacts, and forms.

The example of South African blue yodels points also to the importance of the phonograph in spreading musical styles from the United States to Africa. The cross-racial and cross-national syncretism of South African blue yodels was enabled by the multinational distribution networks of record labels. While Mseleku's Zulu yodels, for example, may well be in part a product of a folk tradition, their ultimate form was midwifed by the influence of records produced by the U.S. culture industry (largely via English record companies). One effect of the widespread availability of American cultural products in South Africa was "the confident assertion of a racial and cultural identity between blacks in South Africa and those in the United States."[113] Ballantine points to phonograph records as a vehicle for a cross-national racial identification; South African artists strove to reproduce styles and tunes they learned from American records.[114] Exported African American cultural products provided models for black South African cultural expression. Jazz, for example, was held by many South Africans to be "a modified and cultured form of . . . bantu music and dance," and blacks in the United States were understood to be "Africans in America."[115]

The distribution of American popular music in Africa via British record companies illustrates the phenomenon Arjun Appadurai describes, whereby "electronic mediation transforms preexisting worlds of communication and conduct." Appadurai identifies media and migration as the two fundamental forces affecting what he calls "the *work of the imagination* as a constitutive feature of modern subjectivity."[116] The reception of Rodgers's music in Africa both illustrates and complicates this notion. For Appadurai, the effects on modern subjectivity of the circulation of media operate primarily in the realm of images, through film and television. In South Africans' affective identification with Rodgers's records, on the other hand, we see instead the work of the imagination through aural rather than visual media. The disembodiment of Rodgers's music in the form of gramophone records dissociates it from the visual logic of race that might otherwise overdetermine its reception, enabling new cross-racial identifications.

While at first glance the incorporation of Rodgers's music into emerging black South African musical performance styles may seem incongruous, the shared history of vaudeville and the popularity of American cultural products—including music—in non-Western markets renders it less surprising. Still, it is not clear exactly how Rodgers fits into this cross-cultural transaction. According to Ballantine, Rodgers and a few other white artists became popular "because they were—rightly or wrongly—identified with the music made by the 'Africans in America.'"[117] This explanation suggests that Rodgers's records sounded "black" to South African listeners, that his music sounded attractively *African* American. At any rate, musicians and record buyers seem to have identified with "Jeemee Roe-Jars" in a way that collapsed national and racial distinctions. These responses fulfilled the promise of an ad for "Waiting for a Train" in the bilingual (Zulu and English) *Umteteli wa Bantu:* "Unga qabuka sowungu JIMMY [*sic*] RODGERS ngokwako" (You can feel like Jimmie Rodgers himself!) (see fig. 2.4).[118]

Precisely such an identification is at work in Boetie's narrative. "Waiting for a Train" is sung from the perspective of a narrator trying to hobo his way home:

> I'm on my way from Frisco,
> I'm going back to Dixieland
> Though my pocketbook is empty
> And my heart is full of pain,
> I'm a thousand miles away from home
> Just waiting for a train.

The song's narrator is kicked off the train by an unsympathetic brakeman in "Texas / A state [he] dearly love[s]":

> I walked up to a brakeman
> To give him a line of talk

Figure 2.4. Advertisement for gramophone records by Jimmie Rodgers, including "Waiting for a Train." From *Umteteli wa Bantu: The Mouthpiece of the Native People*. Johannesburg, South Africa, November 22, 1930.

He says "If you've got money,
I'll see that you don't walk."
"I haven't got a nickel,
Not a penny can I show."
"Get off, get off, you railroad bum"
And he slammed the box car door.

Boetie crafts a similar narrative: after another stint in a reformatory, his narrator hitches a ride on a fast train bound from Cape Town to Johannesburg. When he is apprehended by two white policemen, he explains that he is coming home from Cape Town: "'You mean,' spluttered the other policeman, 'you travelled a thousand miles from Cape Town like that?'"[119] Rodgers's song is replete with evocative place names: "Frisco," "Texas," "Dixieland." Boetie's narrative echoes Rodgers's, substituting Cape Town for "Frisco" as the land of frustrated opportunity, and Sophiatown—a suburb of Johannesburg and a hub of black culture—as the home to which the narrator longs to return.

Boetie's narrator identifies the song that so entrances him as "'Waiting for the [sic] Train' with guitar accompaniment," echoing the description on the label of his 78-rpm record. The song's instrumentation actually comprises, in addition to guitar, a range of other instruments. It opens with Rodgers's singing (in falsetto) in unison with a train whistle. The opening melodic theme is played by a cornet, which is soon joined by a Hawaiian lap steel guitar, itself an artifact of an earlier cross-cultural musical exchange. Rodgers's signature yodel after the first verse is immediately answered by a Dixieland-style breakdown, as the cornet and a clarinet solo simultaneously. The instrumentation and arrangement of "Waiting for a Train" share many affinities with the contemporaneous music being made by "Africans in America." In addition to the appeal that the song's narrative seems to have held for Boetie, these musical affinities offered a means for sympathetic black South African listeners to identify with Rodgers's record—to "feel like Jimmie Rodgers himself!"

A better-known yet more perplexing instance of Rodgers's reception in Africa is the reported popularity of Rodgers's records among the Kipsigis tribe of Kenya in the 1950s. The details of the Kipsigis's appreciation of Rodgers's music are sketchy, but accounts of it begin with ethnomusicologist Hugh Tracey's recordings of three Kipsigis songs, released in South Africa in 1950 as part of the Sound of Africa series from the International Library of African Music (ILAM), and later rereleased commercially in England and by Smithsonian Folkways in the United States. Tracey labeled the three songs as "Chemirocha" I, II, and III and indicated in the 1950 record's notes that "the name 'Chemirocha' is their pronunciation of 'Jimmy [sic] Rodgers' whose gramophone records were the first to be heard in the district."[120] In a spoken introduction recorded for a commercial 1952 pressing, he elaborates: "There were no records in their own language, of course, but the one that took their fancy was a guitar solo by the well-known cowboy singer, Jimmie Rodgers."[121] Which of Rodgers's records so fascinated the Kipsigis is unfortunately not reported, but in Tracey's account, their appreciation of it was intense. He continues: "'What a magnificent *chepkong* player,' they thought. 'Why, no one's ever played the *kipukandet* like this man,' Chemirocha, as they called him. The men of the district said, 'Perhaps he's a fine new dancer who's touring the countryside.' But the girls said, 'Ah ha no, this is no ordinary creature—this is a fawn, half-man and half-antelope.' So they sing this song of welcome to Chemirocha, inviting him to come and dance with them. Who could refuse such an invitation as this?"

At first, Tracey's narration seems like some sort of colonial fever dream, and the embellishments and minor implausibilities in Tracey's original account and in later repetitions of it do little to mitigate this impression. In one early version, Paul Oliver identifies "the 'legendary Jimmie Rodgers'" as "a demi-god to the Kipsigi [*sic*] tribe."[122] Nolan Porterfield describes the songs as part of "a female puberty rite" and cites Tracey's recordings as "exotic evidence of [Rodgers's] visceral magnetism."[123] Porterfield especially focuses on "Chemirocha III," emphasizing the erotic appeal he imagines Rodgers wields over the female singers.

I have so far been unable to find a Kipsigis speaker to translate the three songs' texts, so I don't know what, precisely, the songs are actually about. Tracey's spare and indifferently punctuated notes, therefore, provide the only clues. "Chemirocha III," according to Tracey's notes, does seem to provide some of the titillation that Porterfield emphasizes, as the girls singing the song urge him "to do the leaping dance familiar to all Kipsigis so energetically that he will jump clear out of his clothes." "Chemirocha II" is based on the similarities between Rodgers's guitar and "the local lyre" (both *chepkong* and *kipukandet* are names for the five- or six-string lyre played by the Kipsigis). According to Tracey, "the similarity of the two instruments [the guitar and "the local lyre"] . . . has given rise to the legend of this wandering player whose records have been heard but whose presence is a mystery."

Whatever the accuracy of Tracey's account and subsequent elaborations of it, equally important are the mystifications at work in this story. Tracey's notes to the original 1950 ILAM release provide some insight. He writes of "Chemirocha I": "The main theme of this song is affection for the Kipsigis country. [The singer] also asks 'why the whitemen should have taken over the country,' which incidentally they themselves took from others in the past. . . .

The name 'Chemirocha' is . . . now synonymous for anything strange or new." Writing at the cusp of the Mau Mau uprising against British rule in Kenya, Tracey (himself an Englishman living in Rhodesia) sounds a nervous note about the legitimacy of British occupation of African lands. "Chemirocha," then, is not only a mythical musical stranger or a figure of disembodied sexuality, but also a specific exemplar of a system of colonial exploitation and global exchange. This system of exchange brings Jimmie Rodgers's records to South Africa and to Kenya, where his music is appropriated and recontextualized by musicians whose own understandings of the records that so appeal to them remain obscure.

The defamiliarizing uncertainty elicited by these instances of cross-cultural transmission is valuable, I think, in that it short-circuits the process by which we ascribe racial value to musical performances or artifacts. If we cannot know how Jimmie Rodgers's records sounded to South Africans in the 1920 and 1930s or to Kipsigis in 1950, their resonance with these far-flung listeners suggests that the entrenched association of country music with the souls of white folk has more to do with our own country's complex relationship with whiteness than with the sound of the music itself. The disembodied voice of Jimmie Rodgers on the 78-rpm records that circulate throughout Africa, transformed during their travels into "Jeemee Roe-Jars" or "Chemirocha," short-circuits the overdetermined visual logic of race, paving the way for surprising cross-racial, transnational musical exchanges.

Back in the United States, Carrie Rodgers's insistence that Jimmie and his music were Irish, Abbe Niles's bemusement at a white man who sounds black, folk song collectors' failure to recognize the significance of Rodgers's participation in a musical tradition understood as providing transparent access to the nature of "the Negro," and Lomax's insistence that his African American informant provide him with evidence of racialized musical difference all give voice to the anxiety about the boundaries between white and black that Du Bois identifies (in a later version of "The Souls of White Folk" that appeared in *Darkwater* [1920]) as underlying the "discovery of personal whiteness."[124] The resulting racialized thinking about cultural forms has proven remarkably resilient, and if anything the whiteness of country music is as likely to be perceived as self-evident now as it ever was. The challenge is not only to examine and correct the racist tautologies that delimit separate white and black musical spheres but also to treat seriously the musical evidence when we consider the overlap of music and other cultural forms.

CHAPTER THREE

Plantations, Prisons, and the Sounds of Segregation

In the previous chapters, we saw how the recordings John Lomax made of Blind Willie McTell in November 1940 reveal a history of minstrel fantasies of southern blackness that emerged in the post-Reconstruction South and a sophisticated engagement with these fantasies on the part of African American musicians in the twentieth century. We will pick up the story here with a set of recordings that Lomax made later the same day that he recorded McTell in Atlanta. The McTell recordings have been available for decades on a number of commercial LPs and CDs and have been widely discussed.[1] The master recordings—copies of Lomax's original acetate disks—are housed in the American Folklife Center at the Library of Congress. On the reverse side of the tape are unreleased recordings that Lomax made later that day in Cherokee County, about forty miles north of Atlanta. Among them are songs sung by a group of men identified in Lomax's notes as "Cherokee County Negro Convicts."

The first voice we hear on these recordings is Lomax's: "The songs on this record were sung by a group of boys on Cherokee camp—Cherokee work camp—near Canton, Georgia, on November 5, 1940, for the Folksong Archive of the Library of Congress in Washington." Informed that the men want to sing a spiritual, he asks them where they learned it. "Camp Morris was the leader of this song. Camp, where did you learn this song?" Lomax asks hopefully. Morris answers, "On the radio," to which Lomax replies, audibly disappointed, "On the radio? You didn't . . . It's not a Georgia song, then?" "No, it's not a Georgia song," Morris replies.[2]

Clearly, the song that Morris provides is not the kind of material Lomax was seeking. He explains his reason for visiting prisons and work camps like the one in Cherokee County in a 1933 report he wrote for the Library of

Congress: "Negro songs in much of their primitive purity can be obtained probably as nowhere else from Negro prisoners in State and Federal penitentiaries. Here the Negroes are completely segregated and have no familiar contact with the whites. Thrown on their own resources for entertainment, they still sing, especially the long-term prisoners who have been confined for years and who have not yet been influenced by jazz and the radio, the distinctive old-time Negro melodies."[3] Viewed from this perspective, the Cherokee camp recordings were a bust. While Jim Crow may have ensured that Morris and his men experienced "no familiar contact with the whites," the radio proved to be a powerful force that helped undermine the segregation and isolation that Lomax understood to be necessary for the preservation of "primitive" negro folk songs.

Undeterred, Lomax next records a solo performance by one of the men. Again he introduces the performer by name and the song by genre:

LOMAX: Amos Johnson is going to sing a blues. When do you sing this blues, Mr. Johnson?

JOHNSON: It's been seven, eight years ago [i.e., 1933 or 1934].

LOMAX: When would you sing it? When you're out in the field at work? Plowin'? What else would you do in the fields?

JOHNSON: I sung and plowed.

LOMAX: Sung and plowed? Did you pick any cotton?

JOHNSON: Yes, sir.

LOMAX: What did you sing when you picked cotton?

JOHNSON: "Cell Bound Blues." That was my favorite song.

LOMAX: Was it? That's a mighty slow song—you wouldn't pick much cotton singing that song, would you?[4]

Perhaps still struggling to overcome his disappointment at hearing a song from the radio rather than an indigenous folk song from Camp Morris's men, Lomax sounds none too enthusiastic about Johnson's choice, commanding simply, "All right. Sing it." He does, however, appear to know the song, commenting both on its slow tempo and on the fact that this tempo renders it unsuitable as an accompaniment for cotton picking. Given his request to McTell earlier in the day for "complaining songs, complaining about the hard times, and sometimes mistreatment of the whites," we might imagine Lomax's ears perking up as Johnson begins to sing, a cappella, a slow twelve-bar blues: "Hey hey jailor, tell me what have I done / Hey hey jailor, tell me what have I done / You got me all bound in prison, you say I killed that woman's son." Johnson's song appears to have all the attributes that Lomax seeks in a "complaining song"; it is in a musical idiom (the twelve-bar blues) widely understood as "negro," and it appeals to an oppressive white authority (the jailor) to complain of mistreatment (i.e., imprisonment and the withholding of the knowledge of the crime of which the song's narrator is accused). The second verse continues in a similar vein: "All bound in prison, all bound in jail / All bound in prison, all bound in jail / Oh, I'm bound for life, no one to go my bail." The third verse shifts from narration to make a pathetic appeal: "I got a mother and father, livin' in a cottage by the sea / I got a sister and brother, I wonder do they think of poor me." Here, it would seem, in the narrator's "poor me" is a prime example of the "self-pity" Lomax seeks in "complaining songs."

A clue to Lomax's disinterest appears in the sixteen-bar bridge that follows the initial three twelve-bar verses:

I walked in my room the other night
A man walked in and began to fight
I took my gun in my right hand
Told them folks I'm going to kill that man.

This sixteen-bar section is immediately followed by another:

When I said that I crossed my hands
First shot I fired, that man fell dead
The papers came out and told the news
That's why I said I got the cell bound blues.

As Lomax seems to be aware, something is amiss here, and the structural shift in the song from a twelve-bar blues to a sixteen-bar pop song form reveals that the song that Lomax lists in his notes alternately as "Cornfield blues" and "Cornfield holler" is in fact also not "a Georgia song" but, like the spiritual offered by the other men at the Cherokee camp, a popular song, one that Johnson too would have learned from the radio or phonograph. In this case, the song that Johnson sings in the fields is neither a traditional work song nor an improvised holler but rather a popular recording, "Cell Bound Blues," which Ma Rainey, one of the most popular of the first wave of female blues singers, had recorded in New York in October 1924 and released as the A-side of Paramount 12257. Her backing band for that session, credited to "Ma Rainey and Her Georgia Jazz Band," comprised members of Fletcher Henderson's orchestra, including Louis Armstrong—some of the most technically adept and forward-thinking jazz musicians of the day.

Johnson's rendition of the song is remarkably faithful to Rainey's, despite the fact that his is sung alone for a folklorist in a Georgia prison camp while hers is a professional recording with a world-class jazz orchestra. These two performances reveal a potentially interesting (for us) and discouraging (for Lomax) connection between a commercial recording by a female professional singer and the solo performance of a male southern rural laborer. Johnson's fondness for Rainey's recording disrupts the idea of "negro" folk songs, like the hollers Lomax seeks, as autochthonous products of African American laborers' connection with the southern soil. Instead, Johnson—a Georgia farm laborer—establishes an affinity with the disembodied voice and instrumental sounds put down in a New York studio and transmitted via phonograph record. Johnson adopts the music of the New York–based "Georgia Jazz Band" as his own, ironically fulfilling the promise of the group's name. How much more resonant must Rainey's song have appeared to Johnson, given its subject, when Lomax encountered him in hard labor at the Cherokee work camp. While we do not have a record of the particular crime for which Johnson was accused, convicted, and imprisoned, we nonetheless hear in his song a lament about the imprisonment of African Americans that links his experience with that of Rainey's fictional narrator. The hybrid twelve-bar/sixteen-bar form of "Cell Bound Blues" is echoed by its lyrics, which shift from rhetorical lament ("what have I done") to confession ("First shot I fired, that man lay dead"). It would be too simple, though, to read Johnson's fondness for Rainey's song as a product of the imprisoned condition he shares with the song's narrator. After all, it was his favorite song *before* his tenure in the Cherokee work camp ("It's been seven, eight years ago").

Bryan Wagner points out a similar instance from another of Lomax's song-hunting expeditions, a 1936 session at a Florida prison farm. There Lomax recorded a performance of a song he calls "I Been a Bad, Bad Girl," sung by an inmate named Ozella Jones.[5] Like "Cell Bound Blues," Jones's song is also based on a commercial recording (Ed Bell's "Bad Boy"), and like Johnson's performance, Jones's maintains a nearly word-for-word fidelity to the original.[6] Despite this fidelity, Lomax posits Jones's performance as antithetical to the commercial tradition represented by singers like Ma Rainey and Bessie Smith: "If Bessie Smith enthusiasts could hear Ozella Jones or some other clear-voiced Southern Negro girl sing the blues, they might . . . soon forget their idol with her brassbound, music-hall throat."[7] Lomax's editorial comment establishes the white folklorist as arbiter of black musical authenticity. Bessie Smith and her "enthusiasts" traffic in a counterfeit, corrupted form of the blues, one that has lost its connection with agricultural labor and social segregation. It follows from this argument, then, that the imprisoned black singer occupies something like a natural state for the production of black music, and the condition of imprisonment helps preserve the native conditions that allow uncorrupted negro folk songs to thrive. For Lomax, the connection between the segregated, agricultural South and authentic negro folk song is organic and natural. As he explains in his explication of Ozella Jones's song in *Our Singing Country*, a folk song anthology he co-edited with his son, Alan: "The blues, sung by an unspoiled singer in the South, sung without the binding restrictions of conventional piano accompaniment or orchestral arrangement, grow up like a wild flowering vine in the woods. Their unpredictable, incalculably-tender melody bends and then swings and shivers with the lines like a reed moving in the wind. The blues then show clearly their country origin, their family connection with the 'holler.'"[8]

What, though, are the conditions that produce an unspoiled singer of the blues, and what are the corrupting factors that threaten what elsewhere Lomax terms the "primitive purity" of African American folk songs?[9] Lomax details a number of concerns. First, the unspoiled blues are a distinctive product of the South, rendering suspect if not outright counterfeit performances by such performers as Ma Rainey and Bessie Smith, rural southerners' fondness for commercial records notwithstanding. While Rainey was Georgia-born and Smith was from Tennessee, Lomax valorizes singing by "an unspoiled singer *in* the South"; southern-born singers' performances were evidently adversely affected by northern environments, commercial recordings, and interracial audiences. Second, the blues should be sung without "conventional" instrumental accompaniment. However, the actual performance practices of the rural black musicians Lomax encounters do not necessarily adhere to this proscription. Both Amos Johnson's rendition of "Cell Bound Blues" and Ozella Jones's "I Been a Bad, Bad Girl" bear traces of their orchestrated, commercial antecedents. As Wagner explains, "Unlike the prototypical field holler, which was rhythmically free," these performances demonstrate a "relationship to the implied beat" of the commercial recordings they duplicate.[10] In both cases, the singers perform as though they imagine themselves singing with an invisible jazz orchestra, and indeed this would have been the case as they sang along with records by Rainey or Bell. Third, the blues should be unpredictable, rather than standardized, and rural rather than urban, thereby demonstrating a familial (i.e., racial) connection with the "holler," a form understood as ancestral to the blues, emerging from the conditions of plantation slavery and the economic servitude that followed under Jim Crow.

This vision of black musical authenticity is deeply conservative, in multiple senses of the word. It entails a static conception of authentic musical performance, in that the conditions for such performances must preserve the "primitive" conditions of rural and technological isolation that Lomax imagines allowed for the development of hollers and their descendants, the blues, in the first place. Such an understanding necessarily proscribes geographic, social, or economic mobility for African American musicians, and it likewise maintains racial segregation as a positive force in maintaining musical authenticity. While imprisonment in a segregated prison camp in the Deep South is about as undesirable a situation as can be imagined, for Lomax the grim conditions of such camps provided the ideal environment for the preservation of negro folk song. In a 1934 essay, "'Sinful Songs' of the Southern Negro," he explains that he and Alan sought songs of "the 'wor'ly nigger' . . . in their near purity among the most completely isolated Negro convicts, as well as on large, remote cotton plantations and in lumber camps." While prison camps provide the ideal collecting ground for Negro folk songs, other sites of isolated agricultural labor also help preserve the conditions of segregation and hard toil that Lomax understands as providing the ideal conditions both for the preservation of Negro folk songs and for the creation of new songs in the authentic mold of the old ones. Lomax continues: "The black convicts do not work or eat or sleep in the same buildings as do the white prisoners. They are kept in entirely separate units; they even work in separate fields. Thus a long-time Negro convict spends many years with practically no chance of hearing a white man speak or sing. Such men slough off the white idiom they may once have employed in their speech and revert more and more to the idiom of the Negro common people."[11]

Musical authenticity is here understood as being both preserved and reproduced through coercive racial segregation. Lomax lauds prison camps for their role in preserving not only specific Negro folk songs but also the conditions that allow for their authentic performance. By "slough[ing] off the white idiom" accrued under conditions of relative freedom, imprisoned African Americans revert to a more authentic blackness, "the idiom of the Negro common people." I would like to suggest that beneath this idea that authentic blackness can be preserved or recovered through near-absolute segregation lies an anxiety about the collapsing of racial difference that might otherwise follow from any breach of the color line. Lomax places this anxiety in the mouths of the singers of "a Negro song":

Niggers growin' mo' lak white folks.
Niggers growin' mo' lak white folks,
Every day.
Niggers learnin' Greek and Latin,
Niggers wearin' silk an' satin,
Niggers growin' mo' lak white folks,
Every day.[12]

Lomax doesn't gloss these lyrics, although he appears to read them as a lament for the gradual removal of barriers to social and economic mobility for African Americans. Understood from the perspective of the "Negroes" from whom he hears the song, however, they suggest a different interpretation. Their use of the racial epithet aside, a straightforward reading of the lyrics Lomax quotes suggests that far from lamenting the weakening of racial boundaries, they celebrate the fact that after centuries of slavery and decades of Jim Crow, African Americans in the twentieth century had begun to experience some gains, however modest, in access to education and material resources. By tying African American folk authenticity so closely to the oppressive conditions of Jim Crow segregation, Lomax's model of folk song itself ends up as simultaneously reactionary or even oppressive on the one hand and remarkably fragile on the other, threatened by any progressive change in the social or economic condition of African Americans in the South.

Nowhere is the equation of blackness and criminality more clear than in Lomax's descriptions of his most famous discovery, Huddie Ledbetter, aka Lead Belly. In Lomax's telling, criminality forms the core of Lead Belly's racial authenticity. In announcing their impending visit to the East Coast, Lomax proclaimed, "Leadbelly is a nigger to the core of his being. In addition he is a killer. . . . Penitentiary wardens all tell me that I set no value on my life in using him as a traveling companion." To this sensational claim, Lomax adds, wryly, "I am thinking of bringing him to New York in January."[13] Surely this is in part marketing ballyhoo, but the image Lomax constructs of Ledbetter as a violent, barely civilized, criminal music savant is consonant with his understanding of "negro" music as the product of an isolated, primitive, tantalizingly criminal class. Lead Belly, while remarkable in his range and repertoire, represents the unspoiled black folk musicians that Lomax sought in southern prisons.

While Lomax found plenty of material in southern prisons and labor camps, his disappointing visit to Cherokee County illustrates that the music of African Americans, even in the Deep South at the height of Jim Crow and among long-term inmates, was more diverse than he might have hoped. As the librarian at the federal penitentiary in Lewisburg, Pennsylvania, wrote in 1935 in response to Lomax's request for information concerning songs of the prisoners: "Regarding the question of songs and ballads desired by Dr. Lomax; I find no trace of such material here. The songs here are identically the same songs one hears outside of prison. It may be that men here have too short terms to be acquainted with the sort of material Dr. Lomax desires."[14] A similar situation appears to have obtained in Louisiana as well, as the superintendent of the federal jail in New Orleans wrote that same year: "I hear of no prisoners' songs in the New Orleans Federal Jail. . . . In fifteen years as executive head of prison institutions I have never met with any experience which led me to think prisoners, as a class, have musical appreciation which might be described, even roughly, as comparable with so-called folk songs." If anything, the New Orleans official is less willing than his Pennsylvania counterpart to countenance Lomax's theory, explaining: "If the idea of Dr. John A. Lomax regarding prisoners' songs is based on the idea that prisoners, as a class, are different from the general run of humanity in regard to musical taste, I think he will find his idea is not correct. People in prison are a cross-section of society, more nearly than they are any one classification. They have such songs as have the people outside of prisons, and for the same general reasons."[15] As he intuits, the superintendent's thoughtful description of the catholic musical tastes of prisoners in New Orleans is antithetical to Lomax's theory of racial and musical isolation.

Negro Folk Songs as Sung by Lead Belly, Lomax's 1936 account of his experiences with Ledbetter—from their meeting in another Louisiana prison to Ledbetter's release to their visit to the Northeast (including a tour of colleges and a performance at the 1934 Modern Language Association meeting) to their eventual falling out—is more revealing of Lomax's attitudes toward racial difference and musical authenticity than it is an objective account of Ledbetter and his music. It also provides a cautionary tale for what happens when an "unspoiled" singer of the South is uprooted and exposed to foreign sounds and the temptations offered by the relative freedom of the northern city. Lomax's narrative details his attempts and ultimate failure to police Ledbetter's musical choices and social behavior. At the same time that it paints a portrait of himself as Ledbetter's patron or protector, Lomax's story reveals his struggles to establish himself as Ledbetter's "boss" (his word), while the singer's resistance to the white man's control mirrors his gradual refusal to adhere to the rigid boundaries of racialized musical authenticity that Lomax prescribes.

Lomax imagines that Ledbetter—"a nigger to the core of his being" and "a killer"—poses a grave threat to him and his son: "The picture kept coming to my mind of Alan and myself asleep by the roadside in the swamps of Louisiana and Mississippi with this particular black man on his cot near by, and the prospect did not look attractive."[16] Although he qualifies the identification of the threatening "black man" with "this particular," it is nonetheless clear that Ledbetter's blackness is part and parcel of the threat he poses. It is also, though, key to his appeal as a singer of folk songs.

Ledbetter, too, is conscious of the role that his blackness plays in establishing his authenticity with his white audiences. As Lomax observes, "he never failed to delight his audience when he 'passed his hat' at the end of his program. Then he always became the smiling cajoling Southern darky minstrel extracting nickels from his 'White folks.'"[17] At the same time that he observes Ledbetter's "darky" act, Lomax seems unable or unwilling to countenance the idea that Ledbetter deployed a similar strategy in dealing with him. After a disagreement, for example, Lomax complains that "Lead Belly seemed but little like the pleasant, cheerful, helpful person he could be. His face was an ebony mask—glum, dour, and forbidding."[18] Ledbetter's inscrutability, his "ebony mask," is threatening and "forbidding," especially when contrasted with his demeanor at the start of their relationship. "Boss, here I is," Ledbetter announces. Lomax recollects: "I looked up from my newspaper as I sat in a hotel lobby in Marshall, Texas, on Sunday September 1, 1934, to see a Negro man standing timidly by my chair. He had touched my shoulder to draw my attention as he stood there, his face ashen with uncertainty and fear."[19] In Ledbetter's ashen, fear-stricken face Lomax sees what he perceives as a true vision of blackness, that is, confirmation of their prescribed social relationship under Jim Crow. Lomax is the "boss"; Ledbetter will become both his servant and his ward, although he ultimately resists both these roles.

Much as with his advocating Ozella Jones as an authentic original to Bessie Smith's commercial imitation, with Ledbetter too Lomax claims the role of arbiter of musical and racial authenticity. Ledbetter's repertoire was vast, as was his musical appetite, but Lomax strives to keep both within prescribed bounds. "Lead Belly," he explains, "born in 1885, in his early years escaped the influence of jazz, though his inheritance was rich from the Negro minstrel class. Even the 'blues' came later." The first part of this claim is dubious, but Lomax rightly notes that Ledbetter possessed command of a repertoire that included a range of styles other than the blues, many of which originated in the previous century. "[A]s a master of the dance," Lomax continues with some hesitation, "he has been forced to keep up, more or less, with the development of popular music."[20] For Lomax, these two roles—conservator of traditional "Negro" minstrelsy and master of popular music—are at odds. Ledbetter, by all accounts, did not share this view. Lomax observes, exasperatedly, that "[f]or his programs Lead Belly always wished to include 'That Silver Haired Daddy of Mine' or jazz tunes such as 'I'm in Love with You, Baby.'" Presumably Lomax is referring to "Honey, I'm in Love with You," from the 1925 Broadway show *Mercenary Mary;* Paul Whiteman's orchestra released an instrumental version that same year. The black man's playing Whiteman's music did not sit well with Lomax. "But in these he was only a poor imitator," Lomax continues, "though he could never understand why we did not care for them. We held him to the singing of music that first attracted us to him in Louisiana."[21]

Lomax's use of the verb "held" is unintentionally revealing, as it makes clear his role as master or warden of Ledbetter's repertoire. "That Silver Haired Daddy of Mine" was a hit in 1932 for singing cowboy Gene Autry; that Ledbetter never recorded it is a minor tragedy. Historian Karl Hagstrom Miller has unearthed Lomax's notes for *Negro Folk Songs as Sung by Lead Belly*, in which he goes into greater detail: "Many of the songs he sings do not appear in this volume because they are copyrighted. Prime examples are the yodeling blues and ballads of Jimmy Rogers [*sic*] of recent fame, whose ardent admirer Lead Belly still remains."[22] Jimmie Rodgers's relationship with black musical traditions is the subject of chapter 2 of this book; Ledbetter's ardor for his music is unfortunately only evidenced in the negative in Lomax's notes. Of Rodgers's "yodeling blues and ballads," Autry's sentimental pop song, and jazz tunes, Lomax observes bitterly, Lead Belly "sings them so vilely and with such little understanding that he himself cannot enjoy the performances."[23] This is a remarkable claim. Lomax does not merely assert that Ledbetter's performances of hillbilly, pop, or jazz tunes were poor imitations, but that Ledbetter himself was incapable either of understanding or of enjoying these "vile" performances. This claim goes a step beyond Lomax's positioning himself as an arbiter of black musical authenticity, suggesting that he is privy to an understanding of Ledbetter's intellectual and affective relationships to his own performances that Ledbetter himself lacks.

For all his concern with racial segregation as a force for the preservation of African American folk culture, Lomax's account of his relationship with Ledbetter makes clear that what is ultimately at stake is not absolute separation but rather maintaining the proper relationship between black and white. Lomax chastises Ledbetter for performing for other African Americans rather than for the white audiences Lomax has arranged for and from whom he collects payment. Lomax explains this relationship in terms of patronage: "I reminded him that I was trying to help him, that I had made only a few requests of him, and those for his protection in a strange country; that I wanted him to eat good food, to take plenty of rest, not to play and sing for groups of Negroes late at night."[24] Ledbetter, though, is defiant, as Lomax continues: "He silenced me by declaring resentfully that he knew exactly how to take care of himself. 'I ain't goin' to sing no mo' for you neither lessen I want to.'"[25] Once Ledbetter spends all his money, Lomax manages temporarily to reestablish his proper position of mastery, eliciting a penitent confession: "'I'se never goin' to sing for no bunch of niggers no mo'. . . . I always sings too loud an' too long.' Again he had been out the night before, singing for his own color," although Lomax soon realizes that, having tasted freedom, Ledbetter is no longer under his sway.[26] "I had lost control of my 'man,'" Lomax laments. "Never again would he have genuine respect for his 'boss.' For Lead Belly had disobeyed me and had 'got away with it.' He had defied me, and I had no recourse."[27]

In Lomax's account of his dealings with Ledbetter, the dissolution of their relationship mirrors in microcosm the disintegration of black folk culture as a result of shifting social and economic opportunities for African Americans. Ledbetter's repertoire and mode of performance remain authentic so long as they adhere to the strictures Lomax prescribes. Once Ledbetter sheds the musical and social conventions of the South, loses respect for and gets away with disobeying his "boss," he is no longer a representative of the black "folk." Transplanted to the northern city, Lead Belly is corrupted, not by contact with whites, but with blacks who have likewise escaped the oppressive prisons and plantations of the South.

Alan Lomax's Romance of the Color Line

John Lomax's son, Alan, was a junior partner in much of his father's work in the 1930s, and by the end of the decade Alan would assume the mantle of America's premier folklorist. Alan Lomax traveled to the Mississippi delta in 1941, where he recorded future blues stars Son House and Muddy Waters for the first time. Influenced by his father, Alan was intrigued by the notion of the Mississippi delta as a primeval musical environment where African traditions had taken root and blossomed outside the influence of whites and popular culture. His narrative, however, reveals a desire for aesthetic experiences that allow white listeners to traverse the color line and to access the secrets of African American life through the affective experience afforded by the blues. In setting out to document an African American experience born of isolation and social segregation, then, Alan Lomax unwittingly reveals the role that white fantasies of blackness play in both scholarly and popular understandings of the blues.

While Muddy Waters would later become a bona fide star thanks to a decades-long career as one of the undisputed originators and masters of the electrified Chicago blues style that served as one template for rock and roll, he first emerges in the musicological record as part of the Fisk University–Library of Congress Coahoma County Study, conducted by Alan Lomax, Charles Johnson, and John W. Work of Fisk and others in 1941 and 1942.[28] This trip in many ways marked a departure from the work Alan Lomax had begun with his father, exemplified by projects like *Our Singing Country* and *Negro Folk Songs as Sung by Lead Belly*. In *Lost Delta Found: Rediscovering the Fisk University–Library of Congress Coahoma County Study, 1941–1942*, Robert Gordon writes about the political complications of the Fisk–Library of Congress study, in particular the rather unsavory way in which Lomax appears to have wrested control of it from Work, the African American musicologist who first proposed the study.[29] In any case, the project was significant in that it entailed cooperation between white and black investigators and evidences an attempt to understand African American folk culture in a way that moved beyond the racialist stereotypes that infuse *Negro Folk Songs as Sung by Lead Belly* or John Lomax's interview with Willie McTell. As the Library of Congress's guide to *The Library of Congress–Fisk University Mississippi Delta Collection* attests, the project "was the first racially mixed field study in the Deep South." With significant understatement, it continues, "Racial tension was high in the Delta at the time of the study, and cooperation was necessary. . . . Lomax needed the help of black scholars to overcome racial suspicion and to facilitate rapport with informants."[30]

Lomax's retrospective account of the trip in his 1993 *The Land Where the Blues Began* presents a different vision of interracial collaboration, one in which Lomax forges an affective bond with his musical informants across the color line, pushing his African American scholarly collaborators to the margins. While the professed goal of the Library of Congress–Fisk University study is sociological and systemic, Lomax's account instead operates on an individual level. Central to his story is the romantic notion that the affective power of the musical performances he encounters and records allow for the temporary erasure of barriers of race and caste. Patrick B. Mullen argues that, in fact, Alan literally desired to be black; whether or not we accept this psychoanalytic conjecture, Mullen is certainly correct that for Lomax, as for "many other American white men in the nineteenth and twentieth centuries . . . [an] attraction to blackness . . . was . . . created out of imagining blackness and whiteness to be at opposite ends of a spectrum of pleasure and denial."[31]

As it turns out, the trip—despite significant conflict between Lomax and his collaborators—produced recordings that have been crucial to the story of African American vernacular music in the twentieth century. In addition to producing the first recordings of Muddy Waters, Lomax also recorded other important local musicians, notably Son House and David "Honeyboy" Edwards. By doing so, he helped craft a narrative about the delta blues that traced a lineage from House to Waters through Robert Johnson. A relatively marginal figure during his lifetime, Johnson became in the retrospective view of generations of (mostly white) blues aficionados the lynchpin of a delta blues tradition that came to represent the *ne plus ultra* of musical authenticity.[32] As Lomax himself recognized, the recordings he made of Waters, House, and their compatriots were not only important historical, sociological, and musicological documents; in many cases they were also works of breathtaking artistry and emotional power.

While Lomax's comprehensive narrative of the trip would not materialize until a half-century after his visit to the delta, his recordings of Son House and Muddy Waters helped establish the delta blues as a cornerstone of American popular music. Significantly, the embrace of House, Johnson, and Waters by popular music tastemakers helped import into popular culture longstanding folkloristic understandings of African American musical authenticity as the product of social and geographic isolation and the persistence of performance practices rooted in African musical traditions.

On its face, Lomax's endeavor was primarily a sociological one, as the description of the project from a memorandum he wrote for the Library of Congress attests: "The agreed upon study was to explore objectively and exhaustively the musical habits of a single Negro community in the Delta, to find out and describe the function of music in the community, to ascertain the history of music in the community, and to document adequately the cultural and social backgrounds for music in the community. It was felt that this type of study . . . would afford . . . an oral history of Negro music in the South over the past hundred years."[33] While Lomax aimed to document the contemporary performances of African American residents of the Mississippi Delta, he hoped that in doing so he would help unearth a "history of Negro music in the South" dating back to antebellum plantation culture and slavery. Alan Lomax's study, then, shares an undergirding premise with the earlier work of his father, namely, that the music of the African American folk in rural Mississippi was essentially conservative, tending to preserve rather than to innovate. This assumption links the plantations of the rural South to the prison camps in which Alan had recorded with his father. For John Lomax, segregated prison camps provided insulation from the corrupting influences of the radio, the phonograph, and jazz. In the younger Lomax's *The Land Where the Blues Began*, we see an extension of this idea of the prison farm as incubator of black tradition. For Alan, however, not only the prison but the entire plantation South serves as a carceral space, where segregation and the threat of racial violence work to maintain discrete racial musical traditions.

Lomax's *The Land Where the Blues Began*, a romanticized first-person account of his visits to the delta in the early 1940s, was finally published in 1993. Drawn from Lomax's recollections, field notes, and recordings, it describes his encounter with a rural African American community on the cusp of technological and social change. While on the one hand the Library of Congress–Fisk study aimed to document traditions that dated back to the antebellum period, it also provides a snapshot of a rural community enthralled by the commercial popular culture represented by such sophisticated urban performers as Count Basie, Fats Waller, and Louis Jordan and anxious (like the rest of the country) about the portents of the impending world war. Lewis Jones, one of the Fisk scholars involved in the joint Library of Congress–Fisk project, documented all the records on the jukeboxes in Clarksdale, Mississippi's bars. He found that these selections were overwhelmingly those of popular, nationally known artists like Basie and Waller, with only a few isolated local artists scattered among the big national acts.[34]

In interviewing and recording his African American informants, Alan Lomax follows in the footsteps of his father, seeking out musicians from isolated rural communities who provide access to otherwise obscure folk traditions. (Alan Lomax's first recordings of Muddy Waters were conducted less than a year after the session that John Lomax conducted with Willie McTell, discussed earlier.) At times the younger Lomax's voice on the recordings sounds much like that of his father as he asks Waters where he learned a particular song or about the circumstances of a tune's composition. To be sure, Alan is solicitous where John is often imperious; we hear none of the bullying or badgering that is so uncomfortably evident in the elder Lomax's questioning of McTell. Asking Waters about the genesis of his "Country Blues," Alan asks, "Tell me a little of the story of it, if you don't mind, I mean, if it's not too personal. I mean, I want to know the facts and how you felt and why you felt the way you did. That's a very beautiful song."[35]

Lomax is in control of the rhetorical and technological situation in his encounters with Waters and other delta musicians—he does, after all, quite literally control the means of production—but his gentle, respectful querying of his informants suggests a relationship between them that is quite distinct from the one between his father and Lead Belly or McTell, not to mention the "negro saloonkeeper" who first sang "Home on the Range" to the elder Lomax. There is nevertheless something discomfiting in his account in *The Land Where the Blues Began* that emerges from the uneasy position in which Lomax finds himself. The narrative takes great pains to point out Lomax's awareness of the oppressive effects of Jim Crow on the delta's black population. While Lomax himself ultimately enjoys the benefits of whiteness, his account of his interactions with both blacks and whites in Mississippi derives much of its narrative tension from moments in which Lomax appears to have breached the color line. In many cases, this crossing of racial barriers appears in a positive light, as his African American informants accept Lomax into the social and musical fold. Just as important, though, are moments in the narrative in which his consorting with "negroes" renders him suspect in the eyes of the law. Lomax's project, finally, attempts to strike a delicate balance between an affective bond with African American performers that allows him, through the shared structure of feeling the blues provides, to both transcend the color line and cross back across that line, thereby reasserting the privileges of whiteness and escaping the strictures of Jim Crow.

This combination of an affective desire for blackness and the social danger that this desire elicits structures *The Land Where the Blues Began*. In the first paragraph of the preface, Lomax tells us, "A hundred years ago only blacks in the Deep South were seized by the blues."[36] The blues in this formulation is both a musical style ("a way of singing") and "a state of being" that emerges from the uniquely oppressive social conditions faced by African Americans in the Deep South as slavery and Reconstruction give way to Jim Crow at the end of the nineteenth century. The blues as musical form, in other words, is indissociable from the social circumstances from which it emerged. It is what Raymond Williams defines as "a structure of feeling," a set of "social experiences *in solution*, as distinct from other social semantic formations which have been *precipitated* and are more evidently and more immediately available."[37] That black folks in the South "were seized by the blues" as both a way of singing and a structure of feeling suggests something of the violence inherent in this solution of social experiences. For Lomax, likewise, the affective experience of the blues brings with it a concomitant sense of danger.

In the preface's second paragraph, Lomax explains, "In order to hear the blues, when I was very young, my girlfriend and I slipped into the black ghetto of my Southern hometown under the cover of darkness. If we'd been caught there, we would probably have been expelled from the university."[38] Doubtless there is something thrilling and illicit in the young Lomax's slipping with his girlfriend "into the black ghetto . . . under cover of darkness." To do so subjects them temporarily to the danger that the ghetto's black inhabitants experience as a matter of course. While the threat of expulsion from the University of Texas may seem laughable compared to the legal, physical, and psychological threats that Jim Crow posed for African Americans in the 1930s, it does nonetheless seem to represent a conceptual breakthrough for Lomax, as his slipping into the ghetto to hear the blues offers him his first inklings of the affective power of black musical expression. In fact, Lomax argues throughout the preface that the experiences of African Americans under Jim Crow placed them at the vanguard of twentieth-century American culture. "[A]ll of us," he explains, "are beginning to experience the melancholy dissatisfaction that weighed upon the hearts of the black people of the Mississippi Delta, the land where the blues began."[39] The blues, then, both render audible the souls of black folk and provide an affective conduit between black and white.

Remarkably, though, the possibility for cross-racial sympathy and understanding that Lomax celebrates derives not only or even primarily from interpersonal contact, but rather via the technological mediation of the phonograph. The portable recording machines that he and his father used on their song-collecting trips "gave a voice to the voiceless."[40] But beyond a vehicle for self-expression by his black informants, the phonograph too provided Alan with a tool with which to actively access the feelings of blackness that these musicians kept so closely guarded from whites. "Bit by bit," he explains, "I learned to use these early machines to probe into the singers' feelings. . . . Every time I took one of those big, black, glass-based platters out of its box, I felt that a magical moment was opening up in time. Never before had the black people, kept almost incommunicado in the Deep South, had a chance to tell their own story in their own way."[41] As with the trips to the ghetto to hear the blues, these exchanges are also emotionally intense, even eroticized, as Lomax probes black consciousness and handles the "big, black" acetate records with such care and awe.

At the same time, he is aware that perhaps his interviewees did not sufficiently appreciate the opportunity to "tell their own story in their own way," that the color line which separated them from him produced too much static interference. "It was clear," Lomax writes, "that Southern blacks would not readily confide in a white folklorist. Therefore, I approached Fisk University, the Princeton of black colleges, with the idea of doing a joint field study with my department at the Library of Congress."[42] As Gordon and Nemerov make clear, the available documentary evidence does not support this origin story for the Fisk–Library of Congress collaboration, as Fisk's John Work had already begun such a field study before Lomax became involved.[43] Regardless of its factual accuracy, Lomax's account demonstrates an awareness of the problem that the color line posed for his project. Employing African American scholars as collaborators provides one solution to this problem. *The Land Where the Blues Began*, though, suggests another, as it narrates Lomax's attempts to cross the color line himself, to access the heart of blackness that resides in the desperately poor, violently segregated Mississippi delta.

The narrative proper begins with the first chapter's description of Lomax's trip to Memphis, which would serve as a base for his Mississippi collecting trips (Memphis is in Tennessee, of course, but culturally it is the capital of north Mississippi). Immediately he encounters the trouble to be expected for a white man who makes a habit of disrespecting the color line. "[E]ven after having been snubbed, lectured, arrested, and once or twice shot at," he explains, "I still persist in plunging straight for the bottom where the songs live. . . . When I returned to the South in 1942, after a long absence, I made the same mistake and ran straight into trouble."[44] The trouble he runs into is an unexpectedly metastasized version of Jim Crow, one that would deny equal access not only to black southerners but to a white visitor like Lomax. Arriving in Memphis, he recounts, "I walked as if I owned the place. I drove straight to Beale Street and strode into the Monarch saloon."[45] A southerner by birth and raising ("Texas born and bred," he explains), Lomax expects to exercise the privileges of whiteness and to be accommodated by African Americans in a black-run establishment. Instead he finds that, unlike during a previous visit, when the black barman "sail[ed] into action" to serve him, Jim Crow segregation had instead closed off both lanes of interracial social interaction—prohibiting not only black access to white culture but vice versa as well. The barman points to a sign that explains emphatically, "THIS IS A COLORED PLACE. / NO WHITES SERVED. / SORRY," and explains in dialect that borders on minstrelsy that Memphis powerbroker and two-time mayor "Mister [E. H.] Crump say, 'If we gonna segregate one way, we gonna segregate the other.' Yesir, that old gun got two wrong ends now, and you looking straight down the other one!"[46] Grousing that the man "didn't look sorry," Lomax rues the "crazy logic and double injustice" of the situation. He wanders down Beale Street, searching in vain for a black "barman who agreed with me that this new regulation merely multiplied the insanity of the old barrier between whites and blacks," and disconsolately finds himself excluded from "the dance halls and bars where the fun was going on." He concludes this disappointing episode, astonishingly, with the assertion that he had finally "learned what it was like to be a black man in the wrong part of town."

I don't mean to be overly critical of Lomax, whose desire for cross-racial empathy is clear and laudable, but the idea that the consequence of being "a black man in the wrong part of town" in Jim Crow Mississippi is exclusion from "fun" is jaw-dropping. What, then, should we make of this assertion, especially given Lomax's longstanding commitment to civil rights and social justice, his keen awareness of the pernicious effects of Jim Crow? The answer, I think, tells us much about the decades-long project that *The Land Where the Blues Began* documents. Lomax's experiences in the Delta serve as a template for the effect of the blues on the racial and social perceptions of its white listeners via the affective experience of shared injury and sympathy that Lomax's account models. For Lomax, finally, the emotional power of the blues stems from its ability to give whites affective access to the shared structure of feeling that conditions black life in the delta. His own encounters with both the white-dominated power structure and its black victims provides him with privileged access to this structure of feeling, setting the stage for the affective experiences that later listeners will have as a result of hearing the records he makes. In the narrative's first pages, he experiences the epiphanic realization of "what it was like to be a black man" under Jim Crow.

This is only the first part of the story, however, as he soon hears the blues that will assuage this injury and supplement his newfound racial knowledge. "A very thirsty hour later," he continues, "I heard two guitars in quiet conversation behind the screen door of a tailor shop. I didn't dare open the door or say a word. I just leaned against the wall to listen as a whiny, rather humorous tenor voiced my own sentiments."[47] Chastised by his newfound realization that his whiteness does not fully immunize him from the effects of Jim Crow, Lomax no longer "walk[s] as if [he] owned the place," but rather dares neither to open the door nor to speak. Instead, having been humbled in this way, he attunes his ears to hear the black musicians he has discovered, whose music does not merely entertain but instead engages in "quiet conversation," promising secret knowledge that Lomax hopes to access and understand. In fact, he discovers that he is already primed to receive this knowledge, as the black singer he overhears "voice[s] [Lomax's] own sentiments," which the narrative renders as the lyrics to the standard "East St. Louis Blues": "*I walked all / The way from East St. Louis, / From East St. Louis here, / And I got nobody / No one to feel my care.*"[48]

Unlike the unsympathetic black barman who gleefully if perversely acts as an agent of segregation, the musicians Lomax encounters behind the door invite him to cross the color line through the act of listening. One of the men, Willie Brown, who wears "a big black Stetson on his ruff of kinky hair" and a smile on "his black face," asks, "Whyn't you come in where you can hear better, mister?"[49] Lomax's attention to Brown's putatively African physiognomy (he will later describe his "long oval Sudanese face") and Brown's use of the honorific "mister" to refer to the white stranger both suggest that the two men remain sensitive to the color line and the social strictures of Jim Crow, but the invitation itself violates these social and racial barriers. With this invitation the stage is set for a cross-racial musical exchange that will circumvent the structuring cultural logic of Jim Crow. Significantly, however, this interracial musical experience is interrupted by the police, rendering in literal terms the policing of the color line that I discuss throughout this book. As Lomax recounts:

A powerful flashlight shot its beam in my eyes and then played over the faces of my friends.

"What the hell is goin on over there?" said a cracker voice.

"The blues," I yelled.

"Easy, mister," Willie B. whispered. "That police is pointin his gun over here."[50]

The police interrogate Lomax, accusing him of "'Sociatin with niggers," and advising him (somewhat nonsensically, since his African American associates are evidently Mississippi natives) to "take all this nigger crap back where [he] came from." Lomax attempts to show the police documentation of his mission from the Library of Congress, only to be rebuffed with "That ain't no Memphis permit, . . . that's a damn Washington permit."[51] Finally concluding that Lomax and his companions are "a white tramp with a coupla goddam nigger vagrants," the police order the presumed vagrants to disperse and prompt Lomax to visit city hall to get right with the local authorities. "As a Southerner, you ought to understand," a city worker explains, "[o]ur labor is being corrupted. Agitators putting wrong ideas in their heads. . . . They're gettin so uppity, it's dangerous for a white man to go to Beale Street after dark. Some boys down there would kill you for five dollars."[52] He offers to arrange for a plainclothes police escort to keep Lomax safe from threatening blacks, but of course the folklorist declines, instead rejoining his black companions and escaping the city to the relative freedom of a dance hall "in the middle of an enormous Arkansas cotton field."[53]

Clearly, the police and city hall functionaries treat Lomax differently than they do Willie Brown and the other African American musicians whose company renders Lomax suspect. If the musicians invite Lomax to cross the color line, the whites with whom Lomax interacts compel him to reaffirm a racial and geographical identity, not only as white, but also as a southerner. Lomax faces a paradox, then: in order to be free of the harassment and persecution that awaits "nigger lovers" under Jim Crow, he must disavow his cross-racial affiliations and affirm the privileges of southern whiteness. Opting instead to pursue his project, Lomax flees both the city of Memphis and the state of Tennessee, seeking interracial musical experiences in rural Arkansas and the Mississippi delta. Paradoxically, Lomax sees the action of police as solidifying, rather than threatening, the cross-racial affective bonds he is attempting to forge. "The Memphis police had," he writes, "in a few brutal words, swept aside the barriers of shyness and superiority that, as a Southerner, had cut me off from black singers. I saw that, if I could be normally civil out of sight of the 'law,' I could learn from them much that I wished to know."[54] In Lomax's telling, the actions of the police had enabled him to breach the color line, enabling him to forge an extralegal affective bond with black southerners.

A similar scene occurs when Lomax travels next to Tunica, Mississippi. Discovering that the Tunica County sheriff is similarly unimpressed with his institutional credentials, Lomax explains that he "came from Texas and was descended from a long line of Southerners, with two grandfathers who fought on the right side of the rebellion."[55] Again Lomax relies on an intraregional racial solidarity to escape the consequences of his fraternizing with blacks. The sheriff likewise again invokes concern for Lomax's safety and in the same breath decries interracial sociability. Bearing out Lomax's earlier experience, the "normally civil" interactions between him and the black Mississippians he records render him suspect in the eyes of the law. "Now we come to something I can't really believe, now that you tell me that you were raised in the South," the sheriff declares. "I heard you shook hands with a nigger! Is that so or not?" "Oh, no sir, you know I'd never do a thing like that," Lomax replies, "Why, if my family were to hear of my doing that, I reckon they'd disown me." Temporarily mollified, the sheriff offers a peculiar gesture at rapprochement: "Understand, I sympathize with what you're trying to do. There's nobody likes to hear niggers singin as much as I do. You say we've got some talented niggers here in Tunica? . . . What're their names?"[56] Lomax obliges this seemingly benign request, only to find again that his "normally civil" behavior violates the racial protocols of the delta. He refers to one of his musician friends as "Mister Son House," and the use of the honorific spurs the sheriff into near apoplexy. Their own intraracial bond severed as a result of Lomax's faux pas, the sheriff first considers jailing Lomax as an agitator before electing instead to expel him from the county. Angered and chastened, Lomax departs Tunica for Coahoma County, where he encounters a young McKinley Morganfield, aka Muddy Waters, who would eventually escape the delta, move to Chicago, and help electrify the blues. We will return to Alan Lomax's initial recordings of Waters and his romantic visions of the southern plantation at the end of this chapter, but first I want to examine Waters's involvement with a later plantation fantasy, one that sheds a surprising light on the one Lomax provides in *The Land Where the Blues Began.*

Muddy Waters and *Mandingo's* Plantation Fantasy

Mandingo, director Richard Fleischer's 1975 film adaptation of Kyle Onsott's 1957 pulp novel, provides an infamous contemporary reimagining of antebellum plantation life.[57] With its catalog of horrors—incest, rape, torture, infanticide, and all manner of racial violence among them, including the boiling alive of its protagonist, not to mention the taboo of interracial sex—the film spares no opportunity to shock and offend. Lots of viewers have taken the bait; Roger Ebert famously gave the film an unprecedented zero-star review, calling it "racist trash, obscene in its manipulation of human beings and feelings."[58] On the other hand, visual artist Kara Walker has on more than one occasion cited the film as a touchstone for her own provocative explorations of race and the representational legacy of slavery, suggesting that despite or even because of its prurient sensationalism, *Mandingo* offers a useful lens with which to approach the cultural legacy of plantation slavery and its lingering presence in the American cultural imaginary.[59]

Indeed, *Mandingo* represents a turning point in pop cultural representations of plantation slavery. The film's poster art parodies that of *Gone with the Wind*, pointedly undermining the racist nostalgia of that earlier cultural icon, promising to reveal the violence and degradation that underlies the romantic myth of the Old South and Margaret Mitchell's hugely influential and remarkably enduring reimagining of it in the 1930s. At the same time, the exploitative and borderline pornographic aspects of the film pave the way for outright pornography, and *Mandingo* lends its name both to a contemporary male pornographic actor and to a subgenre of interracial porn. It's surprising, then, given *Mandingo*'s arguably justified reputation as semipornographic "racist trash," to hear in the film's opening credits the voice of McKinley Morganfield, better known as Muddy Waters, the Chicago blues legend, singing a twelve-bar blues composition, "Born in This Time." To my mind, at least, there's something unsettling about hearing Waters's voice in this context. What is he doing giving voice to this perverse, exploitative plantation fantasy? Part of the answer is probably financial exigency: Waters's wife had died in 1973, and he assumed custody of some of their many children. In other words, the man had mouths to feed. (A similar circumstance seems to have motivated the participation of James Mason, who plays Warren Maxwell—the plantation's patriarch—as well: he reportedly told an interviewer that he needed money for his alimony payments, although Ebert opines that "surely jail would have been better.")

The first sounds we hear over the film's opening credits consist of a hummed melody that starts on B and resolves on E, establishing the key of the song to follow. What follows is a standard twelve-bar blues in E, sung by Muddy Waters, accompanied at first only by two banjos—one playing rhythm, the other lead. (The voice that we hear humming at first also seems to be Muddy's, but the voice's timbre is different, and it sounds like it was recorded separately from the other vocals.) The lyrics lament the condition of enslavement:

I was born in this time to never be free
Born in this time to never be free
Waited all my time for freedom, now
It's too far up a hill to me
All my feelin' is all I ever owned
Yeah, you know my feelin' (now) is all I ever owned
Well, you know happiness is one thing
I have never known

And so forth. The lyrics are deliberately vague. In what time, exactly, was the song's narrator born? The antebellum South that provides the film's setting? The 1970s, when the story is told? Or the Jim Crow South in which McKinley Morganfield was born in 1913? By using Muddy Waters's distinctive voice as a framing mechanism, the film collapses these time frames, suggesting a continuity between the film's antebellum setting and the twentieth-century context that the blues provides.

The song that Waters sings, "Born in This Time," deliberately collapses nineteenth- and twentieth-century musical aesthetics. The song follows a prototypical twelve-bar blues pattern—with a I–IV–I–V–IV–I chord progression and *aab* lyric structure—made familiar (or even cliché) by decades of blues compositions, beginning around 1912 with W. C. Handy's "Memphis Blues" and Lee Roy White's "Nigger Blues."[60] The recording's instrumentation, on the other hand, is atypical, substituting banjos for the usual combination of guitars, horns, or harmonica. The result is a sort of musical anachronism, whereby the twentieth-century blues form is sounded in a nineteenth-century idiom, the banjo evoking both blackface minstrelsy and African American folk music predating the blues. We might understand the film's featuring Muddy Waters's voice as a legitimizing gesture—the blues is a genre whose reception is grounded in notions of a racially based authenticity, the stamp of which Waters's singing provides the film. On the other hand, we should not too hastily attribute "Born in This Time" to Muddy Waters. Indeed, he evidently had no hand in composing the song. The music is by the film's soundtrack composer, Maurice Jarre (who had won an Academy Award in 1965 for his score for *Doctor Zhivago*), with lyrics by Hi Tide Harris, a California-born blues performer who would also record music for the soundtrack to Gordon Parks's 1976 *Leadbelly* biopic. By the end of the song's second verse, the initial banjo accompaniment is supplemented by Jarre's orchestra, comprising strings, brass, piano, woodwinds, and percussion. As the narrative begins, "I Was Born in This Time" fades out, and for the most part the rest of the film is accompanied by an orchestral score. The melody to "Born in This Time" persists throughout the film, though, providing a key instrumental motif in the score.

One distinctive characteristic of Muddy Waters's musical style is the elasticity of its sense of rhythm and time (a source of difficulty for some of his accompanists); as Waters explains, "My blues look so simple, so easy to do, but it's not. They say my blues is the hardest blues in the world to play."[61] This claim is born out in "Born in This Time," and we hear a tension between the rhythmic flexibility of Waters's style and the rigid time of Jarre's orchestration, particularly in the first verse. The changes come more quickly and precisely than we would expect from Waters's other performances, and he seems to rush his vocal delivery to keep up. Waters was only marginally literate, and his then-manager, Scott Cameron, maintains that this difficulty resulted from the problems Waters had reading the written lyrics to the song: "[I]t required all his effort and he could not simultaneously comprehend the words."[62] Waters's voice emerges from the score at two other points in the film—once an hour and half into it when Hammond Maxwell (the scion of the plantation) leads a band of dejected slaves whom he intends to sell in New Orleans, and again at the end of the film, after its violent dénouement. By the film's close, Waters's vocals have settled into the strict time of the orchestration while the song's lyrics finally give way to wordless humming that echoes the short melody with which the film begins. Waters's vocal performance, then, both frames the narrative and serves as a sort of chorus, punctuating key moments in the plot. By its third iteration during the closing credits, the divide between Waters's performance and the film's score collapses, as his performance of "Born in This Time" merges with Jarre's orchestral score.

I think it's fair to assume that Waters's presence in the film's soundscape is meant to evoke a sense of authenticity that is grounded both in race (blackness) and place (the rural plantation South). The conflation of the twelve-bar blues and *faux*-folk instrumentation, meanwhile, suggests that this racialized southern plantation setting is timeless, divorced from modernity. If Muddy Waters's voice is the key element to the soundtrack's desired effect, the filmmakers could have simply licensed an existing recording. The fact that they did not do so and that Waters instead actively contributes to the soundscape of the imaginary antebellum southern setting created by the film compels us to pay greater attention to his role in the film. By 1975, when *Mandingo* was released, Muddy Waters was a well-established international star, hero to a generation of blues-influenced rock and roll musicians on both sides of the Atlantic (the Rolling Stones, for example, borrowed their name from the title of one of his songs). He was also one of the key progenitors of the rhythmically complex, electrified, full-band Chicago blues style—a thoroughly modern, urban style very different from his performance in *Mandingo*. With his performance on the film's soundtrack, then, McKinley Morganfield is playing a role—that of world-weary bluesman giving voice to an oppressed class—that draws on his persona as Muddy Waters but nonetheless sounds in a different register than his usual role as urbane bluesman. At the same time, Waters's lending his voice to this late-twentieth-century reimagining of plantation life suggests that we should revisit the role that earlier conceptions of the plantation play in the creation of Waters's persona.

Lomax begins his account of his first recording session with Muddy Waters by emphasizing their shared southern identity. "It was barefoot time in the South," he recalls, "and [Waters] was barefoot, so I had an excuse to follow my Southern raising and shed my own shoes."[63] The first song they record is "Country Blues," which Lomax understands both as an exemplary delta blues piece and as something more. One the one hand, it is "a blues track that literally made pop history" by inspiring imitators like the Beatles and the Rolling Stones, who in turn would bring "about a revolution in Tin Pan Alley."[64] This three-and-a-half-minute field recording unleashes a previously unrealized pop potential, one that would afford legions of white musicians and listeners the cross-racial affective experience that so enraptures Lomax. On the other hand, "Country Blues" and Waters's other "pieces were more than blues" for Lomax in another way as well: "they were love songs of the Deep South, gently erotic and sentimental."[65]

Waters's first song, he recalls, "began with a murmurous tenderness, the slide guitar echoing the melancholy and sensuous syllables" of his singing.[66] Lomax carefully traces a genealogy from Son House's "Gypsy Blues" to Robert Johnson's "Walking Blues" that culminates in "Country Blues," in which he claims to hear a blues-pop hybrid.[67] That he holds up such a hybrid as a positive development marks a difference between Alan's conception of folk authenticity and that of his father; it may also be the product of hindsight, as Lomax publishes his account after a half-century of popular music history has elapsed. At the same time, in Lomax's telling, Waters's music is defined not only by its artistry or relation to a local musical tradition but also by its sensuality, its blackness, and its status as a product of "the Deep South"—volatile ingredients in the southern imagination.

Lomax emphasizes Waters's plantation background; the singer tells him that after his mother died, he and his grandmother "settled way out in the country, where there wasn't another house in sight. . . . I've been pretty much brought up on this plantation, lived here for the last nineteen years."[68] The questionnaire Waters's family filled out for the Fisk investigators, Lomax continues, "paints a stark picture of a sharecropper family in a brown four-room shack in the middle of a cotton field."[69] While in Lomax's account Waters is an authentic if exceptionally talented product of the delta, he also acknowledges Waters's desire to escape the delta by using his music as a ticket to the urban North and the relative freedom of Chicago. The affective power of his music, which Lomax is the first to record, provides Waters a way out, while at the same time it affords access to the emotional world of the twentieth-century plantation to white audiences for whom the experience of black life in the delta is foreign.

"[T]he main theme" of Waters's music, as Lomax sees it, is "submerged hostility toward women."[70] "Muddy's songs were loaded with his mistrust of women, his dependency on them, his need to control them. His muleskinning holler was a truly violent fantasy," Lomax asserts, based on such lines as *"I'll take my .32-20 . . . and lay you in your grave."*[71] We hear in this line in particular echoes of earlier songs, notably Robert Johnson's "32-20 Blues" (itself derived from Skip James's "22-20 Blues") and Jimmie Rodgers's "Blue Yodel," which one contemporary reviewer described as "particularly blood-thirsty" (as discussed in chapter 2).[72]

Lomax appears to be sincerely interested in Waters as an individual, but his assessment of the themes of Waters's music unwittingly echoes an often unsavory branch of racial psychology practiced by earlier folklorists such as his father (who maintained that "negro folk-songs [could] afford an insight into the negro mind") and Newman Ivey White.[73] In the headnote to a chapter entitled "Songs About Women" in his *American Negro Folk-Songs*, for example, White maintains that insights into a general "Negro" character can be gleaned from the lyrics of songs sung by African American laborers; "in his songs about women," writes White, "the modern folk Negro reveals the most unpleasing side of his nature. What slight traces of deference and affection are shown by a few songs . . . are obscured by the dominant tone of brutal selfishness."[74] Many of the songs he collected for his anthology, White avers, "are unprintable, as crude and filthy as brutal tastes could make them."[75] In an earlier essay, White is even more bluntly disapproving of what he imagines to be the moral character of the African American singers whose songs he has collected: "In the songs of an ignorant folk-group we need not look for love songs of too much delicacy. . . . From what is generally known about his laxity in sexual matters, we need not expect his songs about women to constitute a very pleasant exhibit."[76]

Despite their political differences, Alan Lomax's treatment of Muddy Waters's music as at the same time sensual and misogynistic, pop-savvy and rooted in the delta faintly echoes the portrait White paints. While for White the supposed violence and cruelty of blues and work songs illustrated the general psychology of a stereotyped caricature of rural African Americans (what in a particularly cringe-worthy phrase White calls "that buoyant and invincibly likeable person, the illiterate Southern 'darky'"), Lomax is careful to point out the delicacy, sensitivity, and individual artistry of Waters's performances.[77] Nonetheless, his conception of Waters's music is permeated both with a sense of violent sexuality and a romantic racialism that ascribes to Waters's modern twentieth-century blues aesthetic characteristics that Lomax describes as "patently African."[78]

Later, Lomax describes encountering Waters during the Poor People's March on Washington in 1968, which he describes as a confluence of black folks "from the slums of Midwestern cities" and, colorfully if implausibly, others who had come from "the Deep South in wagons pulled by mules."[79] The performance that Lomax describes hearing from Waters's band is very different from the sensitive, "gently erotic and sentimental" one he had recorded in 1941. Instead, the music is rhythmic, forceful, and loud, "amplified by big speakers so every crying note, every beat, could be heard a quarter mile away."[80] Waters's music, having helped give birth to rock and roll, here has absorbed its aggression and electric amplification. (The same year, Waters released *Electric Mud*, an experimental fusion of Chicago blues and psychedelic rock.) Despite this aesthetic transformation, though, for Lomax Waters's group is "far more African than any jazz band—an orchestra built around singing, highly rhythmic yet subtly supporting and amplifying the vocal part, going back through Son House to the one-stringed diddley-bow, to the very roots of African-American music in Mississippi."[81]

By 1975, when *Mandingo* was released, Lomax's understanding of Waters's music as charged both with sexuality and authentic blackness had become axiomatic, largely through the imitations and adaptations of Waters's music by white acts like the Rolling Stones and Led Zeppelin (the latter band's first two albums included recordings of songs penned by Willie Dixon, a longtime collaborator of Waters). *Mandingo*, too, presents a fantasy of African American sexuality, although it ultimately charges the white slaveholding class with the sexual immorality that White, for example, ascribes to black folk. The film's depiction of plantation slavery is a grim antipastoral; Falconhurst, the fictional Louisiana plantation where most of the film is set, does not grow cotton or any other agricultural crop but rather makes its money by breeding slaves, which the plantation owners treat as commodity livestock. In some cases enslaved blacks are mated to each other like prized livestock, but the film also depicts the systematic rape of enslaved women by the plantation's men, in particular Hammond Maxwell, Falconhurst's lame scion, who exercises a sort of plantation *droit de seigneur* in raping the plantation's virgins and fathers many of Falconhurst's slaves. The metaphorical impotence suggested by his crippled leg extends to his refusal to have sex with Blanche, his cousin and wife; this refusal is in part due to his revulsion at her having had sex with her brother and in part to the fact that "he wouldn't know what to do with a white lady." In retaliation both for Hammond's neglect and his seemingly romantic relationship with Ellen, an enslaved woman, Blanche forces Mede, Hammond's prized fighting slave—selected for his pure "Mandingo" West African blood—to have sex with her. She later gives birth to a black baby, and the film ends in an orgy of violence, as the infant and Blanche are poisoned, Hammond boils Mede alive, and Warren Maxwell is shot by Agamemnon, his formerly faithful house slave.

The film's apocalyptic ending not only depicts the collapse of Falconhurst but also the systematic dismantling of the racist stereotypes of plantation romance. The film depicts the supposedly sexually wanton black "wenches" (to use the film's term) as victims of sexual violence at the hands of white men; the loyal, docile house servant becomes an agent of black vengeance; the sexually pure white woman (whose very name, "Blanche," suggests both racial whiteness and moral purity) is revealed as a sexual predator; and most importantly we see the virile, violent, "buck" Mandingo slave as an unwilling object of whites' pornographic fantasies. Blanche's rape of Mede upends the image of the violent black rapist, and his murder at Hammond's hand reveals the myth of black male virility as a projection of white male impotence. *Mandingo*'s seemingly exploitative trafficking in racial and sexual stereotypes of the plantation only to undermine and explode them provides the narrative context for Muddy Waters's performance of the film's theme song.

I suggested earlier that the filmmakers likely included Waters's music in the film to lend it an air of authenticity. But in fact he and the film may be working at cross-purposes here. Waters's participation in *Mandingo* instead helps reveal the artificiality of plantation mythology. "Born in This Time" is cut from a different cloth than the raucous, electric, thoroughly modern music Waters had perfected over the course of a decades-long career; it is an artificial simulacrum of folk authenticity, one that, like *Mandingo* and the plantation romances the film parodies, ventriloquizes white fantasies of rural southern blackness rather than expressing a racialized folk culture. In doing so, it helps us better appreciate the role that white fantasies of black folk life play in the work of such folklorists as John and Alan Lomax. Like Willie McTell in his performances for John Lomax, Waters plays a prescribed role as an avatar of southern black folk culture, but does so in a way that suggests an awareness of the constructedness of that role. Both musicians mirror back white fantasies of black folk authenticity and at the same time reinvent and transform folk traditions in novel ways. The next chapter examines in more detail the related work of African American artists, writers, and intellectuals to reclaim a usable folk tradition from the stereotyped representations that both folklorists and the culture industry had established.

CHAPTER FOUR

The New Negro Looks South

In *The Souls of Black Folk* (1903), W. E. B. Du Bois describes the arrival of the first Africans in America:

> [S]treaming from the death-ship and the curving river is the thought of the older South,—the sincere and passionate belief that somewhere between men and cattle, God created a *tertium quid*, and called it a Negro,—a clownish, simple creature, at times even lovable within its limitations, but straitly foreordained to walk within the Veil. To be sure, behind the thought lurks the afterthought,—some of them with favoring chance might become men, but in sheer self-defence we dare not let them, and we build about them walls so high, and hang between them and the light a veil so thick, that they shall not even think of breaking through.[1]

More precisely, Du Bois's concern here is not primarily actual African people but rather the "thought" or idea of the "Negro." Writing at the turn of the twentieth century, Du Bois identifies this idea of the "Negro" as a *"tertium quid"*—as neither beast nor fully human, defined through a fictional but nevertheless absolute and unbreachable difference from whites—with the system of plantation slavery upon which the New World's economy was based. Its legacy would define the mind-set of "the older South" whose passing Du Bois celebrates but whose cultural effects persist into Du Bois's time and into our own.

As Du Bois suggests, this "older South" predates the United States and extends beyond its current borders. The culture of slavery extends from the west coast of Africa to the Caribbean to the United States, from the mid-seventeenth-century establishment of the plantation colonies that transformed the transatlantic economy to a few years before Du Bois's birth. Its cultural effects, of course, have lasted much longer and are still manifest in a whole range of cultural forms. Paul Gilroy, for example, argues succinctly that "black musics . . . , produced out of the racial slavery which made modern western civilization possible, now dominate its popular cultures."[2] While granting Gilroy's point that these musical forms are the products of "the racial slavery" that begat modernity, I have endeavored throughout this book to complicate the identification of them as simply "black" (or "white," for that matter) by paying attention to the interracial dynamics—often coercive and exploitive, but productive nonetheless—that helped produce them. The "black" musics that Gilroy mentions—ragtime, blues, jazz, rock and roll, reggae, hip-hop, etc., as well as white-identified forms such as country and bluegrass—are all decidedly impure, hybrid forms. None of them could have come into being outside the realm of cross-cultural, multiracial, and transnational contacts that have characterized the culture of the Americas since its inception, and all bear the marks of this heterogeneous origin.

While the thrust of Du Bois's argument in *Souls* has to do with the relationship of "the Negro" to America as a whole—"to merge his double self into a better and truer self. . . . to be both a Negro and an American"—the passage quoted above highlights the importance of the South to this project.[3] In *Souls*, Du Bois reckons with the legacy of slavery, the failed promises of emancipation and Reconstruction, and the promise of industrialization to the nation in general, and to the South in particular. *Souls* combines strands of cultural nationalism with a keen understanding of the significant role that interracialism plays in forging twentieth-century American identities. In "Of the Sons of Master and Man," for example, Du Bois avers that "we have in the South as fine a field . . . as the world affords" for the study of the contacts and interrelations of white and black, "the sons of master and man" of the chapter's title.[4] And he famously declares in his chapter on "The Sorrow Songs": "They came out of the South unknown to me, one by one, and yet at once I knew them as of me and mine."[5] Du Bois's emphasis on the South's centrality to struggles over black identity in *Souls* sets the stage for African American intellectuals' attempts to grapple with the legacy of the South's history to conceptions of black people and the music associated with them, from slave songs to minstrelsy and the popular music that followed.

"Strange Harmonies"

The Autobiography of an Ex-Colored Man, James Weldon Johnson's 1912 novel, tells the story of a musician who moves back and forth across the color line. The son of a light-skinned African American woman and a white father whom he but dimly recollects, the future ex-colored man travels at an early age from his native Georgia—where he was "born in a little town . . . a few years after the close of the Civil War"—to Connecticut, where as a child he lives an existence free of the burden of black life under Jim Crow.[6] This raceless existence cannot hold, of course, and the nameless protagonist is jarringly initiated into an understanding of racial difference at school. He at first experiences this initiation into knowledge of his racial identification as a traumatic act of violence: "Like my first spanking," the narrator recalls, "it is one of the few incidents in my life that I can remember clearly."[7] Music in the novel functions as salve for this traumatic experience of racial difference, and throughout the narrative the ex-colored man alternately gravitates to and flees from the U.S. South, which serves in his imagination—as it does for so many of the other figures discussed in this book's previous chapters—as a repository for an authentic, racially defined folk music tradition, one that the ex-colored man eventually hopes to cultivate and refine into high art, reclaiming his own African American cultural heritage in the process.

The concerns of Johnson's novel and of his narrator are remarkably prescient, and they anticipate debates concerning the relationships of music, race, and nation that would animate the New Negro Renaissance of the 1920s.[8] Several of the narrator's pronouncements concerning spirituals and ragtime appear nearly verbatim in the novel and in the preface to Johnson's *The Book of American Negro Poetry* (1922), which is itself a foundational text for the New Negro Renaissance. What are we to make of the nearly identical ideas articulated first by the novel's nameless protagonist and a decade later by Johnson, who was then the head of the NAACP? How does the ex-colored man's ambivalence about his own racial identification and the relationships of racial and national identities with musical forms influence his theories of music and race? To what extent do Johnson's understandings of these same questions overlap with those of his fictional narrator? To answer these questions, we need to understand both the narrative context in which the ex-colored man elaborates his musicological ideas as well as the larger cultural context in which Johnson himself participates. In the novel, the narrator's statements concerning music and race are imbricated with discussions of African Americans' relationship to the nation as a whole, and to the South in particular. The ex-colored man literally embodies these conflicts, as he attempts to position himself first as an American in Europe and secondly as a "negro" in America through his musical activities.

The narrator's first experience with music, in the novel's opening chapter, involves his mother "pick[ing] out hymns" from a songbook or, alternately, playing by ear "simple accompaniments to some old southern songs which she sang."[9] The narrator recalls that he would "annoy her by chiming in with strange harmonies" and wryly recalls that he "had a particular fondness for the black keys."[10] Importantly, these early descriptions of hymns and "old southern songs" are not racialized, and they ventriloquize the narrator-as-young-boy's preracial perspective, as at this stage in the narrative he has not yet been initiated into the world of racial difference. The "strange harmonies" he plays prefigure the racial ambiguity with which he struggles throughout the narrative, and his "particular fondness for the black keys" anticipates the presumably racial aptitude that he hopes to harness as he embarks on his musical career. The "old southern songs," though, are—significantly—as yet unraced. Whether they are African American spirituals or the sentimental antebellum fantasies of blackface minstrelsy, for the narrator-as-child, they are neither black nor white but rather "southern." The future ex-colored man's initiation into the racial order of Jim Crow arrives by the end of this first chapter as he is identified as "colored" in a traumatic incident at school. Confronting his mother with this new information, he asks, "Tell me, mother, am I a nigger?" "No, my darling," she replies, "you are not a nigger; . . . If anyone calls you a nigger, don't notice them." The narrator continues: "But the more she talked the less I was reassured, and I stopped her by asking, 'Well, mother, am I white? Are you white?' She answered tremblingly, 'No, I am not white, but you—your father is one of the greatest men in the country—the best blood of the South is in you—.'"[11]

This is a complex scene, but perhaps most significant here is the narrator's mother's absolute refusal to countenance "nigger" as a valid racial category. If her son's self-conception at this point in the narrative is preracial, hers is something else—maybe proto-postracial—as she resists the identification the epithet would bestow upon her and her child. Her relationship to the racial category of whiteness is more vexed; whiteness appears to be unavoidable—at least in the negative—as she reluctantly tells her son, "No, I am not white." In attempting to describe her son's identity, however, she substitutes a logic of region for one of race: "the best blood of the South is in you." The problem this opening chapter sets up is explicitly Oedipal, and that Oedipal drama plays itself out later in the novel as the narrator encounters his white father and half-sister in Paris. At the same time, while it does not explicitly disavow the racial logic of Jim Crow, the novel's opening chapter complicates the cultural logic of segregation and suggests that the South—ironically, given what happens later in the novel—offers the possibility for racial identities and cultural productions that frustrate the binary logic of black and white.

After his initial encounter with knowledge of racial difference, the narrator travels first from his Connecticut home to Atlanta and then to Jacksonville, where he is initiated into what he calls "the freemasonry of the race."[12] As he travels first to New York—where he first hears and soon masters the exciting new music of ragtime—and then to Europe, his identity becomes increasingly dissociated from the racial logic of Jim Crow. Meanwhile, an encounter with a German pianist inspires him to move beyond playing ragtime pieces and "ragging" classical music. As he recalls, the German musician "seated himself at the piano, and taking the theme of my ragtime, played it through first in straight chords; then varied and developed it through every known musical form. I sat amazed. I had been turning classical music into ragtime, a comparatively easy task; and this man had taken ragtime and made it classic."[13] This encounter prompts the ex-colored man to resolve to do the same: "The thought came across me like a flash.—It can be done, why can't I do it? From that moment my mind was made up. I clearly saw the way of carrying out the ambition I had formed when a boy."[14] He sets out "to go back into the very heart of the South, to live among the people, and drink in my inspiration first-hand. I gloated over the immense amount of material I had to work with, not only modern ragtime, but also the old slave songs,—material which no one had yet touched."[15]

Despite his assertion that ragtime and slave songs comprise an untapped resource, the fictional ex-colored man is not alone in this endeavor. As the renowned Czech composer Antonín Dvořák explained in 1893: "I am convinced that the future music of [the United States] must be founded on what are called Negro melodies. These can be the foundation of a serious and original school of composition, to be developed in the United States. These beautiful and varied themes are the product of the soil. They are the folk songs of America and your composers must turn to them."[16] Dvořák is but the most famous example, as such a project was attempted by such African American composers as Henry T. Burleigh, William Grant Still, and John Wesley Work, each of whom put into practice—with varying degrees of success—the idea that Johnson's narrator describes. For the ex-colored man, this project is personal, racial, and national in scope. By translating the folk music of African Americans into the idiom of "classic" symphonic music, he attempts to bring African American music to the fore of the larger musical culture of America, while at the same time reconciling the two halves of his personal identity— the legacies both of what he later calls his "mother's people" and that of his absent white father.[17]

The ex-colored man's ambition is thwarted, however, when, having returned to the South to gather African American folk music for his compositions, he witnesses the horrific spectacle of a black man being lynched and burned. As he recounts the experience: "A great wave of humiliation and shame swept over me. Shame that I belonged to a race that could be so dealt with; and shame for my country, that it . . . should be the only civilized, if not the only state on earth, where a human being would be burned alive."[18] His shame—like his musical ambitions—also manifests at the levels of the individual, the racial, and the national, as his personal shame expands first to shame for his race, then for his country. The narrator's emphasis on his own emotional state ("humiliation and shame") highlights the importance of affect to his musical ambitions. The shame elicited by the horror of the lynching is an inversion of the ecstasy that music provides him. While the affective experience that music provides promises to forge a transcendent multiracial identity, lynching destroys this possibility by violently reinforcing the racial logic of Jim Crow. The lynching, and his response to it, prompt the ex-colored man to cross back across the color line, this time permanently. This abandonment of his idea of forging a "universal," classical music from southern, "negro" folk material, and his crossing the color line to live as white, forsaking his "birthright for a mess of pottage," are central to plot of the novel.[19] The narrator's goal of personal and racial reconciliation with the nation as a whole is short-circuited by an act of racial violence.

But while the ex-colored man abandons this project, James Weldon Johnson does not. And this brings us to the passages I alluded to earlier, which appear nearly verbatim in Johnson's 1912 novel and a decade later in his preface to *The Book of American Negro Poetry*. Echoing both Dvořák and Du Bois, Johnson in the preface argues "that the Negro . . . [is] the creator of the only things artistic that have yet sprung from American soil."[20] As evidence for this claim, he lists the same four examples that the ex-colored man offers to "refute the oft-advanced theory that [African Americans] are an absolutely inferior race": "the Uncle Remus stories, collected by Joel Chandler Harris"; "the Jubilee songs" (the ex-colored man's term) or "the 'spirituals' or slave songs" (in Johnson's later reformulation), "to which the Fisk [Jubilee] Singers made the public and the skilled musicians of both American and Europe listen"; the cakewalk; and ragtime. For the ex-colored man, "[t]hese are lower forms of art, but they give evidence of a power that will some day be applied to higher forms."[21]

The repetition of this material from the *Autobiography* in the 1922 preface is intriguing for a couple of reasons. First is the simple fact that Johnson and his novel's narrator occupy radically different political and social positions. The ex-colored man's musicological excursus appears in the context of his book-length apologia for crossing the color line, forsaking "his birthright for a mess of pottage," as the novel concludes.[22] A decade later, when he publishes *The Book of American Negro Poetry*, Johnson is a prominent

African American political and cultural leader—the head of the NAACP and a leading figure in the emerging New Negro Renaissance. Their positions, in other words, could hardly be more different. Nevertheless, both argue that the Uncle Remus stories, spirituals, ragtime, and the cakewalk demonstrate African Americans' contributions to the culture of the nation and the world. The stakes of their arguments too are remarkably similar: for the ex-colored man, these cultural contributions "refute the oft-advanced theory that [African Americans] are an absolutely inferior race," while for Johnson, these artistic productions are important because "[t]he world does not know that a people are great until that people produce a great literature and art. No people that has produced great literature and art has ever been looked down upon as distinctly inferior."[23]

Second, I think it's important to recognize the very different position of African American vernacular music in the public consciousness in 1912 (when the novel was first published anonymously), 1922 (when Johnson published *The Book of American Negro Poetry*), and 1927, when the novel was republished under Johnson's name. Johnson's writings, from *Autobiography* to *The Book of American Negro Poetry*, mark a transition from one conception of African American vernacular music to another. His valorizing the "Jubilee songs" as a uniquely American cultural form echoes W. E. B. Du Bois's assertion in *The Souls of Black Folk* that "[t]here is no true American music but the wild sweet melodies of the Negro slave. . . . [A]ll in all we black men seem the sole oasis of simple faith and reverence in a dusty desert of dollars and smartness." Du Bois asks rhetorically, "Will America be poorer if she replace . . . her vulgar music with the soul of the Sorrow Songs?"[24]

Johnson's work, like Du Bois's, responds to a century of minstrelsy, attempts by white authorities to deny the existence and importance of African American culture, and an emerging culture industry that expropriated and exploited the musical creations of African Americans. The critical status quo engendered by the confluence of these factors centered around two mutually contradictory but nonetheless coextensive claims: that African Americans had no musical culture on the one hand, and that actual performances by African American musicians attested to the innate inferiority of "the negro" on the other. By the 1920s the cultural form that spoke loudest against this double-bind in the popular imagination was no longer spirituals, but jazz.

That Johnson as well as such key figures in the New Negro Renaissance as Alain Locke remained invested in the spirituals well into the 1920s and 1930s, long after jazz and the blues had supplanted the spirituals as paradigmatic forms of black musical expression, indicates the difficulty inherent in their attempts to resolve the contradictions that underlay popular and scholarly conceptions of African American musical culture. For writers like Du Bois, Johnson, and Locke, the spirituals represent an antithesis to the calumnies of blackface minstrelsy and to the commercially motivated musical interracialism manifested in the products of the culture industry. For all three writers, the spirituals are both racially characteristic of "the negro" and fundamentally American. This conception of the spirituals wed aesthetics to an ideology of race, nation, and class. At stake are questions of origins and the direction of the spirituals' aesthetic development. Locke, like Du Bois, works to define the spirituals as distinctly African American—the product of the unique experience of Africans and their descendants in the United States—and calls on the "spiritual kinship" that "the Negro musician" holds with this tradition to help guide their development into an art music.[25] In his chapter on "The Sorrow Songs" in *The Souls of Black Folk*, Du Bois identifies "[t]en master songs, more or less . . . of undoubted Negro origin and wide popular currency, . . . particularly characteristic of the slave."[26] Such songs, which in their "primitive" forms are racially characteristic, are subject to elaboration and development by sympathetic musicians, black and white. "Side by side" with such positive development, however, "has gone the debasement and imitations— . . . a mass of music in which the novice may easily lose himself and never find the real Negro melodies."[27]

Locke draws on Du Bois's description of the development and corruption of the sorrow songs in his prescription for those who would seek to elaborate them into orchestral forms. The composer seeking to develop African American folk materials into formal art music faces a quixotic set of restrictions: "So long as the peculiar quality of Negro song is maintained, and the musical idiom kept unadulterated, there is and can be no set limitation."[28] The contradictions evident in this prescription are daunting, as Locke calls for folk forms to be developed into more formally complex, refined distillates (with the symphony as the ultimate goal) while keeping "the musical idiom . . . unadulterated." Before such a project could even begin, though, the spirituals would first have to be reclaimed from those who would deny that African Americans played a leading role in their creation.

Spirituals in Black and White

In the midst of a heated argument among a group of black intellectuals in Wallace Thurman's 1932 novel, *Infants of the Spring*, a fictionalized treatment of Harlem during the previous decade's New Negro Renaissance, Cedric Williams, a prominent African American poet, proclaims that "[t]o talk of an African heritage among American negroes is unintelligent. . . . Your primitive instincts among all but the extreme proletariat have been ironed out. You're standardized Americans."[29] Another member of the salon, Carl Denny, counters by invoking Countee Cullen's well-known poem "Heritage," summarizing that "Negroes are the only people in America not standardized. The feel of the African jungle is in their blood."[30] Williams dismisses this response as "a pretty sentimental fiction" and twists the knife by claiming that the "spirituals are mediocre folk songs, ignorantly culled from Methodist hymn books."[31] The question of the racial significance of the spirituals is invoked earlier in Thurman's novel when another character, who aims for a career as a concert singer despite his unremarkable talent, refuses to sing spirituals because he has "no relationship with the people who originated them."[32] He goes on to dismiss them as "bastard bits of doggerel" and disclaims such cultural materials as antithetical to his artistic and social aspirations, declaring, "I'm no slave and I won't sing slave music."[33]

The sentiment that Williams asserts in Thurman's novel—that the "spirituals are mediocre folk songs, ignorantly culled from Methodist hymn books"—serves primarily as an opportunistic, incendiary jab at the romantic racialism of appeals to "African" blood, but his provocative assertion recapitulates arguments that had been raging among black intellectuals and their white antagonists and allies since the previous century. It echoes, for example, the claims of George Pullen Jackson, who published several articles and two books maintaining essentially this claim. In "The Genesis of the Negro Spiritual," which appeared in H. L. Mencken's *American Mercury* in 1932 (the same year that Thurman's novel was published), Jackson argues that the spirituals were derived exclusively from nineteenth-century Methodist camp meeting songs. Drawing on other academic scholars such as Newman Ivey White and Guy B. Johnson, Jackson purports to provide "proof of the essential identity of the camp-meeting songs and the Negro spirituals."[34] The idea that both African American spirituals and religious songs associated with whites derive in part from integrated camp meetings is itself uncontroversial; the central question at stake is what Jackson calls the "direction of the influence": black to white or white to black. According to Jackson, the former possibility is allowable only due to "[t]he inertia of faith."[35] Jackson insists that the alternative that he proposes (that the "direction of the influence" is unidirectional, from white to black) is, by contrast, motivated not by prejudice but rather by hard musicological evidence. Ironically, he continues, suggestions that religious songs sung by white people may have had their origins in the songs of African Americans are motivated by prejudice against poor whites. He explains that "the professional Southerners of big-plantation presumptions . . . would do anything to lower the stock of the poor white trash, and were thus willing to discount their black retainers' indebtedness to their upland white neighbors."[36]

In previous chapters, I discussed how in the 1920s and 1930s ethnic English, Anglo-Saxon, and Irish identities were invoked to account for the exotic modal and rhythmic elements not only of the folk music of whites but of blacks as well, at the same time denying the possibility that whites could have adopted musical practices originated by African Americans. Jackson invokes a version of this argument here, arguing that "the whites of the mountains and the hard-scrabble hill country" were (like African Americans) also "musical and oppressed." Their status as a "natively musical and sorely oppressed race," Jackson explains, accounts for the plaintive beauty of their songs.[37] With this move, Jackson thus rather audaciously appropriates and ascribes to whites the discourse of musicality as a racial trait borne of suffering established by writers like Frederick Douglass and W. E. B. Du Bois and developed by James Weldon Johnson and Alain Locke.

This controversy concerning the racial significance of the spirituals helps structure New Negro Renaissance theories of the relationships between race and art. For Alain Locke, "[t]he Spirituals are . . . the most characteristic product of Negro genius to date"; furthermore, "the ultimate destiny" of "the song of the Negro" is recognition as "America's folk-song."[38] In this idea, Locke echoes W. E. B. Du Bois's famous assertion that "the rhythmic cry of the slave . . . stands to-day not simply as the sole American music, but as the most beautiful expression of human experience born this side of the sea."[39] Williams's jibe in *Infants of the Spring* challenges both parts of this assessment, disclaiming both the beauty that both Du Bois and Locke attribute to the spirituals and, even more trenchantly, disavowing the spirituals' status as what Du Bois calls "the greatest gift of the Negro people."[40] For Williams (as for Jackson), the spirituals, far from "the rhythmic cry of the slave"—sublime artistic expressions of racial oppression and a longing for freedom—are instead imperfect appropriations of songs originated by whites, and passed on to African Americans at Methodist revival meetings. In disavowing both the spirituals' artistic merit and their status as products of a racially defined folk, Williams seeks to undermine a project of African American cultural expression based on such folk sources. A key aim of much of Johnson's and Locke's writings on race and music is to counter claims like Williams's (and White's and Jackson's) and to legitimate a theory of musical expression as a racial product.

The view that Williams and Jackson espouse was one that, by the time of Thurman's novel, had been debated for three decades. Dena Epstein identifies Richard Wallaschek as the first influential advocate of the position that the spirituals were appropriated wholesale from existing white sources. Wallaschek's assessment of the slave songs in his *Primitive Music; an Inquiry into the Origin and Development of Music, Songs, Instruments, Dances and Pantomimes of Savage Races* (1893) anticipates not only the general claim but also the specific language of Williams's objection: "I cannot think that these [songs] deserve the praise given by the editors [of William Francis Allen's 1867 *Slave Songs of the United States*], for they are unmistakably 'arranged'—not to say *ignorantly borrowed*—from the national songs of all nations."[41] Wallaschek opines that "these negro songs are very much over-rated, and . . . as a rule they are mere imitations of European compositions which the negroes have picked up, and served up again with slight variations."[42] Tellingly, Wallaschek had never traveled to the United States, nor had he heard the music he describes. His analysis is based entirely on transcriptions of slaves songs in Allen's volume and on Edwin P. Christy's *Plantation Melodies*, a volume of minstrel songs. Crucially, Wallaschek "draws no distinction between minstrel songs and spirituals."[43] Nevertheless, his assessment would go largely unchallenged for a decade.

Du Bois's "The Sorrow Songs," in *The Souls of Black Folk*, may be read productively as a corrective to the line of thinking exemplified by Wallaschek. In response to claims that, in effect, African Americans had no musical culture—that African American music was merely a pale imitation of European sources—Du Bois argues instead that, not only were the spirituals (which he rechristens "Sorrow Songs") a distinctive product of African Americans under the conditions of slavery, but that, "as the sole American music," this music constituted a basis for a national musical culture that transcended its racially specific origin. Du Bois famously asserts that the sorrow songs constitute "the singular spiritual heritage of the nation and the greatest gift of the Negro people."[44] But what precisely is the nature of this gift? While on the one hand affirming a racialist logic that would attribute the sorrow songs to "the Negro people" as a whole, Du Bois at the same time deftly insinuates "the Negro" into the very core of "the nation." In effect, he sets up a dialectic in which a strategic racial essentialism serves as one term and cross-racial affinity as the other. This dual construction enables Du Bois to counter the racist accusation that the songs of "the Negro" were "ignorantly borrowed" from those of Europeans by positioning them instead as "distinctively Negro," and at the same time to deny Wallaschek's insistence that the distinctiveness of African American performance practices points to a hierarchical racial difference that affirms white supremacy.[45]

Du Bois's understanding of the sorrow songs allows for the aesthetic autonomy of African American cultural forms while simultaneously insisting upon the consanguinity of blacks and whites within a national framework.

"Actively we [African Americans] have woven ourselves with the very warp and woof of this nation," Du Bois writes, "we . . . mingled our blood with theirs. . . . Our sound, our toil, our cheer, and warning have been given to this nation in blood brotherhood."[46] From the perspective of historians like Wallaschek, who would seek to deny African Americans the creative capacity to develop original musical forms, the "gift of the Negro people" represented by the sorrow songs is in fact a Trojan horse, a means to breach the wall that barred African Americans from what Du Bois called "the kingdom of culture."[47] In reconceiving the diverse songs of southern slaves as a unified body of sorrow songs, Du Bois places the music of African Americans at the center of the cultural life of the United States. This move both validates African American cultural expression and displaces the stereotyped representations of blackface minstrelsy that occupied a central place in the nineteenth-century racial imaginary.

As Locke would later, Du Bois exhibits an anxiety about the ever-present threat of the debasement, contamination, and racist expropriation of this music. He laments that "[c]aricature has sought again to spoil the quaint beauty of the music, and has filled the air with many debased melodies which vulgar ears scarce know from the real."[48] In this concern, too, Du Bois subtly refutes Wallaschek, who conflates the folk songs of African Americans (Du Bois's sorrow songs) with the "so-called negro-songs" of the minstrel stage.[49] Du Bois maps out diverging forms of development for the "primitive" music of African American slaves: the degrading appropriation of black music by white parodists in the form of minstrelsy and coon songs on one hand; their formal distillation and development by such choral groups as the Fisk Jubilee Singers and respectable composers like Stephen Foster on the other. The difference between "debased melodies" and "the real," then, is not simply a question of folk purity versus aesthetic transformation, since both the Fisk Singers and Foster transformed and arranged their source materials for different audiences. Neither is the music's authenticity strictly bound by the race of its arrangers and performers. Du Bois cites Foster's appropriation of "whole phrases of Negro melody" approvingly as a final step in the development of the slave songs into a refined artistic product at the same time that he disparages "many of the 'gospel' hymns."[50] Locke shares with Du Bois this valorization of the musical output of an idealized folk coupled with a suspicion of the politically and aesthetically compromised productions of actually existing black folk.

In "The Sorrow Songs," finally, a strategically deployed romantic racialism serves as a corrective to Wallaschek's insistence that African Americans lacked the capacity for musical invention, but Du Bois's racialism is coupled with an idea of emotional transparency that allows for an affective response to the sorrow songs that transcends the color line. Crucial to his intervention is the idea that both the aesthetic beauty and the meaning of the slave songs are audible to white listeners: "these weird old songs" are the means through which "the soul of the black slave spoke to [white] men."[51] Not only does "the true Negro folk-song" live on "in the hearts of the Negro people," but also, crucially, "in the hearts of those who have heard them truly sung."[52] For Du Bois, the sorrow songs elicit an affective response across the color line that affirms the humanity of African Americans by establishing their affinity with the nation as a whole. This dual identification of the sorrow songs as at the same time distinctively "Negro" and characteristically American is Du Bois's key intervention into the ongoing musicological conversation about African American folk music. Henry Edward Krehbiel, whose *Afro-American Folksongs* (1914) is a keystone text for Locke's later musicological undertakings, explicitly invokes Du Bois's "The Sorrow Songs" in his chapter on "Songs of the American Slaves." "Why are not the songs of the American negroes American folksongs?" he asks rhetorically. "Can anyone say?"[53] For Krehbiel, the spirituals are fundamentally "American folksongs," just as Du Bois's chapter on the sorrow songs is exemplary "'American' prose."[54]

While Krehbiel's appreciative reading of Du Bois points to *The Souls of Black Folks*'s influence on musicological thinking, the work of Newman Ivey White illustrates the recalcitrant racism of the critical mainstream. George Pullen Jackson's claim that African American music was derived wholesale from white sources represents one part of the racist double bind that Du Bois and Locke work to escape; White's arguments that "Negro folk songs" attest to African American inferiority represents the second. White's "Racial Traits in the Negro Song," published in 1920, reveals its prejudices up front, as it purports to derive from an examination of collections of African American folk songs "a few of the characteristics of that buoyant and invincibly likeable person, the illiterate Southern 'darky.'"[55] White rejects as "demonstrably false" the contention that the spirituals represent "the negro's expression of suffering under slavery and of his joy at liberation." Indeed, "[o]ne does not find so much pathos in these songs as they are conventionally supposed to possess."[56] To account for this misapprehension, White insists on a disjuncture between the musical properties of slave songs and their emotional content: "a strain of supposed melancholy is a common property of folk-songs everywhere and does not always reflect a melancholy mood."[57]

White emphatically denies the emotional transparency that Du Bois and Krehbiel ascribe to the spirituals; rather than offering a means through which the soul of the black slave could speak to sympathetic listeners, for White, slave songs instead attest to African Americans' emotional simplicity and sensuous atavism. At the outset of his piece, White outlines a quasiscientific methodology: "[S]urely we may regard a large body of negro songs as fit material out of which may be evolved some conclusions as to the lives and characters of the singers."[58] The songs of a folk group, in this conception, serve as a window into the character of that group. Almost immediately, though, this method is revealed as tautological. To counter the idea that the supposed "melancholy" of the spirituals' musical form speaks to an emotional melancholy or despair, White argues that "the negro, outside of his songs, is not of a brooding and pensive disposition."[59] Rather than deriving "the negro's" character from an analysis of his songs, in other words, White analyzes the songs through the lens of racial stereotype. For White, as for Wallaschek, analysis (almost exclusively textual, not musical) of "negro songs" reveals the character of "the negro." Unsurprisingly, the character thus revealed is, White proposes, that of "the illiterate Southern 'darky'" (i.e., a minstrel stereotype). Ignoring the warning that Du Bois had issued almost two decades earlier, White willfully conflates caricatures and "debased melodies" with actual African American folk songs.

While Locke follows Du Bois and Krehbiel in his valorization of the spirituals as keystones of African American cultural expression, he ultimately suggests that his readers look elsewhere to find an accurate representation of the "racial traits" that musicologists such as White claim to derive from a mixture of folk songs and the products of minstrelsy. Locke does not reject the racial essentialism that links such disparate thinkers as Wallaschek, Du Bois, and White—in fact he embraces it—but at the same time he differentiates the "New Negro" from the "Old Negro" of stereotype: "a stock figure perpetuated as an historical figure partly in innocent sentimentalism, partly in deliberate reactionism."[60] While White would argue that the characteristics of "the negro" could be accurately discerned from the products of minstrelsy, Locke counters in his foreword to *The New Negro* that "[w]hoever wishes to see the Negro in his essential traits, in the full perspective of his achievement and possibilities, must seek the enlightenment of that self-portraiture which the present developments of Negro culture are offering."[61] Despite this confident declaration, however, "the present developments of Negro culture" would pose their own challenges for advocates of the New Negro.

Popular Melodrama and the Culture Industry

White's assertion that the caricatures of minstrelsy accurately reflect the "racial traits" of "the illiterate Southern darky" points to the legacy of a century of minstrelsy, which strongly colored the reception of African American artistic production by the 1920s. The deeply ingrained presence of the minstrel show—the "stock figure" of the "Old Negro"—in American popular culture helps account for Locke's and other New Negro Renaissance–era figures' complex and ambivalent relationships with the products of the culture industry. This ambivalence is key to understanding Locke's influential conception of the relationship between musical authenticity and racial identity. Locke's ideas about this relationship, which he painstakingly worked out in a series of writings spanning more than a decade, center on the racial significance of vernacular musical forms. In "The New Negro," his introductory essay to the 1925 volume of the same name, Locke issues a hopeful proclamation concerning the New Negro's emancipation from the racist conventions that had constrained representations of African Americans in popular culture and literature since the previous century. In so doing, Locke aims to supplant the image of the mythical, sentimental figure of the "Old Negro" with that of the "New Negro," whose artistic and political representation would be self-defined and free of the minstrel overtones of the old. Locke aims to exorcise the stereotyped figure of the "Old Negro" with the literary project inaugurated by *The New Negro:* "The day of 'aunties,' 'uncles,' and 'mammies' is . . . gone. . . . Uncle Tom and Sambo have passed on. . . . The popular melodrama has about played itself out, and it is time to scrap the fictions."[62]

These fictions proved to be remarkably persistent, however, much to the chagrin of Locke and other cosmopolitan black intellectuals. Eugene Gordon, writing in the *American Mercury* in 1928, laments:

> Most of the Aframerican's native attributes—the inclinations, talents, tastes, preferences, prejudices and predilections that an All-wise Creator implanted in him—are fast oozing out of him. Standing in the glare of Caucasian ridicule, he has become sensitive, secretive, and hypocritical, and full of inhibitions—in fact, a sad Freudian case. He is afraid to be seen eating a pork chop, or even a wing of fried chicken. The sight of a watermelon sets him to blushing. When he sings his spirituals, it is in an affected and "artistic" manner: the old innocent gusto is gone.[63]

As Gordon's criticism suggests, "the popular melodrama" that Locke refers to is both literal and figurative. The legacy of the minstrel caricatures that Locke decries extends well beyond the stage, permeating African American popular culture as well as both white conceptions of blacks and African Americans' own self-conceptions.[64] The New Negro movement as conceived by Locke was to serve as a bulwark against minstrel-derived popular representations (and self-representations) of African Americans. Locke, like Du Bois, John-

son, and other writers before and after him, decries the stereotyped representations of African Americans propagated by the minstrel show, though he
does not reject wholesale minstrelsy's influence on African American performance. He acknowledges, for example, that blackface minstrelsy provided for
the widespread circulation of black or black-derived cultural forms.[65] Also,
the advent of African American minstrels (themselves in blackface) after the
Civil War led later to significant African American involvement on the vaudeville stage and in the realm of popular music. Locke, citing James Weldon
Johnson, notes that the performances of black minstrels were largely constrained by the "performance pattern" established by their white antecedents.
African American minstrels inherited a set of conventions that had been put
in practice by their white predecessors in the nineteenth century and refined
over the following decades. This observation points to the fact that the origins of African American popular culture—at least as represented on first the
minstrel and then the vaudeville stage—lie in the complex spectacle of blacks
imitating whites imitating blacks.[66]

This history provides a context for Locke's complex and largely antagonis-
tic relationship with a popular culture born out of nineteenth-century minstrelsy. This antagonism in turn helps explain the classicism that characterizes
New Negro Renaissance intellectuals' attitudes toward the African American
popular music that was rapidly evolving in the early decades of the twentieth. As Arnold Rampersad notes, *The New Negro*, a seminal document of
the renaissance, recognizes the historical importance of the spirituals, briefly
acknowledges jazz, and completely ignores the blues.[67] By "the blues," Rampersad refers to "classic" female blues singers such as Bessie Smith, whose
work owes at least as much to vaudeville as it does to black folk culture. By
the time Locke was putting together *The New Negro*, the blues, together
with jazz, was well on its way to dominating American popular music. The
omission of the blues and the minor presence of jazz in this seminal anthology, then, are puzzling. Arthur P. Davis (a former student of Locke's) recalls
that he "could and did talk brilliantly on many things . . . folk songs, blues,
African art, and modern painting. Incidentally, Locke was the first person I
heard who discussed seriously the blues and other folk material."[68] Davis's
recollection suggests that we should understand *The New Negro*'s omission
of the blues as a tactical decision rather than as an oversight or accident. The
motivations for this decision can no doubt be traced in part to Locke's own
prejudices and preferences, but it nonetheless speaks to the complex relationship between the types of artistic, musical, and literary production advocated
by *The New Negro* and the myriad other cultural productions taking place
in the popular realm.

The musical world that concerns Locke, both in *The New Negro* and in *The Negro and His Music*, is that of the "rising Negro bourgeoisie," whose musical forms were shared with white bourgeois society. In his "Blueprint for Negro Writing," published a year after Locke's *The Negro and His Music*, Richard Wright faults the previous generation of African American artists and intellectuals (i.e., Locke, Johnson, and their contemporaries) for their division of African America into two "separate cultures": "one for the Negro masses, unwritten and unrecognized; and the other for the sons and daughters of a rising Negro bourgeoisie, parasitic and mannered."[69] Wright's assessment brings into sharp focus the limitations of Locke's conception of African American culture. Locke echoes Johnson in his aim to put black folk sources to new uses, although in the end Locke, unlike Hughes or Wright, seems to have little faith in the uses to which "the Negro masses" were putting this material. He states in "The New Negro" that a "new spirit is awake in the masses" and that "the rank and file . . . are leading, and the leaders . . . are following," but this populist rhetoric is not borne out elsewhere in the essay or in Locke's other work, at least where music is concerned.[70] His pinning his hopes of improved race relations on increased contact between "the more intelligent and representative elements of the two race groups" suggests that what Locke has in mind is instead a sort of bourgeois vanguard.[71] Locke presents the challenges of progressive interracialism in explicit class terms, contrasting racial contacts at "the unfavorable and . . . the favorable levels."[72] This class valence in Locke's thinking carries with it significant implications for African American art and music and points to a key difference between the bourgeois New Negro Renaissance Locke envisioned and the dynamic cultural exchanges facilitated by interaction among those at the "unfavorable" levels of black and white society.

Such skepticism about musical and cultural exchanges at these lower levels marks a point of divergence between Locke's thinking and that of James Weldon Johnson, who anticipates Locke's dismissal in *The Negro and His Music* of ragtime and jazz as "petty dialect."[73] "Of course, there are those who will deny that Ragtime is an artistic production," Johnson writes. "[They] dismiss it with a contemptuous word. But this has long been the course of scholasticism in every branch of art. Whatever new thing the people like is pooh-poohed; whatever is popular is regarded as not worth while."[74] Johnson, too, holds that ragtime (a popular form par excellence) should be refined by African American musicians "of not only musical talent, but training," but in his formulation they should refine it so that they, rather than white "adulterators and imitators," can benefit from the commercial exploitation of such source material.[75]

Johnson precisely anticipates and dismisses Locke's criticism, both in the preface to *The Book of American Negro Poetry* cited above, and in a nearly identical passage from *The Autobiography of an Ex-Colored Man* ten years earlier: "Whatever new thing the *people* like is pooh-poohed; whatever is *popular* is spoken of as not worth the while."[76] In the 1922 preface, he emphasizes the folk origins of ragtime: "The earliest Ragtime songs," he writes, "'jes' grew.'"[77] Only later did "a number of colored men" come along who were able to translate the popular songs into a written form and to write new tunes using the "jes' grew" songs as models.[78] Significantly, it is at precisely this point that Johnson himself makes an appearance in this narrative of musical evolution, as he discusses his involvement (along with J. Rosamond Johnson and Bob Cole) in the commercial development of what, at least in this account, had heretofore been largely a folk music. Thus Johnson models a conception of African American musical development that differs substantially from Locke's. Locke discusses both ragtime and jazz at length, but both finally are valuable precisely to the extent that they are folk expressions rather than popular debasements. Their value as folk music, in turn, lies in their potential as the basis for classical compositions that emulate "the universal speech of formal art music."[79] For Johnson, on the other hand, ragtime itself has already achieved the universality that marks "great and enduring" music.[80] The *Autobiography*'s narrator reports that the compositions of a musically illiterate but naturally gifted ragtime musician are "properly proportioned and balanced." Had this natural musician been formally trained, the narrator speculates, "he might have become, at best, a mediocre imitator of the great masters," rather than a proponent of a distinct and characteristically national and racial musical form.[81]

Critics operating with the benefit of hindsight often collapse the jazz culture that was so important in Harlem and elsewhere in the 1920s into revised constructions of the New Negro Renaissance, and these revisions often differ substantially from Locke's conception. In "Music of the Harlem Renaissance," for example, musicologist Samuel Floyd Jr. both points out and perpetuates this tendency: "The necessity of Renaissance leaders to extol some aspects of black culture while denying and suppressing others was natural, since the idea was to integrate with white society." He goes on to claim that, despite Locke's protestations to the contrary, "[t]he fact was, however, that the 'primitive' and 'degenerate' secular music of the period manifested the aesthetic of the movement better than any other resource available."[82] Floyd's claim that "'degenerate' secular music" (i.e., jazz and blues) was consonant with "the aesthetic of the movement" differs substantially from the views articulated in the work of writers associated with the New Negro Renaissance.

Floyd accounts for this discrepancy by claiming that "Renaissance leaders did not understand, or would not acknowledge, the fact that all of the black musical genres belonged to a single cultural and aesthetic tradition, that they were bound together by a common body of musico-aesthetic principles and characteristics."[83]

Both parts of this claim—that all African American music constitutes "a single cultural and aesthetic tradition," and that Locke, Johnson, and others believed otherwise—are questionable. Johnson, in particular, conceives of the development of African American music that incorporates both "folk" and commercial elements. Locke draws on this history in *The Negro and His Music*, but places more emphasis on the ostensible division between folk forms and the products of their commercial exploitation. Nevertheless, both terms in Floyd's summary appropriately and accurately suggest the terms with which Locke, Johnson, and the rest of the intellectual wing of the New Negro Renaissance conceived of the African American–derived music that began to dominate American popular culture in the 1910s and 1920s. The immediate meaning of the "secular" label is clear enough; the supposed antagonism between the blues and the music of the black church is a well-worn subject. Nonetheless, in both *The New Negro* and *The Negro and His Music*, Locke emphasizes the ostensible division between folk forms and the products of their commercial exploitation. The idea that popular forms such as ragtime and jazz represent debased or degenerate forms of African American folk music appears repeatedly in Locke's writings on music. To collapse these distinctions as Floyd does risks misrepresenting the role of music in the renaissance by painting a portrait based too heavily on our current retrospective understanding of the ways in which African American music and literature would continue to intersect after the renaissance.

Unlike later conceptions, like Floyd's, that would attempt to synthesize the cultural products of popular and mass culture with the aims of the New Negro Renaissance, the ideology of the folk at work in Locke's writings credits "the masses" as the source of the raw materials for African American art but divests them of the capacity for rendering this raw material into respectable aesthetic products. Locke states this thesis frankly early in *The Negro and His Music*: "One of the handicaps of Negro music today is that it is too popular. It is tarnished with commercialism and the dust of the market-place. The very musicians who know the folk-ways of Negro music are the very ones who are in commercial slavery to the Shylocks of Tin Pan Alley, in artistic bondage to the ready cash of our dance-halls and the vaudeville stage. . . . On the other hand, our musicians with formal training are cut off from the people and the vital roots of folk music."[84]

Perhaps unconsciously (or perhaps not, given his description of "Shylocks"), such descriptions sound an anti-Semitic note as they bemoan the commercial prostitution of pristine African American folk music by Jewish exploiters. Locke's disparagement of Tin Pan Alley's "Shylocks" resonates in peculiar ways with ideologies seemingly quite different from any that could be encompassed within the rubric of the New Negro Renaissance. Locke's term echoes the then-current notion of Tin Pan Alley as a Jewish-controlled cabal that degraded and corrupted folk sources. Particularly egregious examples may be found in several pieces that appeared in Henry Ford's *Dearborn Independent* in 1921, for example. One article, "Jewish Jazz Becomes Our National Music," reports on a federal antitrust case against seven Jewish-controlled Tin Pan Alley music publishers. This case, the article continues, offers an answer to the question of "whence come the waves upon waves of musical slush that invade decent parlors and set the young people of this generation imitating the drivel of morons."[85] The answer is clear: *"Popular Music is a Jewish monopoly.* Jazz is a Jewish creation. The mush, the slush, the sly suggestion, the abandoned sensuousness of sliding notes, are of Jewish origin."[86] So intent is this anonymous author in attributing to Jews "exploitative finance," "theatrical degeneracy, "liquor propaganda, "the menace of the Movies," and finally "this miasma of so-called popular music, which combines weak-mindedness with every suggestion of lewdness," that the African American origins of jazz are completely elided, except in a few transparently racist formal descriptions (e.g., "[m]onkey talk, jungle squeals, grunts and squeaks").[87] The author of another article, "How the Jewish Song Trust Makes You Sing," advances arguments that are uncomfortably close to those Locke would make concerning the differences between folk expression and commercial corruption of this expression. Popular songs before the Jews hijacked them, according to the article's anonymous author, "were not the product of song factories, but the creation of individuals whose gifts were given natural expression."[88] Gradually, "the popular lilt slid into ragtime, and ragtime has been superseded by jazz. Song topics became lower and lower until at last they were dredges of the slimy bottom of the underworld."[89] Likewise, for Locke, "the Negro's musical heritage" has been "prostituted by the vaudeville stage [and] Tin Pan Alley."[90]

The surprising similarities between Locke's laments about the commercial exploitation of African American musical forms and the anti-Semitic rantings of the *Dearborn Independent* speak to the pervasiveness of concerns about the relationships between folk expressions and their commercial distillates during this period. In fairness to Locke, such a viewpoint was not restricted to anti-Semitic propagandists like the *Dearborn Independent*'s editorial staff. Simon Raphaelson writes in his preface to the stage version of *The*

Jazz Singer (which predates the film): "Jews are determining the nature and scope of jazz more than any other race—more than the negroes, from whom they have stolen jazz and given it a new color and meaning."[91] Raphaelson's assessment of the effects of Jewish intervention in African American music lacks the negative associations of Locke's. Nonetheless, the rhetoric of debasement and corruption that Locke deploys resonates with earlier and contemporaneous arguments.

Locke's concerns about the commodification of jazz, for example, coincide with similar sentiments in Theodor Adorno's essay "On Jazz," published the same year as Locke's *The Negro and His Music*. Like Locke, Adorno bemoans the "mechanical soullessness" and "licentious decadence" of commercial jazz, which he argues is characterized above all by "an inexorably rigid stereotypology."[92] This stereotypology holds "mechanical soullessness" and "licentious decadence" in dialectical suspension; this dialectic is what characterizes jazz's "decidedly modern character."[93] While we may be tempted to read Adorno's critiques of the machinations of the culture industry as of a piece with Locke's warnings about the exploitive commodification of African American musical productions, their two critical projects demonstrate crucial differences. The most obvious difference, perhaps, is Adorno's seeming insensitivity to questions of race, which for Locke are paramount. Adorno writes that "[t]he extent to which jazz has anything at all to do with genuine black music is highly questionable; the fact that it is frequently performed by blacks and that the public clamors for 'black jazz' as a sort of brand-name doesn't say much about it, even if folkloristic research should confirm the African origins of many of its practices."[94] For Adorno, James Buhler argues, "the idea that jazz is fundamentally a form of African-American folk music is ultimately pernicious . . . to the extent that it occludes the fundamental fact of commodification."[95] Adorno himself addresses this question in 1939: "[T]he actual existence of a clear-cut distinction between spontaneous folk music and commercialized mass production is as problematic as it is alluring." Abstracting jazz from "commodity production," he continues, "is prone to fall prey to that type of romanticism which is fostered by the music industry in order to increase its sales figures."[96] Locke, presumably, would beg to differ.

Such controversy over the racial status of jazz recapitulates the earlier and ongoing debates concerning the spirituals discussed earlier in this chapter. Less obvious but no less salient is Adorno's criticism of jazz as characteristic of the alienation of the bourgeoisie. For Adorno, jazz is symptomatic of the bourgeoisie's "pleasure in its own alienation." As a response to this alienation, the bourgeoisie employs "community ideologies of the most varied forms. . . . That which is alienated is endurable to them only as long as it presents itself as unconscious and 'vital': that which is most alienated is what is most familiar."[97] Adorno's diagnosis provides one explanation for the racialist elements in Locke's thinking on music (a "community ideology"), as both Locke's class status and aesthetic temperament would seem to indicate an alienation from "the vital roots of folk music," while his anxieties about mechanization and commercial exploitation compel him to seek a remedy in these folk roots.[98] Locke explains the latter phenomenon in a 1928 essay, for example: "The modern recoil from the machine has deepened the appreciation of hitherto despised qualities in the Negro temperament, its hedonism, its nonchalance, its spontaneity."[99] Adorno's critique highlights the class anxiety that infuses Locke's writings on jazz and other African American musical forms. For Adorno, "the inexorability of social authority . . . is transfigured in jazz into something original and primitive, into 'nature.'"[100] Class anxieties, then, become racialized, leading the urbane, sophisticated Locke to call for a celebration of a "Negro" hedonism and spontaneity rooted in the folk culture of the South—what Adorno terms "*Negervitalität*."[101] The challenge for Locke and other New Negro Renaissance intellectuals was how to channel this racialized essence into the correct aesthetic forms—forms that would help counter both the lingering traces of minstrelsy and the new debasements threatened by the culture industry.

Refining the Folk

As I have argued, the central place that the spirituals occupy in the pantheon of African American art constructed by New Negro Renaissance–affiliated intellectuals from Du Bois to Locke can productively be understood in part as a corrective to the calumnies of both blackface minstrelsy and of "students of racial qualities" like Newman Ivey White.[102] The attendant emphasis on the spirituals' development also helps account for the limitations that these ideological constraints placed on the New Negroes' understanding of the significance that the radical interventions in American culture that the ascendancy first of ragtime, then of jazz held for African American artistic production. That the folk music of African Americans was burlesqued, parodied, and travestied by blackface minstrels and singers of coon songs is undeniable, but the reserved outrage suggested by Du Bois's description of the spirituals' debasement gives way in Locke's later writings to a more complex and problematic aesthetic theory. This theory is given a specific if theoretically imprecise formulation in "The Negro Spirituals," one of Locke's contributions to *The New Negro*. The spirituals, according to Locke, are "nationally as well as racially characteristic," "a classic folk expression," and universal. This "universality" persists despite both "the corruptions of sentimental balladry" and "the neglect and disdain of second-generation respectability." Finally and crucially, they have escaped from the "fragile vehicle of folk art" and achieved the apotheosis of "formal" (i.e., classical) music.[103] In Locke's formulation, the spirituals are a wellspring of folk purity and creativity, subject either to aesthetic development along classical lines or to commercial degradation and exploitation.

Locke's conception draws in important ways upon the earlier work of Henry Edward Krehbiel, whose *Afro-American Folksongs* he lauds as the "first serious and adequate musical analysis" of the spirituals.[104] In the preface to *Afro-American Folksongs*, Krehbiel notes: "Though for scientific reasons I should have preferred to present the melodies of these songs without embellishment of any sort, I have yielded to a desire to make their peculiar beauty and usefulness known . . . and presented them in arrangements suitable for performance under artistic conditions."[105] Locke's appropriation of these arrangements furthers the project of adapting these source materials for "artistic" purposes. Krehbiel's hierarchical understanding of "folksong," popular song, and art music is mirrored in the complex schemas of Locke's *The Negro and His Music*. Krehbiel resorts to German to differentiate between "folksong" (*das Volkslied*) and "popular song" (*volksthümliches Lied*).[106] "Folksong," in Krehbiel's conception, as in Locke's, must be conceived of separately from the "degraded and degrading . . . music hall ditties" signified by the term "popular song."[107] A similar anxiety permeates Locke's discussion of the spirituals and adaptations of them. This anxiety is conditioned by ideologies of racial and aesthetic purity. Neither Krehbiel nor Locke defines folk purity in positive terms. Rather, both define it negatively against subsequent dilutions, alterations, and corruptions. Locke asserts that "[f]olk elements do not necessarily make folk music. Only when pure and in the form originally used by the people for themselves, do they yield us true folk music."[108] Locke's account traces the history of the spirituals through their public introduction in the concert programs of the Fisk Jubilee Singers in the 1870s. The adaptation of the spirituals to the concert stage clearly represents a transformation, but for Locke, "[o]nly with the original Fisk Singers was their real simplicity and dignity maintained."[109]

Nevertheless, he does not advocate that the spirituals be maintained in a state of stasis. In fact, they must be transmuted into art music, much as, according to Locke, the folk forms of Europe have formed the basis for its various classical traditions. Locke calls for an analogous transformation of African American folk sources into classical forms based on European models. This call echoes James Weldon Johnson's description of ragtime in the 1922 preface to *The Book of American Negro Poetry:* "Ragtime music [and the cakewalk] may be lower forms of art, but they are evidence of a power that will someday be applied to the higher forms."[110]

In *The Negro and His Music*, Locke painstakingly codifies his model for understanding African American music. Black music, he writes, comprises three basic categories: folk, popular, and classical. Following Krehbiel and Johnson, he posits folk music as "the precious musical ore" to be mined by classically minded composers, as well as a source that is corrupted by its transformation into popular forms.[111] These two lines of development—classical and popular—are in Locke's model directly opposed. Folk music's value lies in its potential for development as a characteristically "racial" strain in a larger classical idiom. This process, he argues, is universal; Negro composers should follow the models of Liszt, Brahms, Dvořák, and Smetana in incorporating "the characteristic folk spirit" (of their respective folk—Hungarian for Liszt, German/Austrian for Brahms, Czech for Dvořák and Smetana) into their music without losing "its rare raciness and unique flavor."[112] Refined and adapted to conform to European models, Negro folk music would achieve parity with these other national traditions. Locke places great stock in Dvořák's supposed incorporation of melodies from the spirituals into his "New World" Symphony. As Paul Burgett points out, the extent to which Dvořák incorporated African American folk melodies into his work is not particularly important; rather "[t]he real issue seems to involve an attitude about Negro music. In this instance, that attitude is reflected in Locke's attempts to vindicate the value of Negro folk music . . . by pointing out their use in a musical form not endemic to the spiritual's culture of origin but, rather, [in] a highly valued form of western European culture, i.e., the symphony."[113]

Burgett convincingly describes Locke's desire for African American artists to transform folk materials into formal art based on white models as conditioned by a "vindication syndrome." In other words, African American folk music is "vindicated" to the extent that it is appreciated by knowledgeable (usually white) critics, particularly those who recognize its affinities with European art music. Locke cites both James Weldon Johnson's and Henry Krehbiel's formal analyses of the spirituals but defers to Krehbiel over Johnson, due to the latter's "more academically balance[d]" approach.[114] Again, the peculiar quality of this unadulterated musical idiom is most easily recognized in the negative. Locke is remarkably consistent on this point, as the same proscriptions appear nearly verbatim in "The Negro Spirituals" and *The*

Negro and His Music. Too much emphasis on melody leads to the "sentimental ballad *à la* Stephen Foster." Overemphasis on harmony leads to the "cloying sentimental glee" characteristic of barbershop choruses, which Locke seems to hold in particular disdain. Perhaps most dangerous of all, development of rhythm to the exclusion of the other elements leads to a secularized "syncopated shout."[115] Locke's anxiety is clear: too much rhythm leads to jazz.

In an attempt to provide an example of the successful development of folk sources into refined concert distillates, Locke reifies the Fisk Jubilee Singers' concertized renditions of the spirituals as examples of their "pure" state. The Fisk Singers commenced their first tour in 1871. Descriptions of African American sacred music from just over a decade earlier sound much like the "syncopated shouts" that Locke decries as a degradation of the pristine spirituals: "'Interested, and yet at the same time shocked' at a 'spectacle' observed at a black church in Chattanooga in 1859, the Reverend Robert Mallard wrote: 'The whole congregation kept up one loud monotonous strain, interrupted by various sounds: groans and screams and clapping of hands.'"[116] The music that Mallard describes bears little resemblance to the pristine folk music that Locke imagines will provide the source material for symphonic development. Viewed skeptically, the body of songs he seeks, as for Du Bois and Krehbiel, is perhaps best understood as an invented tradition, revealing more about its twentieth-century champions than its nineteenth-century practitioners. Zora Neale Hurston suggests as much when she asserts that "[t]here has never been a presentation of genuine Negro spirituals to any audience anywhere." The work of African American composers like "Harry T. Burleigh, Rosamond Johnson, Lawrence Brown, Nathaniel Dett, Hall Johnson and [John Wesley] Work" is "[a]ll good . . . and beautiful, but *not* the spirituals."[117] Hurston goes on to describe a performance that differs significantly from the Fisk Singers' concert renditions of what Hurston identifies as "magnificent song—but not *Negro* song": "The first notes just burst out and the rest of the church join in—fired by the same inner urge. Every man trying to express himself through song. . . . Hence the harmony and disharmony, the shifting keys and broken time that make up the spiritual."[118]

The tradition that Mallard describes, which has a better claim to "folk" status than do the Fisk Jubilee Singers' concert arrangements, continued in Holiness churches in the 1890s and in the Pentecostal churches of the early twentieth century, and probably bears a significant formal and genealogical relationship with the performance Hurston describes. Examples of this music made it on to record, often alongside minstrel skits and coon songs. While Locke is right to distinguish between the religious songs and the minstrel-derived material that accompanied it on record company rosters, the distinctions between the performance practices and musical styles of gospel and later African American popular music like blues and jazz are much more difficult to maintain and to justify.

Locke attempts to circumvent this problem by separating the spirituals from the ecstatic religious music described above. Likewise, he separates "classic" jazz, which he maintains is a characteristically racial product, from commercial imitations, degradations, and dilutions. In rehabilitating jazz as both a folk and a classical music, Locke leans heavily on its approval by white critics such as "Kreisler, Rachmaninoff, Koussevitzky, and Stokowski," who are "certainly names authoritative enough."[119] Here too Locke defers to European authorities: Kreisler was Austrian; Rachmaninoff and Koussevitzky were Russian; Stokowski was English. In a bid to establish the legitimacy of jazz, Locke begins his chapter on "Jazz Classics" with the claim that "the important distinction is not between jazz and classical music, but between the good, mediocre, and bad of both varieties."[120] "Classic" jazz, as Locke elaborates it, is that which shares formal affinities with European classical music, and thus is subject to appreciation in aesthetic terms inherited from that tradition. Such a view cannot help but appear unsatisfying from a contemporary perspective. Paul Burgett in his discussion of Locke's "vindication syndrome" offers a rather weak justification for Locke's position: "The Negro Renaissance was a phenomenon of another time."[121] This explanation is unsatisfactory for a number of reasons, not least of which is that Locke's classicist viewpoint ran contrary not only to that of his successors (e.g., Richard Wright) but also to those of his contemporaries (e.g., Langston Hughes and Zora Neale Hurston) and even his predecessors.

It is in their approach to jazz and other musical forms derived from African American vernacular traditions but mediated and disseminated by the culture industry that Locke's ideas of the relationship between folk materials and contemporary artistic production diverge most radically from that of Floyd and other current scholars. In other words, it marks a key point of divergence between the New Negro Renaissance that Locke imagined and the one we consider in retrospect. In essence, the program that Locke advocates presupposes and reinforces a division between folk culture and its "refined" formal distillates on the one hand and the degraded products of commercial interests on the other. The transformation of African American folk culture into a universal high culture would be conducted, he attests, by "the thinking few."[122] Ultimately, the New Negro's project is an alliance not between educated blacks and other African Americans but between the black bourgeoisie and their white counterparts. In fact, Locke protests that the members of the black bourgeois vanguard are unfairly equated with the Negro masses in an "unjust and . . . ridiculous" fashion.[123] This is a peculiar form of class consciousness. This statement, like Locke's lament that "the races . . . have touched too closely at the unfavorable and too lightly at the favorable levels," indicates his vexed relationship with black vernacular culture as well as a profound discomfort toward the interracial musical exchanges that had long been going on among those outside the purview of *The New Negro*.[124]

CHAPTER FIVE

Rethinking Music and Race in Jean Toomer's *Cane*

When it was first published in 1923, *Cane*, Jean Toomer's landmark modernist amalgam of poetry and prose, was heralded as a cornerstone text of the New Negro Renaissance. Critical discussions of this challenging, often frustrating work have long revolved around the twin poles of music and race, and these terms are certainly crucial to understanding it. At the same time, *Cane* also treats subtly but revealingly the sexual anxieties that underlie so much of the discourse on race and culture in the twentieth century. The stories Toomer tells in *Cane* anticipate those of Wright and Ellison, and they also suggest the link between the anxious eroticism and the perpetual, barely contained threats of racial violence that pulse through Alan Lomax's account of his visit to Mississippi. Working through the interpretive challenges of Toomer's book, then, can help us better understand the racialized structures of feeling that undergird those other narratives. *Cane* reveals the meanings of musical performances to be fraught with complications of racial identities and sexual anxiety. The music that features so centrally to the book is the product of both racial violence and sexual desire, and these phenomena, as in Wright's and Ellison's narratives, are inextricably intertwined. Music, like the women around whom many of the book's narratives are structured, far from expressing some sort of static racial essence, instead gives voice to the relationships between men, between men and women, of North and South, and of black and white. Toomer's book, then, continually sounds the color line in a way that lays bare the commingled threads of race, sex, and violence that run throughout twentieth-century discourses about vernacular music.

We see the initial connection between music and race in Toomer's own famous account of the book's genesis, in which he laments the loss of the

133

purity of expression embodied in the "Negro folk-songs" he had encountered in rural Georgia:

> There was a valley, the valley of "Cane," . . . a family of back-country Negroes had only recently moved into a shack not too far away. They sang. And this was the first time I'd ever heard the folk-songs and spirituals. They were very rich and sad and joyous and beautiful. But I learned that the Negroes of the town objected to them. . . . They had victrolas and player-pianos. So, I realized with deep regret, that the spirituals, meeting ridicule, would be certain to die out. With Negroes also the trend was toward the small town and then toward the city—and industry and commerce and machines. The folk-spirit was walking in to die on the modern desert. That spirit was so beautiful. Its death was so tragic. Just this seemed the sum of life to me. And this was the feeling I put into *Cane*. *Cane* was a swan-song. It was a song of an end.[1]

This is a complicated sentiment: part elegy, part romantic racialist lament. In *Cane*, not only does the "folk-spirit" die "on the modern desert"; so too do the black folk themselves, whether through amalgamation, migration, or murder. Toomer identifies the Victrola as an exemplar of a technology of commodification and mechanical reproduction that threatens not only the survival of "folk-songs and spirituals" but also a unified African American identity grounded in this rural southern folk culture. The "Negroes of the town," having adopted urban consumer culture, hold these humble but "rich and sad and joyous and beautiful" products of the folk in disdain.

Cane was initially marketed and received as a paradigmatically "Negro" text, despite its engagement with avant-garde modernist formal experimentation and Toomer's personal and literary relationships with such writers as Waldo Frank and Sherwood Anderson. Anderson articulates the idea of the text's blackness bluntly in a 1923 letter to Toomer: "[Y]ou are the only negro . . . who seems really to have consciously the artist's impulse."[2] Again and again, the text's musicality was understood as part and parcel of its blackness. John McClure, the editor of *Double Dealer*, in which parts of *Cane* were originally published, wrote to Anderson that Toomer should focus on lyric poetry, which McClure understood to express a racial aptitude. "If Toomer follows that African urge, and rhapsodizes," McClure argues, "he will be a commanding and solitary figure."[3] Paul Rosenfeld wrote that Toomer "tunes his fiddle like a tavern minstrel."[4] Michael North identifies the nadir of this line of thinking in Alfred Kreymborg's praise of Toomer's employment of the "frankly lyrical strain native to the darky everywhere,"[5] while Toomer himself identified as among his assets "that lyricism which is so purely Negro."[6]

Not all of Toomer's literary admirers subscribed to this sort of racialist thinking. Waldo Frank, for example, advised Toomer: "The day you write as a Negro, or as an American, or as anything but a human part of *life*, your work will lose a dimension. How typical that is of most recognition: the effort immediately to limit you, to put you in a cubby hole and stick a label underneath."[7] This sentiment anticipates arguments that Toomer himself would later make concerning the racial significance of his work. The marketing and reception of Toomer's book as distinctively "Negro" and the emphasis on its musicality as emblematic of this racial designation are consonant with the culture industry's segregation of musical forms, genres, and performances along racial lines. Nonetheless, despite the manifest racialism (and even racism) of many of these formulations, they do identify an important connection between ideas of racial blackness and a certain musical lyricism that pervades the text. Part of *Cane*'s artistic accomplishment lies in its mastery of both formal and vernacular diction (as Ellison writes of Mahalia Jackson), "almost of the academy one instant and of the broadest cotton-field dialect the next," even if one feels (as I do) that its direct representations of "cotton-field dialect" are less successful than its sublation of them into lyric verse and lyrical prose.[8]

Cane follows a tripartite structure: its first section comprises ten lyric poems and six prose narratives, the lyricism of which at times veers into prose poetry. Several of these narratives/prose poems incorporate songlike lyric refrains. The narratives and lyrics in the book's first section are set in rural Georgia—"the valley of 'Cane'" that Toomer mentions in the long quotation at the beginning of this chapter. The book's second section includes a similar mixture of lyric poetry and narrative prose poems. The narratives of this second section are set in urban settings: Washington, D.C., and Chicago. The protagonist of the book's third section, "Kabnis," is an African American from the North who returns to rural Georgia. Toomer describes *Cane*'s structure in a letter to Waldo Frank as "a circle. Aesthetically, from simple forms to complex ones, and back to simple forms. Regionally, from the South up into the North, and back into the South again."[9] Together, the stories and poems that make up *Cane* trouble the generic lines between poetry and prose (and drama, in "Kabnis"), regional lines between North and South, and, most pointedly, racial lines between black and white.

Other recent readings tend toward a contradictory interpretation, viewing the book's treatment of race as deconstructive or performative. J. Martin Favor, for example, argues that in *Cane*, "catholicity of performance begins to deconstruct the larger rubric describing race," and that Toomer "begins to question the adequacy of any discourse of black identity at all."[10] Most recently, in their exhaustively researched introduction to a new edition of the book, Rudolph P. Byrd and Henry Louis Gates Jr. seek answers in Toomer's own racial self-identification, answering finally in the affirmative what they pose as a central question regarding Toomer and his most famous work: "Was Jean Toomer a Negro who passed for white?"[11] Despite the wealth of critical attention afforded *Cane*, from Toomer's own pronouncement to Waldo Frank's foreword to the original edition to Byrd's and Gates's introduction to the recent Norton edition, *Cane* itself evinces a resistance to the varied and contradictory racial logics of this critical tradition. Indeed, this resistance forms the core of the book's concerns. I agree with Favor that *Cane*, like the "industry and commerce and machines" whose influence Toomer appears to lament, ultimately works to trouble and test—if not to undermine completely—the binary logic of race with which it engages. Any understanding of *Cane*'s lyricism as expressing a racial aptitude for music is complicated by Toomer's eventual ambivalence and outright resistance to his being cast as a "Negro" and *Cane* as a "black" text. Even as Toomer's publishers and supporters were emphasizing what Gorham Munson described in a letter to Toomer as the latter's "negroid lyricism," Toomer was moving toward his eventual disavowal of such a racial identification.[12] He later wrote that while he was working on *Cane*, "I read many books on the matter of race and the race problem in America. Rarely had I encountered the nonsense contained in most of these books. It was evident to me, who had seen both the white and the colored worlds, and both from the inside, that the authors of these writings had little or no experience of the matters they were dealing with."[13]

In response, Toomer "wrote a poem called, 'The First American,' the idea of which was, that in America we are in the process of forming a new race, that I was one of the first conscious members of this race."[14] As Alice Walker puts it in her influential essay on Toomer, "*Cane* was . . . a double 'swan song.' He meant it to memorialize a culture he thought was dying [the folk culture of African Americans in the rural South], . . . but he was also saying good-bye to the 'Negro' he felt dying in himself."[15] At work in all of these conceptions, including Toomer's, is an essentialist understanding of race. Toomer's own conception of his racial status was famously vexed, and by the 1930s he had determined categorically, "I am not a Negro."[16] Toomer's stated goal of inaugurating a new race, with himself as the "the result of racial blending here in America which has produced a new race or stock," does not disavow racial difference or racial essentialism.[17] That is, the fact that Toomer purports not to be "a Negro" does not mean that he disavows the category of "Negro" or that he is unwilling to ascribe this racial identification to others. *Cane* is populated by characters described as "Negroes," "Negresses," and "niggers," though of course none of the myriad perspectives on race articulated in the book is necessarily identical with Toomer's own. Still, he claims to have drawn on the racial wellspring of his "Negro" heritage in writing *Cane*. In a 1922 letter to the *Liberator*, Toomer argued that he embodied a pluralistic racial identity, comprising at least "seven blood mixtures: French, Dutch, Welsh, Negro, German, Jewish, and Indian."[18] This heterogeneity of "blood," however, is reduced to a binary formulation of black and white: Toomer had "lived equally amid the two race groups. Now white, now colored." His "growing need for artistic expression," he continues, pulled him "deeper and deeper into the Negro group. And as my powers of receptivity increased, I found myself loving it in a way that I could never love the other. It has stimulated and fertilized whatever creative talent I may contain within me."[19] Importantly, Toomer deploys metaphors of organicism and of affect to explain this racial identification. Above all, his trip to the rural South, where he "heard the folk-songs come from the lips of Negro peasants," catalyzes his "Negro" blood into artistic expression: "And a deep part of my nature, a part I had repressed, sprang suddenly to life and responded to them."[20] For all its complications, *Cane* not only allows for but in fact requires the existence of a racialized southern "Negro" peasantry, one whose existence is threatened by encroaching modernization, new technologies, and racial amalgamation.

Race in the book, then, is neither purely essential nor entirely contingent. What I wish to propose instead is that musical performance in *Cane* is the primary site through which racial identities and racial difference are negotiated. Rather than expressing a racial essence, instances of musical performance in the book instead articulate what Claudia Tate calls "the residual surplus meaning of unconscious desire."[21] Understanding "unconscious desire" as figured through "residual surplus meaning" offers a way of negotiating the impasse between readings of the text that impose a racial essentialism and those that understand race strictly in performative terms. In other words, musical performance undermines narrowly essentialist assumptions of racial being while at the same time pointing to an idea of race that is nevertheless constitutive of an economy of desire. Taking this question of desire seriously also allows us to see how music functions in *Cane* and, perhaps, in the culture writ large; like race, it is figured in terms of excess and affect. A logic of desire, finally, binds music and race in the book. Throughout *Cane*, Toomer couples poetic and musical lyricism with acts of racialized violence; key scenes depict this violence as the outcome of transgressive interracial erotic desire. Two striking qualities of the book are its manifest musicality and its deep concern with race and structures of desire. I want to elaborate some of the ways that these two qualities operate in concert; the structures of desire at work in the book manifest themselves repeatedly through the dual figurations of race and musical performance. Eve Kosofsky Sedgwick's definition of "desire"—signifying not "a particular affective state or emotion" but rather "the affective or social force, the glue, even when its manifestation is hostility or hatred or something less emotively charged, that shapes an important relationship"—is clearly operative in *Cane*, as it negotiates racial antagonisms and cross-racial affinities.[22]

Many such instances are marked by songs or fragments of songs. In some cases these musical interjections serve as elegies for individual victims of violent death, and this correlation suggests that we read the book's musicality in relation to the narratives of racial and sexual violence it represents. This elegiac function is echoed on a larger scale—songs of mourning for the passing of the "song-lit race of slaves" Toomer invokes in "Song of the Son."[23] Music, rather than expressing some sort of essentially "negroid lyricism," is instead a key means through which the text articulates and negotiates racial difference and racialized desire. This shift in perspective renders lucid some key moments in *Cane* where race and desire intersect—moments that would otherwise remain opaque. I will elaborate this notion by focusing on several narrative scenes from the book. "Becky," "Fern," and "Blood-Burning Moon" are included in the book's first section, set in rural Georgia. "Bona and Paul," from the book's second section, is set in Chicago; "Box Seat" takes place in Washington, D.C. Together, these scenes illuminate the logic of music and race present throughout the book, a logic that I will argue is reducible neither to racial essentialism nor to performance. Race in *Cane* may well be arbitrary and imposed from without, but it is nonetheless real on an affective level.

Toomer invokes African American folk songs—both traditional spirituals like "Deep River" (which appears at the end of "Rhobert") and new pieces of Toomer's own creation—as the lyrical substrate for many of the book's other poems and narratives. Toomer deploys other conventional poetic forms in *Cane*, such as the blazon ("Portrait in Georgia" and "Face" are two examples).[24] "November Cotton Flower," for example, is a sonnet that echoes language in "Karintha," the book's first story. The book's first section includes a number of poems that emulate folk song forms. "Cotton Song" is a ventriloquized work song that also evokes a spiritual: "Come, brother, come. Lets lift it / Come now, hewit! roll away! / Shackles fall upon the Judgment Day."[25] While the poem adopts the basic form of the work song, unlike conventional representations of African American folk song rendered in stylized dialect, it is written for the most part in standard English (except for its omission of contractions, a formal characteristic it shares with many of the narratives in *Cane* as well as the work of other modernist writers, notably Faulkner). The last line of the third stanza and the entire fourth stanza, however, are rendered in dialect and offset by quotation marks:

"We aint agwine t wait until th Judgment Day
Nassur; nassur,
Hump.
Eoho, eoho, roll away!
We aint agwine t wait until the Judgment Day!" (lines 12–16)

Through this move, the poem both adopts the form of an African American folk song and distances itself from this source material by demarcating its boundaries through the use of dialect. In so doing, it suggests a relation between the poem and its folk antecedents but at the same time emphasizes linguistic difference. This linguistic difference is the mechanism through which racial difference registers. The poem's orthographic distinction between the poetic frame (standard diction) and folk source (dialect) makes legible an ostensible aural difference. The poem's dialect attempts to represent racial difference by translating audible linguistic difference into a legible form.

A starker instance of this relation is evident in other poems. "Song of the Son," first published in the *Crisis*, is an elegy for a "song-lit race of slaves," whom the poet implores to "[p]our O pour that parting soul in song" (16; lines 12, 1). The adjective "song-lit," which the narrator uses to describe the "race of slaves" whose passing the poem commemorates, economically collapses the visual and aural logics at work in "Cotton Song." The poem's subjects are explicitly racialized (they are a "race of slaves"), and the racial difference through which they are defined is illuminated through song. A musical and aural logic, then, complicates and supplements a racial logic of visible difference. The poem mourns the passing of this "song-lit race" and at the same time claims a filial relationship between them and the narrator: "Now just before an epoch's sun declines / Thy son, in time, I have returned to thee" (lines 8–9). The dying folk culture that the slave songs represent provides a kernel for new artistic expression: "Negro slaves, dark purple ripened plums" provide a "seed," which "becomes // An everlasting song, a singing tree / Caroling softly souls of slavery" (lines 16, 19, 20–21). The narrator's metaphorical identification of "Negro slaves" with seeds and trees suggests that musical expression becomes both embodied and heritable. The poem, then, narrates an experience akin to the biographical story Toomer recounts concerning his visit to "the valley of 'Cane'"; "Song of the Son" can productively be read as a microcosm of *Cane* in its invocation of a dying folk heritage that the poet transmutes into modernist literary art. Unlike "Cotton Song," which partially emulates its source material in both form and content, "Song of the Son" distances itself formally from the songs sung by "Negro slaves." The poem is written in unbroken iambic pentameter, and its stylized, formal diction distinguishes it from the songs whose passing it evokes. Despite this formal distance, however, the lyric poems in *Cane* evoke a musical sensibility drawn from their antecedents in African American folk song. This lyrical musicality not only pervades the book's lyrics but also plays a significant role in structuring its prose narratives.

"Blood-Burning Moon": Music, Desire, and Racial Violence

In many of *Cane*'s short stories, including "Karintha," "Fern," and "Blood-Burning Moon," black women are the objects of both interracial and intraracial erotic desire; in each instance, this equation of feminine desirability and blackness is figured through music and song. The narrator's description of Karintha echoes the song that precedes it: "[E]ven as a child, Karintha . . . carr[ies] beauty, perfect as dusk when the sun goes down." She is desired by men both young and old whose wish "to ripen a growing thing too soon . . . could mean no good to her." Karintha's voice is figured as excessive, akin to the erotic excess she provokes in her male admirers: "At dusk, . . . before any of the women had started their supper-getting-ready songs, her voice, high-pitched shrill, would put one's ears to itching. But no one ever thought to make her stop because of it." The sexual longing Karintha provokes is figured in the form of a song that emphasizes her erotic blackness: "Her skin is like dusk, / O cant you see it / Her skin is like dusk, / When the sun goes down."[26] While the dark beauty of Karintha's skin is evidently at the heart of her desirability in the story, this desire is strictly intraracial; there are no white people in the story.

"Fern" paints an even more complex picture of this musical figuration of an eroticized racial desire. Again, the desirability of the woman at the story's center is figured through the trope of music: "If you have heard a Jewish cantor sing, if he has touched you and made your own sorrow seem trivial when compared with his, you will know my feeling when I follow the curves of her profile, like mobile rivers, to [Fern's eyes,] their common delta." Like Karintha, Fern succumbs to the desire she elicits in men, even if she does not reciprocate this desire ("Something inside of her got tired of them"). Sexual desire in "Fern" is both racialized and localized: "That the sexes were made to mate is the practice of the South. Particularly, black folks were made to mate." The narrator assures us that the men who desire Fern are black: "[I]t is black folks whom I have been talking about thus far. What white men thought of Fern I can arrive at only by analogy. They let her alone."[27] Despite this somewhat strange assurance that sexual desire had obeyed the racial strictures of Jim Crow, the narrator again invokes the songs of a Jewish cantor to evoke Fern's compelling appearance: "[A]t first sight of her I felt as if I heard a Jewish cantor sing. As if his singing rose above the unheard chorus of a folk-song." Earlier the narrator says that "the whole countryside seemed to flow into her eyes. Flowed into them with the soft listless cadence of Georgia's South." This seemingly incongruous juxtaposition of Jewish religious song and the "cadence of Georgia's South" at first seems to analogize the "Sorrow Songs" of the African American folk with the songs of sorrow represented by the Jewish cantor. Music, then, becomes the common ground through which analogous histories of suffering become audible.

Two instances at the end of the story, though, trouble this neat analogy. Having observed that "[w]hen one is on the soil of one's ancestors, most anything can come to one," the narrator looks on as Fern seems to become possessed by something that is ultimately expressed through song: "She . . . [f]ell to her knees, and began swaying, swaying. Her body was tortured with something it could not let out. Like boiling sap it flooded arms and fingers till she shook them as if they burned her. It found her throat, and spattered inarticulately in plaintive, convulsive sounds, mingled with calls to Christ Jesus. And then she sang, brokenly. A Jewish cantor singing with a broken voice. A child's voice, uncertain, or an old man's. Dusk hid her; I could hear only her song." The narrator provides little explication of this scene, though he seems to attribute it to a religious experience: he "[s]aw her face flow into [her eyes], the countryside and something that I call God." The story ends, though, with a sudden indication that the connection between "a Jewish cantor" and Fern is in fact genealogical rather than merely analogous: "Her name, against the chance you might happen down that way, is Fernie May Rosen."[28] Fern, then, is a product of an interracial union but has been assimilated as African American, as a member of the southern black folk. The song that possesses her, though, as well as the source of the fascination she holds for the narrator, is the product of a racial difference that becomes audible through her singing. At the end, Fern disappears as an object of erotic visual fascination as the narrator can "hear only her song."

"Blood-Burning Moon," the final story in *Cane*'s first section, is structured around a similar interrelation of music, racial difference, and sexual desire. "Blood-Burning Moon" invokes explicitly the sexual anxiety that undergirds the racial anxiety in "Fern" as well as other stories such as "Karintha" and "Becky," and, as in these other narratives, an eroticized racial difference is expressed through song. The story is structured around an interracial love triangle. Louisa, a young black woman, is desired by two men: Bob Stone, the white son of the owner of the factory that employs the town's black men, and Tom Burwell, a black laborer. Stone confronts his romantic rival, who slits Stone's throat and is, predictably, lynched and burned by the white townspeople in return. As with many of *Cane*'s other stories, this narrative is telescoped lyrically into a song refrain that punctuates it: "Red nigger moon. Sinner! / Blood-burning moon. Sinner! / Come out that fact'ry door." This refrain is sung three times in the story, serving as a chorus at the end of each section of the narrative. It ends the first short section, as Louisa considers her desire for Tom and for Bob, and theirs for her: "Separately, there was no unusual significance to either one. But for some reason, they jumbled together when her eyes gazed vacantly at the rising moon. And from the jumble came the stir that was strangely within her." As with Fern, the song Louisa sings is uncontrollable and compelled from within: "Her lips trembled. The slow rhythm of her song grew agitant and restless."[29] Dogs begin to howl, chickens cackle, roosters crow, and the women of the factory town sing, joining Louisa in chorus "as if heralding a weird dawn or some ungodly awakening."

Louisa's song echoes Fern's in its emergence from a commingling of racial difference and sexual desire. This connection is even more explicit in Louisa's case, as her song arises from "the jumble" of the desire for her that Bob and Tom share. Its significance lies not only in the transgression of the color line implied by Bob's desire for her, but also—and more importantly—by the commingling of black and white men's desire, with Louisa as a shared object. This situation is, of course, impossible to sustain; Louisa's sexual entanglements involve multiple transgressions. The first and most obvious are the prohibitions against miscegenation that also underlie "Becky." The disapprobation that Becky's interracial family meets from both "white folks" and "black folks" reveals that these prohibitions are present on both sides of the color line. The real transgression in "Becky," of course, is a white woman's sexual involvement with a black man. By contrast, the right of white men to sexual access to black women is a touchstone for Bob: "He passed the house with its huge open hearth which, in the days of slavery, was the plantation cookery. He saw Louisa bent over that hearth. He went in as a master should and took her. Direct, honest, bold. None of this sneaking that he had to go through now. The contrast was repulsive to him."[30] Bob's nostalgia for the regime of racial and sexual domination that characterized his family's former relations with their African American slaves infuses his desire for Louisa. Paradoxically, despite its binary racial logic, the regime of white supremacy whose passing Bob bemoans was enforced through the rape of black women;

his desire for Louisa is inflected with the loss of this power of racial and sexual domination.

The story's refrain appears again at the end of the second section, after Tom has professed his love for Louisa and warned that if Bob Stone lays claim to her, he will "cut him just like a nigger." He asks her to sing, and the section ends with "Louisa and Tom, the whole street, singing" the refrain. The apocalyptic imagery of the "ungodly awakening" that prefaces the first appearance of the story's sung refrain is repeated at the end of the story, after Tom has killed Bob and has been lynched in return. Here, as at the beginning, Louisa's singing is a response to an imperative: "The full moon, an evil thing, an omen which she must sing to."[31] The song that Louisa, Tom, and other African American townspeople sing to the "[r]ed nigger moon" serves as an aural marker of racial difference produced by the racial terror and violence that the story narrates. The white lynch mob, by contrast, is characterized by "[t]aut humming. No words." The song that Louisa sings contrasts with the yell of the mob: "Its yell echoed against the skeleton stone walls and sounded like a hundred yells. Like a hundred mobs yelling." The mob's yell is the sound of white racial terror; juxtaposed, it and Louisa's song sound the color line that organizes the life of the town.

Despite or perhaps because of the force of this violently policed color line, Louisa's race is far from incidental to Bob's desire for her. In considering their affair, he figures himself consciously as white ("his mind became consciously a white man's") and fetishizes her racial otherness: "She was lovely—in her way. Nigger way. What way was that? Damned if he knew. Must know." Bob self-consciously recognizes Louisa's blackness as the object of his desire: "Beautiful nigger gal. Why nigger? Why not just gal? No, it was because she was nigger that he went to her." For Bob Stone, this quality—"nigger"—is both racial and sexual; it motivates his desire and yet remains illegible: "Was there something about niggers you couldnt know? Listening to them at church didnt tell you anything. Looking at them didnt tell you anything. Talking to them didnt tell you anything . . . unless they wanted to talk. Of course, about farming, and licker, and craps—but those weren't nigger. Nigger was something more. How much more?"[32] The fetishization of Louisa as racially Other here follows a psychoanalytic logic of desire. Racial difference motivates desire and serves as its object; that is, racial difference provokes desire and is produced by it. At stake in Tom's questions to himself is not just desire but knowledge. Louisa is both object of desire and presumed bearer of knowledge for Bob. Bob presupposes Louisa as the bearer of racial knowledge accessible through sexual pleasure. In psychoanalytic terms, she is the "subject presumed to know," in possession of the racial and sexual knowledge that is inaccessible to Bob: "Was there something about niggers you couldnt know?" She is also "the subject presumed to enjoy," whose enjoyment (*jouissance*) is central to Bob's obsessive, racially motivated desire for her.

Slavoj Žižek identifies this "supposed jouissance" as "one of the key components of racism: the Other . . . is always presumed to have access to some specific enjoyment, and that is what really bothers us."[33] Bob, of course, is really bothered by the possibility that Louisa is enjoying Tom, who also represents this terrifying jouissance: "Nigger was something more. How much more? Something to be afraid of, more? Hell no. Who ever heard of being afraid of a nigger? Tom Burwell."[34] Tom is, from Bob's perspective, a "subject presumed to desire," the perception of which marks Bob's progression from obsession to the hysteria that leads to both his and Tom's violent deaths. Again the narrative evinces a psychoanalytic logic, narrating a hysterical desire whose workings Žižek elaborates: "[T]he question to ask is not 'What is his object of desire?' [in this case Louisa] but 'Where does he desire from? Who is the other person through whom he is organizing his desire?' The problem for the hysterical subject is that he always needs to have recourse to another subject to organize his desire."[35]

Bob's obsessive contemplation of his desire for Louisa is organized around the desire of Tom, the other subject around whom Bob's desire is organized: "Cartwell had told him that Tom went with Louisa after she reached home. No sir. No nigger had ever been with his girl. He'd like to see one try."[36] The triangulated relationship between Bob, Louisa, and Tom and his obsession with the possibility of a sexual relationship between Louisa and Tom suggests that we understand Bob's statement that "[h]e'd like to see one try" as something other than an idle boast. Rather, his fascination with the prospect that Tom "had . . . been with his girl" reveals that not only is Louisa's blackness integral to Bob's desire, but that Tom's is as well. Although I do not mean to imply necessarily that Bob's desire is a desire *for* Tom in any direct sense, it is nonetheless clear that Tom's presumed sexual access to Louisa plays a critical role in structuring Bob's own desire, illustrating what Eve Sedgwick calls "the slippery relation . . . between desire and identification."[37] Or, as Freud puts it, "identification is the expression of there being something in common, which may signify love."[38] At any rate, the desire for Louisa that Bob shares with Tom allows him to identify with Tom's masculinity, exemplified by the prerogative of sexual access to black women that Tom exercises and whose loss Bob laments. At the same time, this identification is complicated by Bob's conscious desire for mastery over both Louisa and Tom.

The paired figures of Louisa as the subject presumed to enjoy and Tom as the desiring subject are the twin axes around which Bob's desire revolves. Louisa's desire is significantly absent from the story, manifesting itself only as the "strange stir" to which her song gives voice, while at the same time her presumed sexual enjoyment is the object-cause of Bob's desire.[39] The text provides some indication that this desire is reciprocated; despite Bob's fantasies of sexual and racial domination of Louisa and her relationship with Tom, "[b]y the way the world reckons things, [Bob] had won her. By measure of that warm glow which came into her mind at thought of him, he had won her." Tom, by contrast, is less successful: "Somehow, he never got along." For Louisa, the desire expressed by both Bob and Tom results in stasis: Tom's "black balanced, and pulled against, the white of Stone, when she thought of them." This description is as close as we get to Louisa's emotional universe, which is otherwise only accessible through her singing, as an incantation. Thinking of Bob and Tom, "she sang softly at the evil face of the full moon." She is not alone in this endeavor; other "Negro women improvised songs against its spell" as well. Louisa's song—"Red nigger moon. Sinner! / Blood-burning moon. Sinner! / Come out that fact'ry door"—telegraphs the violent consequences of the interracial desire that structures the narrative. The repetition of the word "Sinner" echoes the vague but evocative religious imagery in "Becky" ("Pines whisper to Jesus"), while explicitly invoking the transgression of racial and sexual taboos that structures the narrative. The assonant rhyme between "nigger" and "Sinner" emphasizes the racial valence of this transgression.

Blackness for Bob is figured not as qualitative difference but as quantitative excess, "something more." This idea of racial essence as excess underlies the way music functions in the text. In "Blood-Burning Moon," as elsewhere in *Cane*, music erupts or is compelled from black characters, defining and giving voice to their blackness, and to whites' desire to access this blackness through acts of sex or violence. Louisa's song articulates the link between Bob and Tom, who are ultimately linked both by their shared desire for Louisa and by the racialized violence in which they both participate, and to which they both succumb. Tom fulfills his promise to "cut [Bob] just like a nigger," violently breaching the color line through an act of physical violence. As the factory workers discuss the inevitable conflict between Bob and Tom over Louisa, they contrast Tom—a "bad nigger" who has "been on th gang three times fo cuttin men"—with Bob: "Blood of th old uns in his veins. . . . He'll scrap, sho."[40] As with Bob's longing for the prerogatives of slave ownership, the black factory workers identify racial privilege in this history. Their invoking the metaphor of blood, however, highlights the irony inherent in this genealogy: the very nature of Bob's nostalgic fantasy—unquestioned sexual access to black women—suggests that the "[b]lood of the old uns" runs not only in his veins but in those of the descendants of the female slaves victimized by this prerogative. Beneath the white-supremacist logic of hierarchical racial difference lies a barely obscured history of consanguinity, and this history erupts in Louisa's song.

"Bona and Paul": Race, Desire, and Difference

"Bona and Paul," the final story in the book's second section, echoes this notion of blackness as inscrutable object of desire. Another narrative of triangulated desire, this one entails four "white" characters: Bona, Art, Art's girlfriend Helen, and his roommate Paul, "whom the whole dormitory calls a nigger." Though the story involves four characters rather than three, their relationships are nonetheless triangulated through two overlapping triangles, each with Paul at the center. One involves Paul, Art, and Helen; the other Paul, Art, and Bona. In each case, the supposition that Paul is a "nigger" motivates the others' desire. As it is for Bob Stone in "Blood-Burning Moon," this quality of "nigger" is for everyone involved an object of fascination, desire, and fear. Bona, Helen, and Art are fascinated with Paul: "[Helen] goes out as often as she can with Art and Paul. She explains this to herself by a piece of information which a friend of hers had given her: men like him can fascinate. One is not responsible for fascination. Not one girl had really loved Paul; he fascinated them. Bona didn't; only thought she did. And of course, *she* didn't."[41]

"Bona and Paul," like "Blood-Burning Moon," articulates a psychoanalytic logic of racial difference as the object of desire. Bona echoes Bob Stone in her association of Paul's blackness with his desirability: "He is a harvest moon. He is an autumn leaf. He is a nigger."[42] This racial identification is undercut with ambiguity and uncertainty, however; Bona reprimands herself for calling Paul a nigger but then asks herself, rhetorically, "But dont all the dorm girls say so?" The peculiar formulation through which Bona figures Paul's racial identity—"harvest moon" / "autumn leaf" / "nigger"—serves too to emphasize the arbitrariness of the epithet, as "nigger" is positioned interchangeably with less fraught terms. This formula is emblematic of the story's negotiation of racial identification, which at times appears to undermine the binary logic of race that structures racist notions of hierarchical racial difference. The story, however, holds such an anti-essentialist notion of race in tension with recurring invocations of racial identifications imposed from without as reflecting an interior racial quality. Importantly, this racial essence is expressed through a conflation of music and desire.

"Bona and Paul" represents a fantasy of escape from the paradoxical but nonetheless binding binary strictures of black and white whose transgression motivates the plot of "Blood-Burning Moon," but this fantasy is ultimately undermined by the reinstantiation of racial difference. As in the other stories set in the urban North, "Bona and Paul" emphasizes links with and transformation of the southern "folk" culture whose passing the first section of the book laments. From his room in Chicago, Paul imagines this connection: "Paul follows the sun to a pine-matted hillock in Georgia. . . . A Negress chants a lullaby beneath the mate-eyes of a southern planter. Her breasts are ample for the suckling of song. She weans it, and sends it, curiously weaving, among lush melodies of *cane* and corn. Paul follows the sun into himself in Chicago." This passage's invocation of a "Negress" stands in stark contrast to the racial ambiguity the story ascribes to Paul. At the same time, the "mate-eyes of a southern planter" imply racial admixture, in another echo of the book's southern stories. Paul's racial status, then, despite its ambiguity, is rooted in the unproblematized racial terminology of the rural South. The song of the "Negress" links Paul to her and to the racial logic of the world she inhabits. Paul imagines himself in a filial, genealogical relation to explicitly racialized southern ancestors. Likewise, the narrator describes "[m]ellow stone mansions [that] overshadow clapboard homes which now resemble Negro shanties in some southern alley."[43] Such ties illustrate how the racial logic of the South as represented elsewhere in *Cane* extends to the Chicago of "Bona and Paul."

Similar connections between African American characters in the North and a southern folk heritage appear elsewhere in *Cane*. In "Theater," for example, once Dorris sheds her bourgeois inhibitions and responds to John's silent injunction to "dance from yourself. Dance!," she does so in a way that evokes an ancestral South: "Glorious songs are the muscles of her limbs. And her singing is of canebrake loves and mangrove feastings." The implicit eroticism of this description is soon made explicit, as "[t]he walls press in, singing. Flesh of a throbbing body, they press close to John and Dorris."[44] John loses himself in an erotic reverie as Dorris dances. After her dance ends as "[t]he pianist crashes a bumper chord," she misrecognizes his having lost himself in his dream as disinterest, and their erotic connection is frustrated and severed (anticipating the eventual outcome of "Bona and Paul").

"Box Seat," another story from the book's second section, set in Washington, D.C., concerns the courtship between Dan and Muriel, neither of whom is explicitly identified as black, though the narrative hints at such an identification through invocations of songs of the South. Dan conceives of Muriel's lips as "flesh-notes of a forgotten song" and declares, "I was born in a canefield" (57). Later this first image is repeated as "Muriel's lips become the flesh-notes of a futile, plaintive longing" (60). In "flesh-notes," the neologism that Toomer uses twice in the story, sexual desire and music are fused through the figurative embodiment of music. In the first instance, they comprise a song; in the second, longing. At the beginning of the story, Dan tries to sing but is stifled by the repressive culture of bourgeois Washington. His repression stands in stark contrast with the organic songs of "niggers" with whom he identifies ambivalently. Muriel fantasizes that Dan's repression will be cast off in an act of sexualized violence: "He cant reach me. He wont dare come in here. He'd put his head down like a goring bull and charge me. He'd trample them. He'd gore. He'd rape"(62). Toomer's portrait of Dan as a repressed neurotic anticipates Eugene Gordon's sardonic diagnosis of the black bourgeoisie in the *American Mercury* five years later: "Standing in the glare of Caucasian ridicule, he has become sensitive, secretive, and hypocritical, and full of inhibitions—in fact, a sad Freudian case."[45] Having followed Muriel to a theater, Dan sits next to "a portly Negress" whom he imagines to possess an organic connection to an ancestral South that he himself lacks. The fantasy that this encounter subsequently provokes directly echoes Paul's imagined southern lullaby: "A soil-soaked fragrance comes from her. Through the cement floor her strong roots sink down. They spread under the asphalt streets. . . . Her strong roots sink down and spread under the river and disappear in blood-lines that waver south. Her roots shoot down. Dan's hands follow them."[46]

The ancestral blackness of the "Negress" troubles Dan, and his affective identification with her leads him to the realization that "[h]e doesn't fit" with the theater crowd surrounding him. This identification is intensified later when Dan notices an old African American man: "Strange I never really noticed him before. Been sitting there for years. Born a slave. Slavery not so long ago. . . . Swing low, sweet chariot" (65). Dan's vexed relationship with a southern, African American folk past is compressed into his invoking this paradigmatic sorrow song, which links the modernity of his world to the ancestral folk world of the old man and the "Negress."

Bona, too, has links with the South, though the narrative provides little in the way of details. Art considers the rumors that Paul is black: "Dark blood; nigger? Thats what those jealous she-hens say. Not Bona though, or she . . from the South . . wouldnt want me to fix a date for him and her" (72; partial ellipses in the original). Contrary to Art's supposition, though, Bona's southernness appears to contribute to her desire for Paul. Paul asks her, "From the South. What does that mean, precisely, except that you'll love or hate a nigger? . . . What does it mean except that in Chicago you'll have the courage to neither love or hate. A priori" (75). Paul diagnoses the dialectic of desire and animosity that characterizes black/white interactions in the book's first section, suggesting hopefully that Chicago will offer an opportunity to escape this southern model. This possibility of escape is both eroticized (Paul fantasizes about "penetrat[ing] a dark pane" that separates him from Bona) and figured ecstatically through music: "But I feel good! The color and the music and the song" (75, 76). The music that accompanies this scene is orchestral jazz, but the lullaby of the "Negress" through which Paul had earlier conceived of his relation to the South recurs and interrupts his soliloquy: "A Negress chants a lullaby beneath the mate-eyes of a Southern planter. O song!" (76). For Paul, as for Bona, the erotic possibilities that Chicago affords are overdetermined by the racial history of the South. Even as Paul considers the possibility of a romance freed from the strictures of racial and sexual domination, this history makes itself audible though the song of the "Negress."

As in "Blood-Burning Moon," race in "Bona and Paul" is figured through metaphors of blood. Art considers Paul's "[d]ark blood; nigger?" and is surprised to find that "Paul, contrary to what he had thought he would be like, is cool like the dusk, and like the dusk, detached" (73). Bona, meanwhile, concludes that Paul is "Colored; cold. Wrong somewhere" (74). For Art and Bona, Paul's dark skin suggests some sort of ineffable internal difference. For Paul, on the other hand, this difference is imposed from without, though he eventually internalizes it. As he, Bona, and Art go to dinner, he feels the eyes of their fellow patrons on him, as they wonder at his indeterminate racial status: "What is he, a Spaniard, an Indian, an Italian, a Mexican, a Hindu, or a Japanese?" Such indeterminacy would seem to point to race as constructed, contingent, and arbitrary, and such a view is in fact consonant with Toomer's own later pronouncements. Within the narrative, however, for Paul this very contingency—the indistinct but nonetheless compelling superficial difference that others perceive—provides a key to unlocking his sense of a real internal racial difference: "Their stares, giving him to himself, filled something long empty within him, and were like green blades sprouting in his consciousness. There was fullness, and strength, and peace about it all. He saw himself, cloudy, but real." By internalizing the difference perceived by others, by seeing himself through their eyes as racially Other, Paul realizes his own racial identity, which, though "cloudy," is nonetheless "real." Paul publicly affirms this identification at the end of the story, and in so doing does away with the ambiguity that had enabled Bona to act on her desire without explicitly transgressing the taboo of an interracial sexual relationship.

Two aspects of this process are particularly salient. The first is the relief that Paul feels at claiming a determinate racial identity, even the silent identification that provides him with "fullness" and "peace." Paul's embrace of this newly determinate racial status precedes his sharing this racial identification or knowledge with others. Art, for one, continues to be bothered by the other diners' stares after Paul's realization: "And those godam people staring so. Paul's a queer fish. Doesnt seem to mind . . . . I could stick up for him if he'd only come out, one way or the other, and tell a feller" (75). Art's frustration derives from his being deprived of the racial knowledge that Paul has just come to possess. Second, Paul considers his externally visible racial difference as an object of desire: "Suddenly he knew that people saw, not attractiveness in his dark skin, but difference" (74). Paul draws an opposition between "attractiveness" and "difference" and thereby misreads the relationship between the two qualities as Bona, Helen, and Art perceive them. Their desire for Paul, like Bob Stone's for Louisa in "Blood-Burning Moon," is a product of Paul's perceived racial difference. "Attractiveness" and "difference" are in fact the same quality.

This confluence of racial "difference" and "attractiveness" is finally what defines "nigger" in the story; what at first seems to be a pejorative racial term in fact diagnoses a relation between a desiring subject and the object of his or her desire. In this story, as in "Blood-Burning Moon" and "Fern," this desire-as-difference is rendered audible through musical performance; this aural component complements and, as we shall see momentarily, complicates the visual. Audible and visible racial differences are operative not only in Bona's desire for Paul but also in Paul's for Art and Art's for Paul. The narrator describes Art in the terms of "attractiveness" and "difference" through which Paul conceives of himself being seen: "Art has on his patent-leather pumps and fancy vest. . . . His face is a healthy pink the blue of evening tints a purple pallor. Art is happy and confident in the good looks that his mirror gave him" (72). Paul's "dark face," meanwhile, "is a floating shade in evening's shadow."

Mid-paragraph the perspective shifts from the narrator's to Paul's, as he "sees Art, curiously. . . . He loves Art. But is it not queer, this pale purple facsimile of a red-blooded Norwegian friend of his?" (73). Paul ruminates on racial difference ("Perhaps for some reason, white skins are not supposed to live at night"), as "Art [sits] on the piano and simply [tears] it down. Jazz." That Art, who is so emphatically racialized as white, plays jazz with such passion is somewhat surprising, given the racialization of musical performance in the book. More surprising, however, is Paul's response: "I've got to get the kid to play that stuff for me in the daytime. Might be different. More himself. More nigger. Different? There is. Curious, though." Paul's grammar here is curious as well, perhaps indicating his struggle to articulate the paradox that this formulation embodies: Art, who is phenotypically white—parodically so ("this pale purple facsimile of a red-blooded Norwegian")—nonetheless possesses an inner quality that Paul defines as "nigger" and that is audible through Art's musical performance.

Paradoxically, Art's counterintuitively racialized musical aptitude both evinces and confounds the binary logic of racial difference, mirroring the evident confuting of racial stereotype in Art's perception of Paul as "cool" and "detached." Art, Paul, and the narrator all use the word "queer" to describe these confusions of racialist logic, suggesting that these transgressions of racial demarcations lead to or reflect transgressions of erotic boundaries as well.[47] Art, considering Paul's reluctance to confirm or deny that he is "a nigger," perceives something "[q]ueer about him." Art could "stick up for him if he'd only come out, one way or another, and tell a feller."[48] The queerness engendered by Paul's racial indeterminacy, and Art's desire for him to "come out," suggest a relation between racial indeterminacy and what Sedgwick calls "[m]ale homosocial desire."[49] Paul reciprocates both this desire and this language of queerness: "He loves Art. But is it not queer, this pale purple facsimile of a red-blooded Norwegian friend of his?"[50] The racial difference that Paul perceives in Art here motivates homosocial desire. Helen, Art's girlfriend, appears to be aware of the situation and invokes Paul's racial difference as a justification for Art to sever ties with him: "She tries to get Art to break with him, saying, that if Paul, whom the whole dormitory calls a nigger, is more to him than she is, well, she's through" (76). Her reaction highlights the dual transgressions that Art's relationship with Paul represents: it both transgresses the color line and poses a threat to the heteronormative relationship between Art and Helen.

The polymorphous configurations of desire at work in the story—Helen's for Paul, Paul's for Art, Art's for Paul, Paul's and Bona's for each other—are momentarily resolved as Bona decides that she loves Paul, and he admits that she interests him: "Don't I, Paul? her eyes ask." This question, which both instantiates what is evidently a cross-racial desire and stabilizes the previously inchoate circuits of desire in the story along heterosexual lines, sets the stage for a final instance of musical performance: "Her answer is a crash of jazz." As Bona and Paul dance, their blood commingles metaphorically and erotically: "The dance takes blood from their minds and packs it, tingling, in the torsos of their swaying bodies. Passionate blood leaps back into their eyes. They are a dizzy blood clot on a gyrating floor. They know that the pink-faced people have no part in what they feel" (77). For a moment, it appears as though jazz has enabled Bona and Paul to transcend the color line through a shared affective response to the music, coupled with an erotic desire for each other. Such a fantasy of racial commingling both recapitulates and complicates the language of blood at work earlier in the book.

Both Dan in "Box Seat" and Paul in "Bona and Paul" conceive of a link to a rural African American folk culture figured through metaphors of blood and music. Bona's disavowal of "the pink-faced people" suggests that an affective response both to jazz and to Paul's racialized "difference" provides her access to this culture as well. Rather than Paul's being "whitewashed"—the neurotic condition that affects Dan—Bona instead gains access to blackness through her connection with Paul: "Their [now-shared racial] instinct leads them away from Art and Helen, and towards the big uniformed black man who opens and closes the gilded exit door." Paul observes that the black man leers at them knowingly ("Too many couples have passed out, flushed and fidgety, for him not to know"). He "leaves Bona and darts back" to confront "the huge bulk of the Negro," to tell him that he is mistaken. Paul insists that what the black doorman sees as sexual desire is actually knowledge: "I came into the Gardens with one I did not know. . . . I felt passion, contempt and passion for her whom I did not know." Their shared response to the music they have heard, Paul argues, has allowed them to transcend the color line and to achieve a racial fusion: "I came back to tell you, brother, that white faces are petals of roses. That dark faces are petals of dusk. . . . That I am going out and know her whom I brought here with me to these Gardens which are purple like a bed of roses would be at dusk" (78).

At least two orders of metaphor are operative in Paul's speech. The first is essentialized and ontological: "dark faces are petals of dusk," while "white faces are petals of roses." These racialized essences are complicated by the final turn, though, fusing into "purple like a bed of roses would be at dusk." In this final metaphor, the racialized essence of whiteness ("petals of roses") is transformed through its contact with blackness. After this conversation with the doorman (during which Paul addresses him as "brother," affirming a racial tie), Paul discovers that Bona is gone, and the story abruptly ends.

Paul's vision in which white "petals of roses" and "dark . . . petals of dusk" merge "like a bed of roses would be at dusk" represents the fleeting, optimistic apogee of *Cane*'s vision of the transcendence of racial difference. This fusion would be accomplished, presumably, by acknowledging difference as the object of desire; by capitulating to an erotic desire triggered by a perception of racialized difference, Paul and Bona hope to transcend that very difference. That the quality of this difference—that of "nigger"—is perceptible not only in Paul but also in Art (the obvious allegorical significance of whose name should not be ignored) through his performance suggests both that the transcendence that Paul hopes for will short-circuit not only the racial logic that shadows his relations with Bona but also the gendered ones that structure his with Art. Art's "jazz," then, serves not as a signifier of an innate racial difference but rather of the dissolution of this difference, as sound is dissociated from the visual logic of race.

The story's ending, however, frustrates this hope. Paul's encounter with "the Negro" resolves the vexed question of his racial identification. Although Paul insists that the black man's perception that he and Bona are enacting a ritual of racial and sexual desire is wrong, and that their "contempt and passion" have been sublated into knowledge, in the end this transcendence is denied. Just as for Bob Stone "there [is] something about niggers you couldnt know," the knowledge that Paul seeks is ultimately unattainable. The transcendence of racial difference whose possibility becomes fleetingly audible in the jazz that Art plays and that motivates Bona and Paul's momentary imagined fusion into "a dizzy blood clot on a gyrating floor" is sundered by the symbolic reimposition of the color line.

Throughout *Cane*, music alternately voices the possibility of transcending racial difference and sounds the color line that forecloses this possibility. In each of the book's narratives, from the southern soundscapes of "Fern" and "Blood-Burning Moon" to the urban milieu of "Bona and Paul," musical performances are intimately tied to questions of racial identity. As my discussion of these narratives has shown, however, race in *Cane* is far from a static property, but neither is it merely arbitrary or purely performative. Rather, race erupts through musical figurations in these narratives as "the residual surplus meaning of unconscious desire."[51] This figure of desire takes on various forms throughout the book but consistently manifests itself through racialized musical expressions. Together, finally, these instances suggest an understanding of race and racial difference that sounds differently from the dominant racial logics with which Toomer struggled and in relation to which his work has been read. Even while dramatizing the continual reinforcement of the color line through means both violent and subtle, *Cane* holds out the possibility of reconfiguring race through sound, confounding the racial logic of the visible.

CHAPTER SIX

Music and Racial Violence in William Faulkner's *Sanctuary*

Written later in the 1920s and from the other side of the color line, William Faulkner's *Sanctuary* further illuminates the interrelations of racial difference and racialized violence, sexual desire, and music that feature so prominently in Jean Toomer's *Cane*. Befitting a novel that he claimed was "a cheap idea," a commercial venture into popular fiction, *Sanctuary* weaves into its narrative fabric a number of popular musical forms.[1] Faulkner reportedly claimed to have "worn out three records of [George] Gershwin's 'Rhapsody in Blue'" in order to "set the rhythm and jazzy tone" of the novel.[2] Faulkner's invocation of Gershwin's piece, first performed in 1924, suggests an analogy between Gershwin's incorporation of vernacular musical forms, particularly jazz, into his compositions and Faulkner's own later uses of such materials. Gershwin, in an essay entitled "Composer in the Machine Age," wrote that in "America [the] preferred rhythm is called jazz. . . . When jazz is played in another nation, it is called American. . . . Jazz is the result of the energy stored up in America. It is a very energetic kind of music, noisy, boisterous, and even vulgar."[3] This description of America's "preferred rhythm" anticipates the significance that Faulkner ascribes to Gershwin's music. Gershwin and Faulkner both attest to an aim of transmuting vernacular sources into the refined distillates of the concerto and the novel, respectively. As Jeffrey Melnick has argued, for Gershwin this aesthetic incorporation also involves a complex racial negotiation—in order for jazz to become distinctively "American," it is necessary for the composer to "loosen jazz from its racial moorings."[4] *Rhapsody in Blue*, then, serves as a musical melting pot in which the artistic products of African American folk culture are amalgamated with other ingredients into a distinctively American high art form.

Faulkner's description of the "rhythm and jazzy tone" that his novel borrows from *Rhapsody in Blue* evokes the celebratory deployment of African American vernacular music in Gershwin's composition. The discourses of racial and sexual violence in the novel are intertwined with its engagement with popular music. The instances of musical performance in the novel not only illuminate the racial politics of Faulkner's fictional world but also shed light on the complex and often contradictory associations of racial identities and musical forms that characterize understandings of vernacular music in the novel's late 1920s cultural milieu. While these subjects have received much less critical attention in Faulkner's work than in Toomer's, we can nevertheless see in *Sanctuary* evidence of how racialized understandings of music (and musical understandings of race) crucially inform the work not only of African American–identified writers like Toomer, Wright, or Ellison but also self-identified southerners like Faulkner.

This chapter focuses on three scenes in *Sanctuary* in which commercial popular records, sung spirituals, and small group jazz, respectively, provide the means through which the novel interrogates the relationships between racial identities and musical forms. The scenes rehearse three alternative understandings of these relations. They reveal the workings of segregation's cultural logic and the stress points at which it breaks down. While the cultural logic of Jim Crow and the violence that attends it establish a musical color line, instances of vernacular music in the novel reflect and catalyze the breakdown of the "dream of the old South" by troubling the binary logic of racial difference upon which it depends. Each of these instances elaborates a scene of death or mourning: the first concerns "ballads" of "bereavement," the second portrays the laments of an African American murderer on the verge of his execution, and the third narrates a funerary scene drawn from popular song. *Sanctuary* first evokes the loss of an agrarian social order, moves on to the songs of African Americans as a response to the pervasive threat of racial violence against them, and then arrives at a funeral scene whose treatment of death through the blues evinces an anxious engagement with musical traversals of the color line. These instances of music in the novel, in other words, both sound the color line and highlight its arbitrary contours.

Ballads

Sanctuary juxtaposes the racially ambiguous music heard on radios and phonographs with the racially marked songs sung by a doomed "negro murderer."[5] Both sets of performances attract a multiracial audience, though the narrator is careful to differentiate its members by race only in the latter case. Significantly, his description of the mass-mediated music that captivates its rural audience assiduously avoids any explicit racial markers at all. As Horace Benbow walks into the town of Jefferson, he encounters "a slow, continuous throng" of visitors from the country, "black and white." The narrator casually mentions the interracial composition of this "throng," but this interracial difference is superseded by the identifiably rural nature of their dress and manner. Though they hope to be taken for "town dwellers," they are instead "unmistakable by the unease of their garments as well as by their method of walking . . . not even fooling one another." The crowd of rural people, likened by the narrator to "streams of ants," "sheep," and "a deliberate current," move not only from country to city but also from a timeless agrarian past into modernity. They function "outside of time, having left time lying upon the slow and imponderable land."[6] The dynamic, modern townscape of Jefferson stands in stark opposition to this static agrarian landscape, and the rural folks' encounter with modernity is mediated through sound:

> The sunny air was filled with competitive radios and phonographs in the doors of drug- and music-stores. Before these doors a throng stood all day, listening. The pieces which moved them were ballads simple in melody and theme, of bereavement and retribution and repentance metallically sung, blurred, emphasized by static or needle—disembodied voices blaring from the imitation wood cabinets or pebble-grain horn-mouths above the rapt faces, the gnarled slow hands long shaped to the imperious earth, lugubrious, harsh and sad.[7]

What are these "ballads" that so captivate the "throng" that gathers to hear them? The narrator identifies the other instances of vernacular or popular music in the novel by some combination of race and genre—as in much of the thinking about race and music during this period, race and genre are nearly synonymous—and in some instances even indicates specific titles. Here, however, the songs played by radios and phonographs are described only as "ballads simple in melody and theme, of bereavement and retribution and repentance." Sean Wilentz and Greil Marcus maintain that ballads "were the dim forerunners of modern commercial popular music," and this description seems partially to match Faulkner's usage.[8] The themes of "bereavement and retribution and repentance" that he describes permeate such popular songs of murder, remorse, and revenge as "Pretty Polly" (Dock Boggs's popular recording was issued in 1927), "Ommie Wise" (aka "Omie Wise," aka "Naomi Wise"; recorded by G. B. Grayson in 1927, Clarence Ashley in 1929, and in numerous other versions), and "Frankie" (aka "Frankie and Johnny," aka "Frankie and Albert"; perhaps the most famous versions of these were recorded by Mississippi John Hurt in 1928 and fellow Mississippian Jimmie Rodgers a year later). Any of these songs could conceivably be heard on the streets of a Mississippi town in 1929, when the action of the novel takes place. Faulkner's use of the term "ballads," though, is complicated by the specifically racial valence that the term had by then accrued through the work of academic folklorists and collectors, as I discussed in chapter 1.

The conflict that Werner Sollors has identified between "contractual and hereditary, self-made and ancestral, definitions of American identity—between *consent* and *descent*" (as discussed in chapter 1) structures and animates much of Faulkner's work, as it does so much of the history of vernacular music in the twentieth century.[9] Such conceptions depend upon a logic of cultural, social, and physical segregation; the proponents of descent-oriented understandings of ballad and song traditions sought out singers from communities that had supposedly been isolated from members of other racial and ethnic groups and, ideally, from the modern world and its culture industries. Despite the conscious attempts by Cecil Sharp, the Lomaxes, and others to collect songs from sources who had been denied intercultural or interracial contact, such folk collectors were consistently mortified to find their informants—white and black—singing songs of hillbilly or, worse, vaudeville, origin. Charles Seeger sums up this idea succinctly: "You have to keep a tight rein on things or else you hear nothing but jazz."[10]

In retrospect, the anxiety that academic collectors seeking "ballads" expressed when finding their subjects singing contemporary hillbilly or blues songs or playing jazz appears to be motivated by a profound misunderstanding of the very folk cultures that they aimed to document and preserve. Advocates of racially bound musical traditions, while misguided in their fear of jazz, were, to a certain extent, accurate in their concern that music they considered culturally foreign might permeate and ineluctably influence the music of the southern folk of such interest to them. Try as they might, such racially minded purists proved utterly incapable of fortifying the always permeable, tenuous, and largely artificial barriers that separated folk and popular, urban and rural, and black and white styles, songs, and traditions.

While at first glance Faulkner (or at least his narrator) might appear to share many of these prejudices, his description of the crowd's response to the recorded music they hear suggests a more complex and sympathetic view. The racialist overdetermination of the term "ballads" is offset by Faulkner's rendering of the scene. On one hand, these "disembodied voices blaring from imitation wood cabinets," "metallically sung [and] blurred," appear as agents of country folks' alienation from the commodity culture that these new recording technologies represent. The members of the rural "throng" are "shaped" to the land through agricultural labor. Seen from this perspective, the mass media technologies of radio and the phonograph stand in synecdochally for the industrial changes transforming the lives of such laborers and driving nails in the coffin of the Old South. That the "disembodied voices" are "lugubrious, harsh and sad" suggests that we read this scene as one of mourning and that we hear the "ballads" as elegies for an agrarian world of master and slave whose passing these songs commemorate.

On the other hand, these songs are not only "blurred" by radios and phonographs but also "emphasized." The throngs who listen do not do so passively or unemotionally; instead, they are held "rapt," "moved" by the simple melodies and themes "of bereavement and retribution and repentance." Though the "ballads" that so move the listeners are described as "lugubrious, harsh and sad," the text provides little clue as to the specific affective response that they elicit. A clue to the nature of this response follows, however; in the next paragraph, we are told that the rural listeners "were back again, most of them, in clumps" the following Monday, even though May was "no time to leave the land." The object of fascination in this latter instance is not a recorded ballad telling a story of death and regret, but rather the dead body of Tommy, a mentally handicapped man who had been shot and killed earlier in the novel. Tommy, like the members of the throng, is described in terms that mark him as from the country: he is "barefoot, in overalls." Some of the spectators, we learn, "had known him for fifteen years about the countryside." Some of the city folk had "on infrequent Saturdays . . . seen him in town, barefoot, hatless, with his rapt, empty gaze."[11] Tommy's bare feet and overalls mark him as a stereotyped rural southerner, while the description of his "rapt, empty gaze" mirrors the "rapt faces" of the rural throng as they listen to the disembodied voices sounding from radios and phonographs of Jefferson's streets. Tommy's identification with the members of the rural throng who come to mourn him is prefigured earlier in the novel through a description of affect: "From time to time he would feel that acute surge go over him, like his blood was too hot all of a sudden, dying away into that warm unhappy feeling that fiddle music gave him."[12] This description provides an insight into the emotions that the visitors to the town experience in response to the music they hear. The "warm unhappy feeling" that fiddle music elicits in Tommy, in other words, anticipates the visitors' affective response to "ballads . . . lugubrious, harsh and sad."

In 1929, the year in which *Sanctuary* is set, the songs heard on radios and phonographs in the South were more likely to be commercial hillbilly or race records than ballads in the folkloristic sense, although as noted, such distinctions were hardly respected by the musicians themselves. Despite, or perhaps because of, the mass media's commodification and reproduction of these "ballads," their affective power is not diminished but rather amplified. This view, implicit in Faulkner's rendering of the scene, can fruitfully be read as anticipating Lawrence Levine's argument in "The Folklore of Industrial Society" that such affective responses frustrate the putative distinction between authentic folk culture and inauthentic popular culture. Levine argues against the notion that popular culture does not emanate "from within the community but [is] created—often artificially by people with pecuniary or ideological motives—*for* the community, or rather *for* the masses who no longer [have] an organic community capable of producing culture."[13] For Levine, to distinguish between such popular, mass-mediated cultural forms and authentic "folk" forms is a mistake, as the "folk" themselves respect no such distinctions.

Faulkner's description of the country folks' affective response to the music they hear through the new forms of mass media likewise reveals a blurring of the boundaries between folk and popular, between lived experience and commodified performance. By 1929, the cultural logic of segregation—and the aforementioned musical color line—had been firmly established in the marketing practices of the recording industry. The major record labels maintained separate "hillbilly" and "race" series for white and black artists, respectively, though these distinctions were in large part artificial. Faulkner's evocation of these records and their audience, however, denies or at least sidesteps these racialized distinctions by eschewing the record companies' generic terminology. This refusal to delineate the songs by genre and race complicates the equation between musical forms and racial identities so prevalent at the time. *Sanctuary* does not indicate the race of the performers whose recordings so enrapture the rural throng. Though both the normative racism of Faulkner's fictional world and that of the folkloristic tradition that had come to define the term "ballad" suggest that people and cultural forms thus unmarked should probably be understood as white, they are therefore literally unraced.

The text itself, though, is ambiguous, and this ambiguity helps undermine the racialist thinking that underlies the strict association of this musical form with white racial identity. The members of the "throng" are identified first as "white and black," though their collective identity appears to be neither, but rather rural and agricultural: "the rapt faces, the gnarled slow hands long shaped to the imperious earth." This description leaves open the possibility of interracial or cross-racial identification, as the voices on the records that fill the air are "disembodied," and the bodies of the listeners are characterized not by racial designations but by the physical markers of agricultural toil that they share. John N. Duvall's analysis of the ways in which the social conditions of agricultural labor in the South generally, and in Faulkner's fictional

Yoknapatawpha County specifically, blur the racial lines between "white" and "black," "to unhinge the Southern binary that would oppose whiteness to 'the Negro,'" provides one way to think through this dynamic.[14] I think that Duvall overstates the case somewhat in his claim that as sharecroppers, "black and white bodies inhabit an *identical* subject position."[15] Nevertheless, we can see in Faulkner's pointedly unraced description of such sharecroppers' rapt engagement with the "disembodied voices" a suggestion that they forge in response a collective identity that supplements, even if it cannot supplant, racial identities defined according to the terms of the white/black binary.[16]

In Faulkner's account, the collective identity thus forged through a multiracial audience's shared identification with the disembodied songs and sounds made available to them through mass media technologies thus supplements and potentially undermines the logic of descent that had accrued via a half-century of scholarly attention to folk balladry, and which subtly underlies Faulkner's own terminology. The scene he describes instead illustrates the short-circuiting of a cultural logic of descent; we may see in its place the emergence of a culture of consent that Sollors posits as descent's antithesis. If the logic of descent undergirds Sharp's notion that the songs of "mountain people" transmit "racial attributes" or Lomax's idea that the culture of "the Negro" is best preserved by the forced segregation of the prison camp, the scene Faulkner describes suggests a very different notion of cultural affiliation through a shared affective response. The individual audience members' affective responses to the "ballads" they hear are defined, not by their ethnic heritage or racial attributes, but rather by their affective identification with disembodied cultural productions that are not limited or defined by race, place, or genre. Racial identification, then, is supplemented by the shared emotional identification that the recorded "ballads" enable.

Spirituals

Such cross-racial moments of cultural consent are limited by social realities, of course, and all such racial ambiguity is dispensed within the novel's next chapter, as the color line is violently reimposed through the execution of "a negro murderer" who had killed his wife by slitting her throat: "He would lean in the window in the evening and sing. After supper a few negroes gathered along the fence below . . . and in chorus with the murderer, they sang spirituals while white people slowed and stopped . . . to listen to those who were sure to die and him who was already dead singing about heaven and being tired."[17] In contrast to the carefully unraced depiction of the throng enraptured by the radio and phonograph at the end of the previous chapter, this description is replete with racial markers. The singer and the songs he sings are clearly identified by race and genre, respectively. The murderer is "a negro," and other "negroes" join him "in chorus." Together they sing "spirituals," a genre generally, if not universally, understood as black.[18] Their audience, on the other hand, consists of "white people."

Unlike the murky ambiguity of the recorded ballads already discussed, the explicit racial and generic marking of the prisoner and his songs posits a direct equation between the race of the singer and the racial significance of his songs. The singer's racial status as "a negro" and the status of the spirituals he sings are of course products of a system of segregation and racial violence. In marked contrast with the disembodied recorded "ballads" that allow for an elective identification that potentially frustrates racial boundaries, the spirituals' literal embodiment in the figure of the "negro murderer" reinforces racial difference and the cultural logic of segregation. Other "negroes" of diverse occupation (they wear "natty, shoddy suits and sweat-stained overalls") identify with the murderer and join in his singing, while whites are silent auditors—a race apart, despite their physical proximity.[19] Underlying this racial division is the pervasive threat of racial violence and death. The "negroes" of the chorus, none of whom have been suspected of any crime, so far as we know, "are sure to die," and the "negro murderer" himself is, symbolically at least, "already dead." A "rich, sourceless" voice mourns that in "Fo days mo . . . dey ghy stroy de bes ba'ytone singer in nawth Mississippi!"[20] The spirituals in the novel emanate from moribund black bodies.

After this scene-setting episode, Lee Goodwin discusses the question of his own presumed guilt with Benbow, his lawyer. Benbow reminds Goodwin that he is "not being tried by common sense" but rather "by a jury."[21] The novel gives no description of any such counsel being afforded to the "negro murderer" before he is condemned to die. By contrast, the crime of which "the negro murderer" is accused is flatly asserted: he "had killed his wife." Likewise, the narrative gives no account of his trial having been decided by a jury; two sentences after his guilt is asserted, he is described matter-of-factly as "sure to die."[22] It seems, then, that he has been tried by what passes for common sense in Jefferson, which is to say by Jim Crow. From his introduction into the narrative until his execution, the negro murderer's singing is explicitly linked with his impending death at the hands of whites: "one night he would be singing . . . the next night he would be gone."[23] Goodwin, meanwhile, awaits his trial, reaping one of the benefits of his whiteness: recourse to "the law, civilization, justice."[24] Benbow's sister Narcissa sardonically fantasizes that the racial distinctions which dictate Goodwin's and the negro's separate and unequal treatment will collapse. "He had better sing fast," Benbow remarks;

"He's only got two days more." Narcissa replies, "Maybe they'll wait and hang them both together."[25] Though she doesn't get her wish, in the end, Goodwin's eventual castration and immolation by a mob for a rape of which he is innocent does put him in the position of a lynched "negro," collapsing the racial distinction between him and his fellow prisoner.

Chapter 17 repeats the scene of "the negro murderer . . . singing in chorus with those along the fence below."[26] The text provides no description of "the negro murderer"; we do not learn his name, nor are we told whether he is tall or short, fat or thin, light-skinned or dark, young or old. Aside from one brief description of "his face checkered by the shadow of the grating in the restless interstices of leaves," he is an unseen presence, represented only by his voice.[27] Though this voice is therefore disembodied, its significance is ultimately determined by a logic of racial embodiment and racial difference. The novel's presentation of the singer as a radically unindividuated figure is consistent with contemporary understandings of "spirituals" as the product of a racialized "folk" consciousness rather than as vehicles for individual expression. The songs that the condemned prisoner sings are transparent to the other negroes, who seamlessly join in singing them, while they appear obscure in both form and meaning to the whites who gather to listen. This obscurity is reflected in the text itself. Paralleling the absence of physical description of the condemned singer, any indicators of his songs' formal properties are likewise lacking. We are provided no descriptions of their tonality, tempo, or form. The words to his songs are never rendered in verse—that is, in a form that would help render them intelligible or accessible as part of a shared musical or poetic language. Instead, they are presented as utterances, as pleas and cries. At first glance, such paucity of description might seem to point simply to a lack of musicological interest or knowledge on Faulkner's part, but it also places the spirituals at a remove from both the prisoner's white listeners and the book's readers.

Such obscure representations of "spirituals" stand in contrast to those in *Sartoris*, published two years before *Sanctuary*, which contains detailed, accurate descriptions and renditions of African American music. For example, Gene Bluestein identifies as a spiritual a song that Elnora, an African American character, sings:

Sinner riz fum de moaner's bench,
Sinner jump to de penance bench;
When de preacher ask 'im whut de reason why,
Say, 'Preacher got de women jes' de same ez I.'

Oh, Lawd, oh, Lawd!
Dat's wut de matter wid de church today.[28]

One might take issue with this identification, as Elnora's song is less a spiritual in the classic sense than it is a specific secular, sardonic critique of a philandering preacher. Thadious M. Davis, for example, argues convincingly that the song Elnora sings in this passage is not a spiritual but rather a blues song: "Though the lyrics might be mistaken for a spiritual, as Bluestein does, they are more of a personal expression of her dissatisfaction, masked as a religious righteousness, and, importantly, the song is of her own making."[29] A similar confusion of spirituals and the blues is at work in *Sanctuary*. Nonetheless, Bluestein's observation that Faulkner has taken pains to represent accurately an instance of African American vernacular song stands. He also points to the earlier novel's description of Elnora's singing as floating "in meaningless minor suspense" and "mellow falling suspense" as evidence of Faulkner's sensitivity to the nuances of African American song: such descriptions catch "nicely the melismatic quality of Negro singing as it moves from tone to tone, rarely stopping on a given pitch."[30] The presence of such precise musical attention in *Sartoris* helps render conspicuous the lack of such attention in *Sanctuary;* this lack is properly read as deliberate and significant. In fact, Bluestein points to a similar elision in *Sartoris*—its inattention to "the singing which would accompany the blues"—as evidence that "Faulkner is still far from understanding fully the meaning or the function of blues in black tradition."[31] This assessment applies equally to *Sanctuary*, which evinces only a superficial engagement with the blues as a popular form, and none at all with the blues as a product of Jim Crow's system of racial difference and racialized violence. The songs that the condemned man and his chorus sing are instead described as "spirituals," though the sparse descriptions of the songs themselves present them not as group expressions of spiritual longing but rather as secular, personal protests against the singer's impending hanging.

The participation of the other "negroes" in the performance of the song suggests that we should consider these utterances as racial, not individual. Like the term "ballads," "spirituals" evokes a history that conceives of a vernacular musical form in racial terms. By the mid-nineteenth century, the term "spirituals" referred to religious songs sung by African American slaves, and the precise contours of the musical field the term denoted would be fiercely contested into the 1940s. In 1870 Thomas Wentworth Higginson proposed that the "Negro Spirituals" he heard from black soldiers during the Civil War were analogous to the Scottish ballads: "a kindred world of unwritten songs, as simple and indigenous as the Border Minstrelsy, more uniformly plaintive, almost always more quaint, and often as essentially poetic."[32] Such a view of spirituals as emotionally powerful folk poetry was elaborated over the course of the next half-century. In an essay in *The New Negro* (1925), Alain Locke asserts that "underneath broken words, childish imagery, [and] peasant simplicity, lies . . . an epic intensity and a tragic profundity of emotional experience."[33] This understanding of the spirituals as expressions of emotional anguish and longing for freedom harks back to Frederick Douglass's 1845 description of slaves' "songs of sorrow," whose "[e]very tone was a testimony against slavery," and to W. E. B. Du Bois's 1903 claim that they constitute "the articulate message of the slave to the world."[34] The negro murderer's songs resonate with this history, as they are pleas for delivery from unequal and unjust treatment under the law, from imprisonment and the lynch mob.

As we saw in chapter 4, by the 1920s the term "spirituals" had taken on a supplementary meaning, denoting a recognizable body of songs that African American intellectuals like Locke, James Weldon Johnson, and composers such as Nathaniel Dett and John Wesley Work hoped to develop into a concert repertoire. At the same time, white scholars like Newman Ivey White, George Pullen Jackson, Dorothy Scarborough, Howard Odum, and Guy Johnson had compiled and cataloged many instances of religious songs sung by African Americans, which White, for example, maintained provided access to "the character of the folk Negro."[35] Both these models suppose a degree of transparency or intelligibility across the color line. For Du Bois, Locke, and Johnson, the spirituals give voice to black subjects. Though their songs articulate a racially specific history of oppression and suffering, their themes are universal. Both in their "pure," presumably unmediated forms and as refined, concertized distillates, the spirituals attest to African Americans' claims to common humanity and provide sympathetic listeners a way to traverse the color line through musical identification. Johnson, for example, argues in his preface to *The Book of American Negro Poetry* that "No persons, however hostile, can listen to Negroes singing this wonderful music without having their hostility melted down."[36] White and his fellow folklorists likewise assume transparency in African American folk songs, though for them such material provides insight into "the negro" less as subject than as object of study. According to White, the texts of the songs he has collected reveal "the negro's" essential character: he is "a most naïve and unanalytical-minded person, with a sensuous joy in his religion; thoughtless, careless, unidealistic, rather fond of boasting, predominantly cheerful, . . . charitably inclined toward the white man," etc.[37] Diametrically opposed to Johnson's view, in which the spirituals are understood to produce an affective response that will eliminate hostility toward the race which produced them, White's view reaffirms invidious racial difference and legitimates discrimination against "the negro," whose inferior nature is made manifest through his music.

Contrary to understandings of spirituals either as expressions of pathos or as articulate messages protesting injustice, in *Sanctuary* the condemned man's songs do not elicit sympathetic emotional responses in white listeners: "white men sitting . . . across the street," for example, "listen above their steady jaws."[38] Goodwin, who is in as likely a position to identify with the condemned man's pleas as anyone, responds instead with irritation: "Damn that fellow. . . . I aint in any position to wish any man that sort of luck, but I'll be damned."[39] Goodwin's irritation at the chorus's singing is echoed toward the end of the novel, as Popeye awaits his own execution: "somewhere down the corridor a negro was singing . . . 'For Christ's sake,' [Popeye] said."[40] Rather than eliciting sympathy from white listeners occupying similar subject positions (that of condemned prisoners), the African American singers' songs—intelligible to other "negroes" and obscure to whites—reinscribe racial difference as they sound the color line. As whites and blacks in the novel hear this music with different ears, their disparate responses ironically recapitulate the relationship that Douglass famously describes in his *Narrative*. The slaves on Colonel Lloyd's plantation would, he writes, "sing, as a chorus . . . words which to many would seem unmeaning jargon, but which, nevertheless, were full of meaning to themselves."[41] To those "outside the circle" (i.e., whites), "these rude and apparently incoherent songs" would serve as "a testimony against slavery, and a prayer to God for deliverance from chains."[42] The transracial sympathy that for Douglass allows the meaning of these songs to penetrate the consciousness of white listeners is absent from the world of Faulkner's novel, short-circuited by the racial violence and hostility engendered by Jim Crow. Rather than eliciting cross-racial identification, the songs of the negro chorus serve instead to solidify racial difference.

Sanctuary includes two instances of the negro murderer's singing. In the first instance, the condemned man exclaims, "One day mo! Den Ise a gawn po sonnen bitch. Say, Aint no place fer you in heavum! Say, Aint no place fer you in hell! Say, Aint no place fer you in jail!"[43] His song is a plea for sanctuary, though one that is sure to be denied. Its second instance is slightly elaborated: "One day mo! Aint no place fer you in heavum! Aint no place fer you in hell! Aint no place fer you in whitefolks' jail! Nigger, whar you gwine to? Whar you gwine to, nigger?"[44] I am confident that the phrase "Ise a gawn po sonnen bitch" does not appear in any collection of spirituals. In fact, the inclusion of this profane preamble suggests that "spirituals" is an approximate and inaccurate label for the songs sung by the murderer and his chorus. While the novel's depictions of the murderer's songs as shared products of a racialized folk square with contemporary understandings of spirituals as folk expression, the songs' profanity and the specific circumstances from which they emerge and to which they speak complicate this identification.

The songs the condemned black man sings are less spiritual pleas to God or heaven than they are laments, remonstrances against the racial violence undergirding the system of Jim Crow. Moreover, they appear not as a part of a general repertoire but rather as products of the singer's specific situation as he counts down the days until his execution. Adam Gussow has argued that "the grievous spiritual pressures exerted on working-class black southerners by the sudden eruption of lynching-as-spectacle . . . help to form . . . a 'blues subject,' who then found ways, more or less covert, of singing back to that ever-hovering threat."[45] The self-identified "gawn po sonnen bitch" whose laments the novel records may be understood as precisely such a subject, and lynching—or at least hanging—at the hands of whites is the specific threat to which his songs sing back. While his songs may be understood as "black spirituals, with their collective subject pursuing a freedom coded as otherworldly," they are more clearly instances of a particular, individual subject longing for worldly freedom.[46] Though Faulkner never uses the word "blues" to describe the condemned man's songs (they are instead always described as "spirituals"), the stage he sets for them is precisely the one that, as Gussow argues, produces the blues as "a cultural form that enabled black people to salve their wounded spirits and assert their embattled individuality" in the face of the racial terror that buttressed Jim Crow.[47] Equally germane here is the distinction that Jahan Ramazani draws between the blues and spirituals as they relate to the process of mourning. Spirituals, according to Ramazani, "tend to be poems of normative mourning, whereas the blues are typically melancholic, un-redemptive and anti-consolatory like many modern elegies."[48] The characteristics that Ramazani ascribes to the blues describe the negro murderer's songs perfectly: far from songs of otherworldly redemption or spiritual consolation, laments like "Aint no place fer you in heavum! Aint no place fer you in hell! Aint no place fer you in whitefolks' jail!" are anticonsolatory and nonredemptive.

The generic substitution of "spirituals" for the blues that I am suggesting is significant in that it parallels a narrative displacement in which the violence of the negro murderer's execution/lynching is completely elided. It is substituted instead by a gruesome description of his wife's death at his hands: he "had killed his wife; slashed her throat with a razor so that, her whole head tossing further and further backward from the bloody regurgitation of her bubbling throat, she ran out the cabin door and for six or seven steps up the quiet moonlit lane."[49] This description of the dying black woman, which lingers over the grisly details of the woman's murder with something close to relish, is followed by the matter-of-fact, almost idyllic, "He would lean in the window in the evening and sing."[50] Through this abrupt tonal shift, the murderer's songs are distanced from his crime. They become the expression of a racial sentiment anchored in the past rather than a response to the here and now. The negro's own death at the hands of whites, by contrast, is not narrated: he "was to be hung on a Saturday without pomp, buried without circumstance."[51] This narrative elision borders on the perverse, given the spectacular nature of the lynching of black men in the Jim Crow South. In stark contrast to this historical and social fact, the black man's death at the hands of whites in the novel is simply a matter of procedure, not even bearing elaboration or description. The description of his songs as "spirituals" helps naturalize the killing of black men by whites as a response to real or imagined violence against women as procedural acts of justice rather than instances of racial terror. The fact that the victim here is an African American rather than a white woman constitutes an additional displacement.[52] If the blues can be understood, as Gussow argues, as a response to such acts of terror, their sublimation into "spirituals" helps obscure this relationship.

Blues

The narrative provides no motivation for the murder the African American singer is accused of, suggesting perhaps that a tendency to such acts of violence, like a proclivity to sing spirituals, is a racial trait. On the other hand, the fact that the victim in this case is the accused murderer's wife implies a sexual jealousy that begets violence, and this plot point resonates with the thematics of the novel as a whole. It also anticipates a scene later in the narrative: the funeral of Red, a gambler whom Popeye first solicits as a sexual partner for Temple, then murders. A scene of ecstatic mourning, Red's funeral elaborates the paradox inherent in the title of Gershwin's *Rhapsody in Blue*. Like the doomed murderer's songs discussed above, the blues in this scene arise from a confrontation with death. The last time we see Red alive, he is shooting craps. The next chapter opens with preparations for his funeral, in the same craps parlor. As the gambling den is converted into a temporary funeral home, the appurtenances of gambling and music-making are intermingled with funerary accoutrements: "Just beneath the orchestra platform the coffin sat. . . . [A] mass of flowers . . . appeared to break in a symbolical wave over the bier and on upon the platform and the piano, the scent of them thickly oppressive." "The negro waiters," meanwhile, "moved with swaggering and decorous repression; already the scene was vivid, with a hushed, macabre air a little febrile," while a "black pall lay upon the crap-table, upon which the overflow of flower shapes was beginning to accumulate."[53] Presiding over this scene is the proprietor; among the guests are a bootlegger, musicians, gamblers, pimps, madams, and prostitutes.

With its craps parlor setting, cast of colorful underworld characters, and central figure of the dead gambler, this scene literally stages a version of the popular ballad / folk song / jazz standard known variously as "Those Gambler's Blues," "St. James Infirmary," and "Dyin' Crap-shooter's Blues." Carl Sandburg's 1927 anthology, *The American Songbag*, includes under the heading "Blues, Mellows, Ballets" two versions of a song it identifies as "Those Gambler's Blues."[54] Sandburg's introductory note to the song observes, "This may be what polite society calls a gutter song. In a foreign language, in any lingo but that of the U.S.A., it would seem less vulgar, more bizarre. Its opening realism works on toward irony and fantasy, dropping in its final lines again to blunt realism."[55] "Those Gambler's Blues" enjoyed a vogue from the late 1920s into the next decade. Probably the best-known version was recorded by Jimmie Rodgers in 1930. It was recorded that same year by Mattie Hite, and a year earlier by the Hokum Boys. It became a jazz standard under the title "St. James Infirmary" via recordings by Louis Armstrong in 1928, King Oliver in 1929, and Cab Calloway in 1930, whose performance of the song features in a surreal 1933 cartoon version of *Snow White*, starring Betty Boop. The variant of the tune that most closely parallels the scene Faulkner paints is "Dyin' Crap-shooter's Blues," best known today from Blind Willie McTell's 1940 and 1949 recordings, but which "was recorded by numerous vaudeville blues singers in the 1920s, notably Martha Copeland, Viola McCoy, and Rosa Henderson."[56] The bulk of the song's lyrics entail the titular crapshooter's instructions concerning his impending funeral, for example,

> I want eight crap-shooters for my pallbearers
> And let 'em be dressed in black
> Nine men going to the graveyard
> And only eight men coming back
> I want a jazz band on my coffin
> Chorus girl on my hearse.[57]

Precisely such unconventional funerary arrangements provoke disagreement during Red's funeral. An "orchestra from a downtown hotel" is enlisted to play for the funeral, but its organizers cannot agree on what sort of music is appropriate:

"Let them play jazz," the second man said. "Never nobody liked dancing no better than Red."

"No, no," the proprietor said. "Time Gene gets them all ginned up on free whiskey, they'll start dancing. It'll look bad."

"How about the Blue Danube?" the leader said.

"No, no; dont play no blues, I tell you," the proprietor said. "There's a dead man in that bier."

"That's not blues," the leader said.

"What is it?" the second man said.

"A waltz. Strauss."

"A wop?" the second man said. "Like hell. Red was an American. You may not be, but he was. Dont you know anything American? Play I Cant Give You Anything but Love. He always liked that."[58]

This is broad humor, borrowing from vaudeville. Its jokes involve a straight man and an interlocutor, musical jokes (e.g., misidentifying "The Blue Danube" as a blues song), and a clumsy, unfunny pun based on an ethnic slur (waltz/wop). "Jazz" and "blues" are both marked in this conversation as excessively libidinal and thus inappropriate for even as unconventional a funeral as this one.

The anxiety expressed by Joe, the proprietor ("dont play no blues"), is justified by the chaos that ensues, as the mourners get "ginned up . . . and start dancing": "They surged and clamored about the diminishing bowl [of punch spiked with liquor]. From the dance hall came the rich flare of the cornet."[59] The link between violence and music pervades the scene: "As though swept there upon a brassy blare of music the proprietor" appears and tries to keep things under control.[60] As the tippling mourners metamorphose into drunken revelers, a fight breaks out. The band continues to play but is "immediately drowned in a sudden pandemonium of chairs and screams."[61] As the fight intensifies, the scene becomes a macabre farce:

[the combatants] bore down upon the bier and crashed into it. The orchestra had ceased and were now climbing onto their chairs, with their instruments. The floral offerings flew; the coffin teetered. . . . They sprang forward, but the coffin crashed heavily to the floor, coming open. The corpse tumbled slowly and sedately out and came to rest with its face in the center of a wreath.

"Play something!" the proprietor bawled, waving his arms; "play! Play!"[62]

This grisly dénouement to Red's funeral is darkly humorous, but it also illustrates an explicit failure to mourn. This failure dramatizes the concept of melancholia that Freud lays out in his 1917 essay, "Mourning and Melancholia," as "pathological mourning."[63] The funeral scene in *Sanctuary* literalizes this melancholia, as both violence and the music that catalyzes and accompanies it prevent successful mourning. The scene itself evinces a pathological disposition: "the hushed, macabre air [is] a little febrile."[64] Red's corpse emerges as a symptom of this pathology, as a thing, and the violent intrusion of its corporeal presence prevents the decathexis that the work of mourning is meant to accomplish. The mourners cannot let go of the dead gambler, since his grotesque reappearance at the funeral—like the blues and jazz whose excessive, libidinal effects the proprietor fears—mocks and parodies the work of mourning. Joe calls for music to repair the damage, to soothe the riled mourners and to facilitate the work of mourning. Instead, the music in this scene is disruptive, an intoxicant akin to the free-flowing gin.

The link between jazz and vice is established earlier in the narrative, where it takes the form of drunkenness, prostitution, and illicit, interracial liaisons. The word "jazz" first appears in the novel as a verb as Ruby, Goodwin's common-law wife, tells Temple about her efforts to get Goodwin out of jail after he had "killed another soldier over one of those nigger women and they sent him to Leavenworth. Then the war came and they let him out to go to it. . . . [W]hen it was over they put him back in Leavenworth until the lawyer got a congressman to get him out. Then I could quit jazzing again."[65] Temple is shocked by Ruby's admission of "jazzing"—that is, of prostitution. This exchange prefigures Temple's future experience in Miss Reba's Memphis brothel. Popeye essentially prostitutes her to Red; this arrangement later sours when Temple tries to leave Popeye for Red, leading to the latter's death by Popeye's hand. The debate over "jazz" at Red's funeral is inflected by this earlier invocation of the term, as the genre is marked as libidinal, mercenary, and illicit.

The link between jazz and prostitution is reinforced elsewhere in the novel in the figure of Clarence Snopes. Snopes discovers Temple in the Memphis brothel where Popeye has imprisoned her, whereupon he contacts Horace Benbow. Snopes correctly surmises that Benbow will be interested in knowing Temple's whereabouts, since Temple's testimony would exonerate Goodwin (whom Benbow is defending) against the charges he faces of raping her and murdering Tommy. Snopes telephones Benbow, and their conversation is punctuated by the sounds of jazz emanating from Snopes's gramophone: "The victrola blared, faint, far away; [Benbow] could see the man, the soiled hat, the thick shoulders, leaning above the instrument—in a drugstore or a restaurant."[66] As Snopes offers to sell his information to Benbow, "[a]gainst Horace's ear the radio or the victrola performed a reedy arpeggio of saxophones. Obscene, facile, they seemed to be quarrelling with one another like two dexterous monkeys in a cage."[67] The technology at work here ("the radio or the victrola") is the same as that in the description of "ballads," though the effects it elicits are substantially different. While the earlier records are "lugubrious, harsh, and sad," these are "obscene, facile," and monkey-like.[68]

In the funeral scene, jazz and the blues are inflected by this conflation of blackness and vulgar sensuality, though the mourner's identification of them as "American" illustrates that vaudeville, records, radio, and film had facilitated repeated cross-racial traversals of the musical color line. The term "blues" functions in this scene not in the folkloristic sense of a rural folk form but rather as one element in a vernacular musical vocabulary associated with vaudeville. The song the jazz aficionado suggests, "I Can't Give You Anything But Love," was featured in *Blackbirds of 1928*, a successful Broadway production.[69] It became a hit for Louis Armstrong in 1929, though he first recorded it in December of the previous year, the day before recording his well-known rendition of "St. James Infirmary."[70] The band settles on "Nearer My God to Thee"—a nineteenth-century hymn—and later "a male quartet engaged from a vaudeville house" sings "Sonny Boy," a sentimental song written for and sung by Al Jolson in the 1928 film *The Singing Fool*.[71] The blues forbidden by the speakeasy / funeral parlor's proprietor differ radically from the earnest hymn and maudlin, sentimental song he insists on, and offer a means of mourning more in keeping with the deceased's wishes. "Red wouldn't like it solemn," the jazz fan insists, "[a]nd you know it."[72] Or, as Copeland's dying crapshooter has it, "Don't be standing around me cryin' / Everybody Charleston while I'm dyin'."[73]

Given Faulkner's well-known antipathy toward jukeboxes, vaudeville, and popular culture in general, this scene is remarkable for the fluency with current pop hits it exhibits.[74] It also suggests a potentially significant connection with the vernacular "ballad" tradition. The gambler's funeral scene in *Sanctuary* elaborates a narrative common to contemporary versions of the "Gambler's Blues" / "St. James Infirmary" family of songs. The novel's echoes of these songs include the plot of a gambler murdered over a woman, the setting ("Old Joe's barroom" in many versions of the song, a speakeasy and gambling den run by a man named Joe in the novel), even specific phrases ("She never had a pal like me" in Jimmie Rodgers's rendition, "he never had a better friend than me" in Faulkner's).[75] In its hundred-year history, the ballad mutates from the story of an unfortunate rake done in by syphilis to the story of a soldier killed in battle to that of a young woman who succumbs to an unnamed but doubtless unsavory affliction to that of a cowboy gunned down by a rival to a dying crapshooter's lament.

Each of these transformations results from a shift of location, time, performance context, or medium. By the time Faulkner is writing *Sanctuary*, it has become thoroughly enmeshed in the popular musical realm that he draws on for the novel's "rhythm and jazzy tone." In the introduction to the 1932 Modern Library edition of *Sanctuary*, Faulkner claimed to have drawn on precisely such popular materials: thinking of "books in terms of possibly money," he writes; "I took a little time out, and speculated what a person in Mississippi would believe to be current trends, chose what I thought was the right answer and invented the most horrific tale I could imagine."[76] Sandburg's description of "Those Gambler's Blues" as "a gutter song" attributes to it the qualities of current popularity and tawdriness that Faulkner purported to draw on in writing the novel. I suggest that we understand Faulkner's use of such material in his novel not merely as commentary on the process of repetition with a difference that this ballad-cum–pop song tradition represents but as a part of it. "Look at its [contents]," Sandburg wrote of *The American Songbag*. "Its human turmoil is terrific. . . . It is a volume full of gargoyles and gnomes, a terribly tragic book and one grinningly comic."[77] The same might well be said of *Sanctuary*, of course, and its use of "ballads" and blues illustrates that in his "cheap idea," Faulkner found a surprising emotional and thematic resonance with the ballads and songs that so captivate and vex his characters.

Race, Region, and the Politics
of Hip-Hop Authenticity

In the introduction, I wrote about the confusion that records by rap artists like the Beastie Boys and Run DMC caused for my adolescent peers and me when they arrived in the rural South in the mid-1980s. That confusion was both generic (we were puzzled by the conflation of rap and rock) and racial: our affective responses to the music were structured by racial (and racist) protocols. Our enjoyment of the music across lines of genre and race and our ambivalence about that enjoyment is symptomatic of the twentieth-century southern culture that structured our responses. Here I want to return to that scene two and a half decades later, now that hip-hop has been fully absorbed into the southern musical landscape.

In his recent book *Dirty South: OutKast, Lil Wayne, Soulja Boy, and the Southern Rappers Who Reinvented Hip-Hop* (2011), journalist Ben Westhoff sets up a framework for understanding the emergence of southern rap in both generational and stylistic terms. As he explains, established East Coast rappers tend to regard southern rap as formally and technically simplistic and inauthentic at best, as furthering demeaning, minstrel-based, "coon" stereotypes at worst. Westhoff quotes an array of New York rappers who all make similar claims regarding southern rap, notably members of the Wu-Tang Clan, whose 1993 album, *Enter the Wu-Tang: 36 Chambers*, set a new standard for lyrically inventive and technically sophisticated New York hip-hop.[1] Robert Diggs, aka RZA, a key member of the group, for example, does not mince words in describing the South as culturally backward: "The South has evolved later than us. . . . I got cousins out there that still live in the South. They have not picked up on the wavelength of where their mind should be."[2] In Diggs's view, his country cousins are stymied by their southern environment, and their music reflects this cultural deficiency.

Westhoff offers as a key example of the type of music Diggs derides "Fry That Chicken," a song and video by Shreveport, Louisiana–based rapper and comedian Ms. Peachez. The lo-fi video for the equally simple musical track features Nelson Boyd in character—that is, in drag—as Ms. Peachez, serving plates full of fried chicken to a group of enthusiastic children who sing along to the song's chorus ("so dumb it's genius," as Westhoff describes it): "Everybody want a piece of my chicken / Southern fried chicken / Finger lickin'."[3] In its gleeful presentation of stereotypes of rural southern African Americans, "Fry That Chicken" has elicited accusations of minstrelsy, of propagating century-old "coon song" stereotypes. As a columnist from the *Washington Post* asked rhetorically, "How can anyone explain black performers willingly . . . perpetuating such foolishness in the 21st century?"[4] Westhoff tracks down those involved in producing the song and video; they in turn express naïve bafflement at the uproar it caused. The song's producer, for example, opines: "The video was pure innocence. It had nothing to do with coonery, no negative vibe at all. The world made it controversial. We're used to seeing stuff like that in the South. We eat fried chicken! We eat watermelon!"[5] Likewise, Boyd (aka Ms. Peachez), defends the song and video as an authentic representation of southern rural life: "I'm from the country, that's how we do. . . . That's our lifestyle, that's a part of our heritage."[6] The song's creators, in other words, counter claims of minstrelsy and coonery with appeals to a locally based cultural authenticity: they're from the country, that's how they do.

Westhoff paints the polarized responses to the music of Ms. Peachez and other southern hip-hop artists in regional terms, and as reflecting a perceived opposition between country and city. Equally important, though, is Riché Richardson's contention in her 2007 *Black Masculinity and the U.S. South* that animosity toward southern rap speaks to anxieties concerning black masculinity. While Richardson focuses primarily on "the assertive masculinist posturing of black southern rappers as 'gangstas' and 'playas' . . . as a defensive response to the conventional exclusion of southern artists in the rap industry," the drag performance of Ms. Peachez's persona, together with other southern forms of hip-hop such as New Orleans' "sissy bounce," represents a potentially more subversive and paradoxical response to "the devaluation and stereotyping of black masculinity in the South."[7] An adequate exploration of the complex gender politics of these performances falls outside the purview of this book, but I do want to close by considering how the participation of white rappers in this emerging southern hip-hop tradition complicates the representational politics of the music and its reception. If, as Richardson argues, southern hip-hop is invested in specific conceptions of black masculinity, what room does the music provide for the kinds of interracial exchange that have been my concern throughout this book?

White rappers are no longer the anomaly they might have appeared to be during hip-hop's early days, although the challenges facing southern rappers in general are certainly complicated by the South's racial politics. As Roni Sarig explains in his 2007 book, *Third Coast: OutKast, Timbaland, and How Hip-Hop Became a Southern Thing*, while Andy Mathis (aka Bubba Sparxxx) was not the first white southern rapper to traffic in tropes of rural southern whiteness (thereby promulgating a subgenre that some wags have termed "hick-hop"), he was the first to have a legitimate shot at becoming "the Southern Eminem."[8] Sparxxx, who grew up in LaGrange, Georgia, achieved widespread recognition through his collaborations with producers Timbaland, Organized Noize, and Mr. Collipark, and his music, though peppered with banjo samples and semi-ironic shout-outs to rural life (his second album is titled *Deliverance*), is grounded squarely in the futuristic, urban aesthetics of these producers. So while Sparxxx's lyrics and self-presentation have usually included country signifiers, sonically his music consists primarily of credible Atlanta club rap. In other words, even while foregrounding his whiteness and rural background, Sparxxx's music sounds, for lack of better terms, "black" and "urban," and the resulting tension is not always fully resolved. The video for his 2001 single "Ugly," for example, pairs cutting-edge musical production with surreal representations of abject white southerners, the cumulative effect of which resembles an avant-garde reimagining of *Hee Haw*. By far the most successful track of Sparxxx's career is "Ms. New Booty," which he recorded with Atlanta duo the Ying Yang Twins and producer Mr. Collipark in 2005.[9] "Ms. New Booty" reached number 7 on *Billboard*'s Hot 100. Despite his status as probably the most prominent "hick-hop" artist, Bubba Sparxxx ultimately achieved popular success with a track that, unlike his earlier recordings, is stripped of cornpone country signifiers. Ironically, then, Bubba Sparxxx—a country boy from LaGrange—seems to have found a successful voice not in "hick-hop" but in straight-ahead Atlanta strip club rap. In other words, Sparxxx establishes his legitimacy as a rapper by performing the stereotyped version of black masculinity that Richardson positions at the center of southern rap.

More recently, though, rural southern rappers have devised new responses to complex demands of racial and regional authenticity. While Bubba Sparxxx is perhaps the prototypical white southern rapper, Gadsden, Alabama, native Michael Atha, aka Yelawolf, is currently at the center of the media spotlight. Like Sparxxx, Yelawolf has also aligned himself with established Atlanta figures: for example, he performs two verses on Atlanta rap superstar Big Boi's 2010 "You Ain't No DJ," about as prominent a guest spot as any rapper could ask for. That track features production from Andre 3000, Big Boi's former partner in OutKast, and an ultramodern beat that sounds like it's from outer space. The hyperstylized video, likewise, opens with sped-up images of a bustling Atlanta. Big Boi's preeminence in contemporary hip-hop is the subject of his first verse: "I double dare; matter of fact, nigga, I double dog dare / Any rapper to take it there with this player here / Let's be clear: I'm a leader, not your peer / Valedictorian of this rap shit every year."[10] With this guest spot Yelawolf aligns himself with the leaders of Atlanta's rap scene. Following Big Boi, he raps, "Roll with pimp scholars, ATLiens / A-L-A-B-A-M-A agains, come and check my weight again." *ATLiens* is the name of OutKast's breakthrough 1996 album that helped establish Atlanta as the center of the hip-hop world; by rhyming that title with a neologism based on his home state of Alabama, Yelawolf both acknowledges Atlanta and reimagines the rural South as an authentic site for hip-hop. In so doing, he contributes to the collective project Richardson describes, whereby southern "rap artists are emphasizing the immediacy and specificity of life in the South, including the rural South, and are constructing the South as an organic and viable here and now in the visual iconography and lyrical content" of their music.[11]

Increasingly, this multimedia art—comprising visual iconography, lyrical content, and sonic production—is key to rappers' self-presentations, as the music industry becomes decentralized and artists take both audio and video production into their own hands. Advances in Internet technology as well as in video and audio production technology have allowed artists like Yelawolf to operate independently from the record labels that have controlled the means of production for most of popular music's history.[12] The video for Yelawolf's breakout hit, "Pop the Trunk," for example, was filmed by Atlanta-based production crew Motion Family in and around Atha's family home outside Gadsden, Alabama.[13] The song's and the video's representations of rural Alabama are worlds apart from Ms. Peachez's version of Louisiana or Bubba Sparxxx's images of Georgia. The song's video pairs a slow, minor-key piano riff with images of a shotgun-toting figure in silhouette, abandoned country streets, and a country shack with broken windows and a yard full of junk and an old work truck. The foreboding rural gothic effect of these opening images intensifies as the video mirrors the action of the first verse, which begins: "Meth lab in the back and the crack smoke spills through the streets like an early morning fog / Mama's in the slaughterhouse with a hatchet helping daddy chop early morning hog." Yelawolf goes on to narrate an incident wherein an intruder breaks into his family's property in an attempt to steal drugs, only to be shot dead by his father: "Stood up in my Crimson Tide Alabama sweat pants and threw my pillow / Looks like daddy caught the motherfucker that tried to sneak in and steal his elbows [one-pound packages of marijuana] / They don't know that old man don't hold hands or throw hands naw he's rough like a brillo / Went to the Chevy and pulled out a machete and a gun as heavy and tall as the midget Willow."

The odd final simile aside (in which Yelawolf compares his father's shotgun with the protagonist of the 1988 George Lucas film, which a commenter at the rap lyrics website *Rap Genius* appositely describes as "a kind of off-brand hobbit"), "Pop the Trunk" does a remarkable job of the work Richardson describes.[14] That is, it "emphasiz[es] the immediacy and specificity of life in the South, including the rural South, and . . . construct[s] the South as an organic and viable here and now in [its] visual iconography and lyrical content."[15] Both the song and the video for "Pop the Trunk" engage with and adapt the conventions of so-called gangsta rap by crafting a narrative of violent retribution grounded in a local environment. In Yelawolf's case, though, that local environment is not an urban corner or project but rather his rural family home. Like much rap music, the song and video stake a claim to verisimilitude. Later in the song, Yelawolf declares: "This ain't a figment of my imagination, buddy; this is where I live: Bama." The video's claims to realism are bolstered by the fact that the man with the shotgun in the video is, in fact, Atha's stepfather. The woman chopping the hog is Atha's mother. The house in the video is his parents' house. Atha maintains that his aesthetic is rooted in Gadsden, in a shared rural experience. As he explains in a promotional video (shot at his "mom and pop's house," he explains) accompanying the release of *Trunk Musik*, the album that includes "Pop the Trunk": "We have a different brand of hip-hop out here, you know, as far as what is rooted here and comes from here. The working class, with the box Chevys. Hustlers, you know? And that's pretty much the story around here." More specifically, he explains: "When you shake up a snow globe of Gadsden, Alabama, you're gonna get sprinkles of crystal meth falling over Walnut Park. You're gonna get ash from burnt trees [marijuana] falling over South Side and Rainbow City."[16] As he told the *Gadsden Times* in 2010, "I was trying to bring rap to Gadsden, trying to rep my city. I just wanted to tell the story of small-town Alabama."[17]

"I Wish," the song that accompanies this video, is another track from *Trunk Musik*. Earlier I referenced Ben Westhoff's idea that southern rap has functioned in large part as the antithesis of cerebral, lyrical East Coast hip-hop, of which the Wu-Tang Clan are central figures. Raekwon the Chef is one of the Wu-Tang's most successful members. As Westhoff points out, Raekwon was one of the first established East Coast rappers to break from the orthodoxy that southern rap was primitive or not worth listening to, guest-rapping on a verse on OutKast's 1998 track, "Skew It on the Bar-B." He is also featured on "I Wish," which is an apologia both for Yelawolf's personal participation in hip-hop and for Alabama as an authentic site for the production of hip-hop. The first words we hear on the track are Raekwon's: "Chill, chill, chill. Let him rhyme, man. You know what it do, man. Just sit back, relax. Yelawolf, what up? Raekwon in the building."[18] On the one hand, this spoken (not rapped) introduction is simply so much throat-clearing. On the other hand, given the history that Westhoff, Sarig, and Richardson describe, it represents a significant racial and regional rapprochement.

Raekwon essentially authorizes Yelawolf to speak, serving (in a neat inversion of the relationship between Lomax and Ledbetter, for example) as a black patron for a white rapper, in the mode of Dr. Dre and the most famous white rapper, Eminem. Raekwon's guest verse bears out the promise of his intro, referencing Raekwon's "clique of murderer niggas who love hip-hop" and threatening:

> You fuck with Yelawolf and them niggas
> Your head gon' pop
> I'm just sincere, fresh cut
> All up in the Lear, listen
> Yo, leave him alone
> He brought me along
> Rap, he got it.

Yelawolf, in other words, has Raekwon's stamp of approval.

Still, patronage is one thing; full participation and artistic independence is another. In this regard, I think it's noteworthy that the video for the remix of "I Wish" replaces Raekwon's verse (although Yelawolf gives him a visual nod by wearing a Wu-Tang Clan shirt) with guest verses by Georgia rappers CyHi the Prynce (from Stone Mountain) and Pill (from Atlanta).[19] On the remix, Yelawolf is not the junior partner to Raekwon's elder patron but rather one member of a cohort of southern rappers who share a musical culture that crosses both color lines and those between country (Gadsden, Alabama, and Stone Mountain) and city (Atlanta). As a final example, we would do well to consider another rural southern rapper, Justin Scott, aka Big K.R.I.T., from Meridian, Mississippi (coincidentally, Meridian is also Jimmie Rodgers's hometown). Like Yelawolf, African American rapper Big K.R.I.T.'s lyrics focus largely on his status as a rapper from the rural South and the challenges resulting from that situation. He and Yelawolf are reportedly working on an album called *Country Cousins*.[20] The album's title is significant, especially when considered against RZA's dismissive description of his own southern cousins as behind the cultural curve ("I got cousins out there that still live in the South. They have not picked up on the wavelength of where their mind should be").[21] On tracks like the remix for Big K.R.I.T.'s "Hometown Hero," the two rappers together work to counter this understanding of the South, particularly the rural South, as backward, and to instead imagine the rural South—including K.R.I.T.'s Mississippi and Yelawolf's Alabama—not as a benighted backwater doomed by its history of racism and segregation but rather as fertile ground for cross-racial musical collaboration and the production of vital new cultural forms. To do so requires that they reject not only the notion of southern inferiority suggested by RZA's claim but also the segregation of music along racial lines.[22] As Yelawolf raps on Big K.R.I.T.'s "Happy Birthday Hip-Hop":

> You see I had to dig to find the Hieroglyphics
> My mama didn't know about Del and Souls of Mischief
> See the Bible Belt gave me the Holy Spirit
> But it didn't give me rap, 'cause I wasn't supposed to hear it
> So I had to walk under them rebel flags
> With my hoodie inside out, with Adidas on the tag.[23]

The Hieroglyphics, Del [the Funky Homosapien], and Souls of Mischief are all hip-hop artists whose records were popular in the early 1990s; for a young Michael Atha, these and the other rap artists he mentions by name—particularly southern artists like Tela, UGK, Skinny Pimp, and Mystikal—provide a counterculture to the "Bible Belt" of Alabama, signified by the ideology of the rebel flag he rejects in favor of the visual iconography and sounds of hip-hop. Likewise, in his first verse on the song, Big K.R.I.T. redefines his relationship both to the rural South and to hip-hop culture writ large: "Old school Chevy, sprayed it Ole Miss Rebel / . . . 808 bassin', haters strut facin' / While you was Kid 'n Playin', I was UGKin'." In a paradoxical twist, K.R.I.T. adopts the iconography of Ole Miss's rebel flag, transforming its significance from a symbol of Confederate nostalgia to part of an interracial culture rooted in the Deep South. He also invokes southern rap standard-bearers UGK, from Port Arthur, Texas, as examples of southern hip-hop's authenticity, contrasting their gritty, proto-gangsta rap from the late 1980s and early 1990s with the pop rap of the duo Kid 'n Play. In so doing, he suggests that not only is southern rap as legitimate as music from other regions but that it is in fact a more real, more authentic form of hip-hop.

In the opening pages of this book I mentioned the confusion and discomfort that the Beastie Boys' *Licensed to Ill* elicited among my friends in rural Louisiana when it was released in 1986. Yelawolf, too, mentions that album as his first exposure to hip-hop. "The first hip-hop that I heard was *Licensed to Ill*," he explains. "And specifically, it was the 'Paul Revere' beat, that reverse 808. . . . That's when I fell in love with the sound of it. Not everyone gets that out here."[24] While my friends responded positively to the familiar guitar sounds the Beastie Boys' songs sampled, Atha instead heard promise in the sound of the Roland TR-808 drum machine that provided the beat to "Paul Revere." This is the same "808 bassin'" that Big K.R.I.T. invokes as a distinctive sound of southern hip-hop. In other words, to return to the framework that Ralph Ellison provides, well before they adopted their rap personas, both Atha and Scott, "who [knew] their native culture and love[d] it unchauvinistically," were "never lost when encountering the unfamiliar" sounds of hip-hop.[25] Instead, they are examples of twenty-first-century southerners who are reimagining what that term might mean through the music they make. If the soundscapes of the twentieth century should be understood as defined by the continual establishment and effacement of a musical color line, artists like these suggest the possibilities that a twenty-first-century musical southern imagination affords for forging new relationships between music, race, and region.

Notes

Introduction

1. Beastie Boys, *Licensed to Ill.*
2. Run DMC, *Raising Hell.*
3. Wolk, "Gay '90s."
4. Du Bois, *Souls of Black Folk*, 13.
5. Ellison, "Living with Music," 236.
6. Ibid.
7. Miller, *Segregating Sound.*
8. Ibid., 3.
9. Radano, *Lying Up a Nation*, 279; see also Ramsey, *Race Music.*
10. Radano, *Lying Up a Nation*, 284.
11. Ibid., 282.
12. See, for example, Wald, *Escaping the Delta;* Waterman, "Race Music"; and Barker and Taylor, "Nobody's Dirty Business."
13. Ivey, "Border Crossings," 11.
14. Kreyling, "Toward 'A New Southern Studies,'" 16.
15. Romine, *The Real South*, 1.
16. Appadurai, *Modernity at Large*, 3.
17. Williams, *Marxism and Literature*, 133.
18. Duck, *The Nation's Region*, 9.
19. Pecknold, "Introduction: Country Music and Racial Formation," 2.
20. Miller, *Segregating Sound;* Filene, *Romancing the Folk;* Hamilton, *In Search of the Blues.*
21. Filene, *Romancing the Folk*, 6.
22. Lomax, *American Ballads and Folk Songs*, xxx.
23. Gitelman, *Scripts, Grooves, and Writing Machines*, 125. Emphasis in original.
24. Wright, *Uncle Tom's Children*, 125. Ellipses and emphasis in original.
25. Ibid., 128.
26. Ibid., 131.
27. Toomer, "The *Cane* Years," 123. See chapter 5.
28. Wright, *Uncle Tom's Children*, 140.
29. Ibid., 131.
30. Ibid., 132.

31. Quoted in Osbeck, *101 More Hymn Stories*, 311.

32. Wright, *Uncle Tom's Children*, 132–33. Ellipses and emphasis in original.

33. Ibid., 135. Emphasis in original.

34. Ibid., 137.

35. Ibid., 138.

36. Ellison, *Invisible Man*, 9.

37. Ibid.

38. Ibid., 10.

39. Armstrong, *Hot Fives & Sevens*, vol. 4.

40. Maxwell, *New Negro, Old Left*, 14.

41. Ellison, *Invisible Man*, 10. Emphasis in original.

42. Ibid., 9.

43. Ibid., 9–11.

Chapter 1. American Balladry and the Anxiety of Ancestry

1. Lomax, *Cowboy Songs*, 1910. The "Collector's Note" from which this and subsequent citations are drawn is unpaginated.

2. Campbell and Sharp, *English Folk Songs*, vii.

3. On the significance of the Child canon to later conceptions of American folk music's relationship to English and Scottish antecedents, including those of Sharp and Lomax, see Filene, *Romancing the Folk*, 9–46.

4. Greenway, "Jimmie Rodgers," 231–34; see also Russell, "Blacks, Whites, and Blues." I discuss Rodgers in depth in the next chapter.

5. Lomax, *Cowboy Songs*, 1910. The preface to the 1910 edition of *Cowboy Songs* is unpaginated.

6. Lomax, *Cowboy Songs*, 1938, xviii–xix.

7. Ibid.

8. Ibid., xv.

9. Ibid., xix.

10. Lomax, "Half-Million," 2.

11. Ibid.

12. Ibid.

13. Ibid. My emphasis.

14. Lomax, "Letter to Mrs. Katherine D. Tucker." My emphasis.

15. Lomax credits Higley with a single stanza, and argues that the song was current before 1867. See Lomax, "Half-Million," 4.

16. Will, "Songs of Western Cowboys," 256–57.

17. Lomax, "Letter to Barrett Wendell."

18. Lomax, "Letter to the Trustees of the Carnegie Foundation."

19. Lomax, "Cowboy Songs of the Mexican Border," 30.

20. Ibid., 35.

21. Sollors, *Beyond Ethnicity*, 5–6.

22. Ibid., 6.

23. Lomax, *Cowboy Songs*, 1938, xviii.

24. Ibid., xxv.

25. Lomax, *Adventures*, 61–64.

26. Ibid., 48. Other specifically named sources in this chapter include Harry Stephens (50–53), Garland Hodges (66), "Texas Jack" (72–73), and Stewart Edward White (73).

27. Lomax, *Cowboy Songs*, 1938, xviii.

28. Ibid.

29. Lomax, *Adventures*, 69.

30. Frost, "Our Contemporary Ancestors," 311.

31. Harkins, *Hillbilly*, 236; See also Williams, *Appalachia*, 11–14.

32. Kincaid, *My Favorite Mountain Ballads and Old Time Songs*, 11: 7.

33. For a detailed overview of the racialist tradition of folk song scholarship in which Lomax and Sharp participate, see Filene, *Romancing the Folk*, 9–46; on Kincaid's participation in this tradition, see Malone, *Singing Cowboys*, 82–84.

34. "Kincaid Says His Songs Are Not Hillbilly."

35. Kincaid, *Favorite Mountain Ballads and Old Time Songs*, 6.

36. Du Bois, *Souls of Black Folk*, 251.

37. Safford, "Bradley Kincaid, a Kentuckian, Became a Noted Singer," 82.

38. Sollors, *Beyond Ethnicity*, 234.

39. Ibid.

40. McDonald, "Muhammad Ali Receives Freedom of Great-grandfather's Irish Home Town," 22.

41. Kincaid, *Favorite Mountain Ballads and Old Time Songs*, 6.

42. Jacobson, *Whiteness of a Different Color*, 46–48.

43. Malone, *Singing Cowboys*, 105.

44. Malone, *Don't Get Above Your Raisin'*, 21.

45. Green, "Bradley Kincaid's Folios," 22.

46. Adams, "Preface," 5.

47. Adams, "Bradley Kincaid and His Houn' Dog Guitar," 49–50.

48. "Old Ballads Hit on Radio."

49. "The Houn' Dog Guitar."

50. "He Makes a Business of Ballads," 33.

51. Quoted in Jones, "Who Is Bradley Kincaid?," 122.

52. Loyal Jones, e-mail message to author, July 29, 2009.

53. Kincaid, interview by Loyal Jones.

54. Morrison, *Playing in the Dark*, 17.

55. Ibid., 46–47.

56. See Lott, *Love and Theft*, 18–19.

57. Quoted in ibid., 56.

58. Ibid., 18.

59. Quoted in Jones, *Radio's "Kentucky Mountain Boy," Bradley Kincaid*, 57.

60. Ibid.

61. Kincaid, "Modern and Up-to-Date History."

62. Kincaid, Interview by Dorothy Gable.

63. Cash, *The Mind of the South*, 40.

64. Kincaid, "Letter to Elizabeth Gilbert."

65. Kincaid, interview by Loyal Jones.

66. Lomax, *Adventures*, 1.

67. Loyal Jones, e-mail message to author, July 29, 2009.

68. Lomax's recordings of "Blind" Willie McTell have been commercially issued on a number of different labels; they are currently available on Blind Willie McTell, *Blind Willie McTell, Complete Library of Congress Recordings in Chronological Order (1940)*.

69. Gray, *Hand Me My Travelin' Shoes*, 267–68; Russell, "Blacks, Whites, and Blues," 195–98.

70. Lomax, "Letter to Mrs. C. S. Prosser."

71. Lomax, "Self-Pity in Negro Folk-Songs," 141.

72. Ibid.

73. Ibid.

74. Ibid.

75. Lomax, *American Ballads and Folk Songs*, 233–34.

76. White, "Racial Traits," 404.

77. Oliver, *Songsters and Saints*, 102.

78. Ibid., 103.

79. Folklorist Newman Ivey White documents a number of variants similar to Chatmon's, which he collected from Auburn, Alabama, in 1915 and 1916. See White, *American Negro Folk-Songs*, 381–82.

80. Russell, "Blacks, Whites, and Blues," 186.

81. I have been unable to find any biographical information about Armstrong, although an item in Emory University's Manuscript, Archives, and Rare Book Library includes the inscription, "A donation from J. Hagood Armstrong, Augusta, Ga.," and is dated "June 28, 1880," suggesting that he was living in Georgia at around the time "It's Hard to Be a Nigger" was published.

82. Lott, *Love and Theft*.

83. See also White, *American Negro Folk-Songs*, 381. White documents a number of variations of the "white folks go to college" line, as well as the couplet about turnip greens that Chatmon incorporates.

84. Du Bois, *Souls of Black Folk*, 13.

Chapter 2. Country Music and the Souls of White Folk

1. Du Bois, "The Souls of White Folk," 339.

2. Ibid.

3. Du Bois, *Souls of Black Folk*, 250–64.

4. See Porterfield, *Jimmie Rodgers*, 2002; Mazor, *Meeting Jimmie Rodgers;* Neal, *The Songs of Jimmie Rodgers;* Davis and Zanes, *Waiting for a Train.*

5. Though "yodelin' songs" are the only "white" musical style McTell specifically identifies, the musical example he provides—an F major arpeggio consisting of short eighth notes—bears no resemblance to such songs, and may be meant instead to evoke a minstrel banjo style. I am indebted to Richard Will for this observation.

6. Quoted in Gray, *Hand Me My Travelin' Shoes*, 250.

7. Quoted in Feder, "Song of the South," 60.

8. Coltman, "Roots of the Country Yodel," 137; Evans, "Black Musicians," 13.

9. Coltman, "Roots of the Country Yodel," 137.

10. Evans, "Black Musicians," 13.

11. See ibid.; Evans, *Tommy Johnson*, 43.

12. Wolfe, "A Whiter Shade of Blue."

13. Evans, "Black Musicians," 13.

14. *Early American Rural Music.*

15. Mazor, *Meeting Jimmie Rodgers*, 54.

16. Rodgers, *My Husband, Jimmie Rodgers*, 7.

17. See Abbott and Seroff, "America's Blue Yodel," 5; Cockrell, *Demons of Disorder*, 152.

18. Abbott and Seroff, "America's Blue Yodel," 5.

19. Rodgers, *My Husband, Jimmie Rodgers*, 91.

20. Russell, "Blacks, Whites, and Blues," 195.

21. Abbott and Seroff, "America's Blue Yodel," 5; on Anderson and "Sleep, Baby, Sleep," see also Russell, "Blacks, Whites, and Blues"; Coltman, "Roots of the Country Yodel," 137; and Mazor, *Meeting Jimmie Rodgers*, 67.

22. Feder, "Song of the South," 57.

23. Brooks, *Lost Sounds*, 171.

24. Ibid., 161.

25. Ibid., 164–65.

26. Ibid., 159.

27. This recording is available from the Cylinder Preservation and Digitization Project at the Department of Special Collections, Donald C. Davidson Library, University of California, Santa Barbara: http://cylinders.library.ucsb.edu/mp3s/4000/4892 /cusb-cyl4892d.mp3.

28. Malone, *Don't Get Above Your Raisin'*, 221. Malone makes this identical point in *Southern Music, American Music* (22) and in *Singing Cowboys and Musical Mountaineers* (64).

29. Russell, "Blacks, Whites, and Blues," 158.

30. Haden, "Vernon Dalhart," 69.

31. Ibid.

32. Porterfield, "Hey, Hey, Tell 'Em 'Bout Us," 17.

33. White, *American Negro Folk-Songs*, vii.

34. Ibid., xxiv.

35. Ibid., v. Though White does not identify it, this song is "Sing, Sing, Darkies, Sing," first published in 1844 (*Minstrel Songs, Old and New* 141–42).

36. White, *American Negro Folk-Songs*, 19.

37. Levine, "Concept of the New Negro," 100, 98.

38. White, *American Negro Folk-Songs*, 25.

39. Ibid.

40. Ibid.

41. White, "Racial Traits," 403.

42. Ibid., 388–89.

43. Ibid., 396–97; White, *American Negro Folk-Songs*, 25.

44. White, "White Man in the Woodpile," 211.

45. White, *American Negro Folk-Songs*, 29–30.

46. Greenway, "Jimmie Rodgers," 232; White, *American Negro Folk-Songs*, 26.

47. Feder, "Song of the South," 110.

48. Porterfield, *Jimmie Rodgers*, 2002, 123–24; Feder, "Song of the South," 110–14.

49. Niles, "Ballads, Songs, and Snatches," July 1928, 566.

50. Ibid.

51. Porterfield, *Jimmie Rodgers*, 2002, 123–24.

52. Feder, "Song of the South," 111.

53. Porterfield, "Hey, Hey, Tell 'Em 'Bout Us," 124.

54. Niles, "Ballads, Songs, and Snatches," September 1928, 77.

55. Ibid.

56. Abbott and Seroff, "America's Blue Yodel," 3.

57. Niles, "Ballads, Songs, and Snatches," November 1928, 328.

58. Niles, "Ballads, Songs, and Snatches," December 1928, 459.

59. Greenway, "Jimmie Rodgers," 231.

60. Ibid.

61. Belden and Hudson, *Folk Songs from North Carolina*, 3: 564; qtd. in Greenway, "Jimmie Rodgers," 231.

62. Greenway, "Jimmie Rodgers," 231.

63. Belden and Hudson, *Folk Songs from North Carolina*, 3: 395–96.

64. Ibid., 3: 396–97.

65. Ibid., 3: 563.

66. Ibid., 3: 371.

67. Ibid., 3: 428.

68. Qtd. in Russell, "Blacks, Whites, and Blues," 193 (emphasis in original). Carlisle had backed Rodgers on steel guitar at a 1931 recording session in Dallas and recorded covers of Rodgers's "Memphis Blues" and "Desert Blues" as well as original compositions like "Rambling Yodeler" that are clearly modeled on Rodgers's recordings.

69. Williamson, *Crucible of Race*, 467.

70. Du Bois, "The Souls of White Folk," 339.

71. See Ignatiev, *How the Irish Became White;* Allen, *Invention of the White Race;* Roediger, *Wages of Whiteness.*

72. See Lott, *Love and Theft,* 29, 35, 67, 71, 94–96, 148–49, quotation is on 29; Cantwell, *Bluegrass Breakdown,* 262–65.

73. Rodgers, *My Husband, Jimmie Rodgers,* 7, 50.

74. Ibid., 7.

75. Cash, *The Mind of the South,* 40.

76. Ibid., 51.

77. Ibid., 40.

78. In a Hollywood studio in July 1930, well into his career as a popular singer, Rodgers recorded a blackface dialogue called "The Pullman Porters." In this atavistic sketch, Rodgers's character, "Hezekiah," serves as interlocutor to his foil, "Hiram." Hiram asks Hezekiah to read a telegram for him. "What's the matter, nigger? Can't you read?" Rodgers's character asks. The skit continues in a similar vein for four excruciating minutes. The recording was not released but is now available on *The Singing Brakeman,* Bear Family Records' box set of Rodgers's complete recordings.

79. Rodgers, *My Husband, Jimmie Rodgers,* 75.

80. Ibid., 25.

81. Ibid., 67.

82. Ibid., 179.

83. Paris and Comber, *Jimmie the Kid,* 10.

84. Porterfield, *Jimmie Rodgers,* 2002, 7.

85. Ibid.

86. Porterfield, "Jimmie Rodgers," 1992, 3, 4.

87. Ibid., 10.

88. Koenig, *Jazz in Print,* 17.

89. Ibid., 67.

90. Ibid., 77.

91. Krehbiel, *Afro-American Folksongs,* 83.

92. See, for example, White, *American Negro Folk-Songs,* 28–29.

93. Cantwell, *Bluegrass Breakdown,* 265.

94. Rodgers, *My Husband, Jimmie Rodgers,* 69–70.

95. Rodgers, "Mississippi Delta Blues."

96. Locke, *New Negro,* 3.

97. Ibid., 5.

98. Cantwell, *When We Were Good,* 31.

99. Melnick, *A Right to Sing the Blues,* 109.

100. Rodgers, *My Husband, Jimmie Rodgers,* 58.

101. Malone, *Don't Get Above Your Raisin',* 21.

102. Ibid., 20.

103. Ballantine, *Marabi Nights,* 207–8. This recording is available on a CD accompanying Ballantine's book.

104. Erlmann, *African Stars*, 94. I am grateful to Erlmann for providing me with copies of these recordings.

105. Mphahlele, *Down Second Avenue*, 12.

106. Belden and Hudson, *Folk Songs from North Carolina*, 3: 428.

107. Boetie, *Familiarity Is the Kingdom of the Lost*, 12.

108. Ibid., 12–13.

109. Ibid., 13.

110. Ibid.

111. Ballantine, *Marabi Nights*, 16.

112. Ibid., 24.

113. Ibid., 20.

114. Ibid., 18–20.

115. Ibid., 29, 30.

116. Appadurai, *Modernity at Large*, 3. Emphasis in original.

117. Ballantine, *Marabi Nights*, 23.

118. Ibid. The ad is in Zulu; the translation ("You can feel like Jimmie Rodgers himself") is Ballantine's.

119. Boetie, *Familiarity Is the Kingdom of the Lost*, 15.

120. Tracey, *Sounds of Africa*.

121. Tracey, *Music of Africa Series no. 2: Kenya*.

122. Oliver, "Jimmy Rodgers," 10.

123. Porterfield, *Jimmie Rodgers*, 2002, 200.

124. Du Bois, *Darkwater*, 29.

Chapter 3. Plantations, Prisons, and the Sounds of Segregation

1. See, for example, Gray, *Hand Me My Travelin' Shoes*, 267–74; Russell, "Blacks, Whites, and Blues," 195–96, 198.

2. Unidentified group, *Judgment*.

3. *Archive of American Folk Song*, 24.

4. Lomax's notes to this recording list it as "(Blues) *Cornfield Blues*—sung by Amos Johnson, with comment Nov. 5, 1940." The typed index card for the recording in the American Folklife Center at the Library of Congress lists the performer as "Manus Johnson." It's unclear whether this is an error or a correction.

5. Wagner, *Disturbing the Peace*, 228.

6. Ibid., 230.

7. Lomax and Lomax, *Our Singing Country*, 364.

8. Ibid., 364–65.

9. *Archive of American Folk Song*, 24.

10. Wagner, *Disturbing the Peace*, 231.

11. Lomax, "'Sinful Songs' of the Southern Negro," 182.

12. Ibid., 186. Italics in original.

13. Quoted in Filene, *Romancing the Folk*, 59.

14. Davenport, "Letter to Dr. F. Lovell Bixby, Asst. Director, Bureau of Prisons, Dept. of Justice, Washington D.C."

15. Amrine, "Letter to Dr. F. Lovell Bixby, Asst. Director, Bureau of Prisons, Dept. of Justice, Washington D.C."

16. Lomax, *Negro Folk Songs as Sung by Lead Belly*, 32.

17. Ibid., 52.

18. Ibid., 58–59.

19. Ibid., 29.

20. Ibid., xi.

21. Ibid., 52–53.

22. Quoted in Miller, *Segregating Sound*, 245.

23. Quoted in ibid.

24. Lomax, *Negro Folk Songs as Sung by Lead Belly*, 59.

25. Ibid.

26. Ibid., 61.

27. Ibid., 63.

28. Lomax's recollections of this seminal recording trip are documented in *The Land Where the Blues Began*. A fuller account that more thoroughly incorporates the perspective of his African American colleagues is provided by Work, Jones, and Adams, *Lost Delta Found*.

29. See Work, Jones, and Adams, *Lost Delta Found*, 12–13.

30. Quoted in ibid., 14.

31. Mullen, *The Man Who Adores the Negro*, 115.

32. The appeal of Robert Johnson and his place in the mythology of twentieth-century American popular music has been much discussed. See, for example, Wald, *Escaping the Delta;* Pearson and McCulloch, *Robert Johnson;* and Guralnick, *Searching for Robert Johnson*. Lomax devotes a section, entitled "Little Robert," of *The Land Where the Blues Began*'s first chapter to Johnson. Lomax, *The Land Where the Blues Began*, 12–15.

33. Quoted in Szwed, *Alan Lomax*, 176.

34. Jones's complete list of these records, along with scholar Tony Russell's later analysis of them, is reprinted in Work, Jones, and Adams, *Lost Delta Found*, 311–14.

35. *Muddy Waters: The Complete Plantation Recordings*.

36. Lomax, *The Land Where the Blues Began*, ix.

37. Williams, *Marxism and Literature*, 133–34. Emphasis in original.

38. Lomax, *The Land Where the Blues Began*, ix.

39. Ibid.

40. Ibid., xi.

41. Ibid.

42. Ibid., xii.

43. Work, Jones, and Adams, *Lost Delta Found*, 11–14.

44. Lomax, *The Land Where the Blues Began*, 3.

45. Ibid., 4.

46. Ibid.

47. Ibid.

48. Ibid., 5. Italics in original.

49. Ibid.

50. Ibid., 6.

51. Ibid.

52. Ibid., 7.

53. Ibid.

54. Ibid., 12.

55. Ibid., 22.

56. Ibid., 23.

57. Fleischer, *Mandingo*.

58. Ebert, "Review of *Mandingo*."

59. Walker, "The Art of War"; Carpio, *Laughing Fit to Kill*, 171.

60. Miller, *Segregating Sound*, 148–51.

61. Quoted in Palmer, *Deep Blues*, 103.

62. Quoted in Gordon, *Can't Be Satisfied*, 363.

63. Lomax, *The Land Where the Blues Began*, 405.

64. Ibid., 405, 406.

65. Ibid., 406.

66. Ibid., 406.

67. Ibid., 410.

68. Ibid., 412.

69. Ibid.

70. Ibid., 415.

71. Ibid., 414. Italics in original.

72. Niles, "Ballads, Songs, and Snatches," July 1928, 566.

73. Lomax, "Self-Pity in Negro Folk-Songs," 141.

74. White, *American Negro Folk-Songs*, 312.

75. Ibid.

76. White, "Racial Traits," 399.

77. Ibid., 396.

78. Lomax, *The Land Where the Blues Began*, 416.

79. Ibid., 420, 421.

80. Ibid., 421.

81. Ibid., 421–22.

Chapter 4. The New Negro Looks South

1. Du Bois, *Souls of Black Folk*, 89.

2. Gilroy, *The Black Atlantic*, 80.

3. Du Bois, *Souls of Black Folk*, 4.

4. Ibid., 164.

5. Ibid., 250.

6. Johnson, *Autobiography*, 2.

7. Ibid., 13.

8. In keeping with the terminology used by African American writers and intellectuals in the 1920s, I use the term "New Negro Renaissance" in place of the more familiar "Harlem Renaissance." The latter term is a later coinage and, in my opinion, risks the false implication that the renaissance was confined to Harlem. As I aim to show, it in fact grew in part out of a profound engagement with the South. For a concise overview, see Graham, "The New Negro Renaissance."

9. Ibid., 4–5.

10. Ibid., 5.

11. Ibid., 12.

12. Ibid., 72.

13. Ibid., 139.

14. Ibid.

15. Ibid., 139–40.

16. Quoted in Abbott and Seroff, *Out of Sight*, 273.

17. Johnson, *Autobiography*, 153.

18. Ibid., 137.

19. Ibid., 20.

20. Johnson, "Preface to the First Edition," viii.

21. Johnson, *Autobiography*, 63.

22. Ibid., 154.

23. Johnson, "Preface to the First Edition," vii.

24. Du Bois, *Souls of Black Folk*, 12.

25. Locke, "The Negro Spirituals," 207.

26. Du Bois, *Souls of Black Folk*, 255.

27. Ibid., 256–57.

28. Locke, "The Negro Spirituals," 208.

29. Thurman, *Infants of the Spring*, 241.

30. Ibid.

31. Ibid., 241–42.

32. Ibid., 107.

33. Ibid., 108.

34. Jackson, "The Genesis of the Negro Spiritual," 244.

35. Ibid.

36. Ibid., 246.

37. Ibid., 248.

38. Locke, *The Negro and His Music*, 18; Locke, "The Negro Spirituals," 199.

39. Du Bois, *Souls of Black Folk*, 251.

40. Ibid.

41. Wallaschek, *Primitive Music*, 61; my emphasis.

42. Ibid., 60.

43. Epstein, "White Origin," 55.

44. Du Bois, *Souls of Black Folk*, 251.

45. Ibid., 256.

46. Ibid., 263.

47. Ibid., 4.

48. Ibid., 253.

49. Wallaschek, *Primitive Music*, 60–61.

50. Du Bois, *Souls of Black Folk*, 256, 257.

51. Ibid., 250.

52. Ibid., 253.

53. Krehbiel, *Afro-American Folksongs*, 27–28.

54. Ibid., 28.

55. White, "Racial Traits," 396.

56. Ibid., 404.

57. Ibid., 397.

58. Ibid., 396.

59. Ibid., 397.

60. Locke, "The New Negro," 3.

61. Locke, "Foreword," xxv.

62. Locke, "The New Negro," 5.

63. Gordon, "The Negro's Inhibitions," 159.

64. Locke, "The New Negro," 3.

65. Locke, *The Negro and His Music*, 43–46.

66. Ibid., 44–45.

67. Rampersad, "Introduction," xx.

68. Davis, "Growing Up," 57.

69. Wright, "Blueprint for Negro Writing," 56.

70. Locke, "The New Negro," 3, 7.

71. Ibid., 9.

72. Ibid.

73. Locke, *The Negro and His Music*, 9.

74. Johnson, "Preface to the First Edition," 15–16.

75. Johnson, *Autobiography*, 73.

76. Ibid., 73; emphasis in original.

77. Johnson, "Preface to the First Edition," 12.

78. Ibid., 13.

79. Locke, *The Negro and His Music*, 9.

80. Johnson, *Autobiography*, 74.

81. Ibid.

82. Floyd, "Music in the Harlem Renaissance," 5.

83. Ibid., 5.

84. Locke, *The Negro and His Music*, 4–5.

85. "Jewish Jazz Becomes Our National Music," 64–65.

86. Ibid., 65; emphasis in original.

87. Ibid., 65.

88. "How the Jewish Song Trust Makes You Sing," 75.

89. Ibid., 78.

90. Locke, *The Negro and His Music*, 4.

91. Quoted in Melnick, *A Right to Sing the Blues*, 103.

92. Adorno, "On Jazz," 470, 472.

93. Ibid., 470.

94. Ibid., 477.

95. Buhler, "Frankfurt School Blues," 106.

96. Quoted in ibid., 106.

97. Adorno, "On Jazz," 474.

98. Locke, *The Negro and His Music*, 5.

99. Locke, "Beauty Instead of Ashes," 24.

100. Adorno, "On Jazz," 474.

101. Ibid., 471.

102. White, "Racial Traits," 404.

103. Locke, "The Negro Spirituals," 199.

104. Locke, *The Negro and His Music*, 20.

105. Krehbiel, *Afro-American Folksongs*, x.

106. Ibid., 1–2.

107. Ibid., 2.

108. Locke, *The Negro and His Music*, 12.

109. Ibid., 20.

110. Johnson, "Preface to the First Edition," 17.

111. Locke, *The Negro and His Music*, 12.

112. Ibid., 130.

113. Burgett, "Vindication," 33.

114. Locke, "The Negro Spirituals," 206.

115. Locke, *The Negro and His Music*, 22.

116. Humphrey, "Holy Blues," 113.

117. Hurston, "Spirituals and Neo-Spirituals," 360; emphasis in original.

118. Ibid.; emphasis in original.

119. Locke, *The Negro and His Music*, 95.

120. Ibid., 93.

121. Burgett, "Vindication," 39.

122. Locke, "The New Negro," 4.

123. Ibid., 6.

124. Ibid., 9.

1. Toomer, "The *Cane* Years," 123.

2. Quoted in Toomer, *Cane* (1988), 160.

3. Quoted in Ford, *Split-Gut Song*, 24.

4. Quoted in North, *The Dialect of Modernism*, 149.

5. Quoted in ibid.

6. Quoted in Ford, *Split-Gut Song*, 14.

7. Quoted in Toomer, *Cane* (1988), 160; emphasis in original.

8. Ellison, "As the Spirit Moves Mahalia," 252.

9. Quoted in Toomer, *Cane* (1988), 152.

10. Favor, *Authentic Blackness*, 75, 79.

11. Byrd and Gates, "Jean Toomer's Racial Self-Identification," lxvi.

12. Quoted in North, *The Dialect of Modernism*, 149.

13. Toomer, "The *Cane* Years," 120.

14. Ibid., 121.

15. Walker, "The Divided Life of Jean Toomer," 65.

16. Quoted in North, *The Dialect of Modernism*, 150.

17. Quoted in ibid.

18. Quoted in Sollors, "Jean Toomer's *Cane*," 33.

19. Quoted in Turner, "Introduction," 128.

20. Quoted in ibid.

21. Tate, *Psychoanalysis and Black Novels*, 9.

22. Sedgwick, *Between Men*, 2.

23. Toomer, *Cane*, 16; line 12. All quotations from *Cane* are from the 2011 Byrd and Gates edition unless otherwise noted.

24. For an examination of Toomer's use of the blazon form, see Ramazani, *Poetry of Mourning*, 351–52.

25. Toomer, *Cane*, 13; lines 1–3.

26. Toomer, *Cane*, 5, 6.

27. Toomer, *Cane*, 18, 19.

28. Toomer, *Cane*, 21.

29. Toomer, *Cane*, 32, 31.

30. Toomer, *Cane*, 34.

31. Toomer, *Cane*, 33, 34, 37.

32. Toomer, *Cane*, 34, 35.

33. Žižek, *Sublime Object*, 187.

34. Toomer, *Cane*, 34.

35. Žižek, *Sublime Object*, 187.

36. Toomer, *Cane*, 34–35.

37. Sedgwick, *Between Men*, 24.

38. Freud, "Mourning and Melancholia," 250.

39. Toomer, *Cane*, 31.

40. Toomer, *Cane*, 35.

41. Toomer, *Cane*, 76; emphasis in original.

42. Toomer, *Cane*, 70.

43. Toomer, *Cane*, 71, 73.

44. Toomer, *Cane*, 53, 54.

45. Gordon, "The Negro's Inhibitions," 159.

46. Toomer, *Cane*, 63.

47. The use of the adjective "queer" to mean "homosexual" was operative by the time Toomer was writing *Cane*. The OED's first citation of such a usage is from 1914, though its cognate noun form was in use by 1894 ("Queer, Adj. 1").

48. Toomer, *Cane*, 75.

49. Sedgwick, *Between Men*, 1.

50. Toomer, *Cane*, 73.

51. Tate, *Psychoanalysis and Black Novels*, 9.

Chapter 6. Music and Racial Violence in William Faulkner's *Sanctuary*

1. Faulkner, "Introduction," v.

2. Blotner, *Faulkner: A Biography*, 754.

3. Gershwin, "Composer in the Machine Age," 227.

4. Melnick, *A Right to Sing the Blues*, 73.

5. Faulkner, *Sanctuary*, 258.

6. Ibid., 256.

7. Ibid., 257.

8. Wilentz and Marcus, *The Rose and the Briar*, 1.

9. Sollors, *Beyond Ethnicity*, 5–6.

10. Whisnant, *All That Is Native and Fine*, 206.

11. Faulkner, *Sanctuary*, 257.

12. Ibid., 233.

13. Levine, "Folklore of Industrial Society," 1370.

14. Duvall, "A Strange Nigger," 106.

15. Ibid., 111. My emphasis.

16. The rhetoric of "disembodied voices" at work here echoes similar language in *As I Lay Dying*. John T. Matthews discusses that novel's depiction of the graphophone (a type of phonograph) as a technology that "represents the displacement of labor and gratification into reified form—into a commodity" (Matthews, "*As I Lay Dying* in the Machine Age," 76). Anticipating the argument I am making here for *Sanctuary*, for Matthews this is an instance of "the disintegrative force of modernization," through which, as "the coherence of the world from the standpoint of certain privileged racial, class and gender positions begins to disintegrate, new voices and subjectivities emerge" (ibid., 84).

17. Faulkner, *Sanctuary*, 258.

18. The debate over the racial significance of the spirituals was at its height during the period in which *Sanctuary* was written and published. See, for example, Jackson, "The Genesis of the Negro Spiritual." Jackson argues that "Negro spirituals" are derived wholesale from mid-nineteenth-century white Protestant hymns. See also White, *American Negro Folk-Songs*, 44–53. Most African American commentators dismissed this thesis. See, for example, Fauset, "Hail the Nordic Spiritual!" For an overview of this debate, see Epstein, "White Origin." For a detailed discussion of the history of the spirituals in American cultural discourse, see Cruz, *Culture on the Margins;* Epstein, *Sinful Tunes and Spirituals*, 191–238.

19. Faulkner, *Sanctuary*, 258.

20. Ibid.

21. Ibid., 270.

22. Ibid., 258.

23. Ibid., 269.

24. Ibid., 270.

25. Ibid., 271.

26. Ibid., 266.

27. Ibid.

28. Quoted in Bluestein, *The Voice of the Folk*, 122.

29. Davis, "From Jazz Syncopation to Blues Elegy," 86.

30. Bluestein, *The Voice of the Folk*, 122.

31. Ibid., 124.

32. Higginson, *Army Life in a Black Regiment*, 197.

33. Locke, "The Negro Spirituals," 200.

34. Douglass, *Narrative*, 27; Du Bois, *Souls of Black Folk*, 187.

35. White, *American Negro Folk-Songs*, 29.

36. Johnson, "Preface to the First Edition," 20.

37. White, *American Negro Folk-Songs*, 29–30.

38. Faulkner, *Sanctuary*, 258.

39. Ibid.

40. Ibid., 394.

41. Douglass, *Narrative*, 27.

42. Ibid.

43. Faulkner, *Sanctuary*, 258.

44. Ibid., 266.

45. Gussow, *Seems Like Murder Here*, 4–5.

46. Ibid., 5.

47. Ibid., 4.

48. Ramazani, *Poetry of Mourning*, 142.

49. Faulkner, *Sanctuary*, 258.

50. Ibid.

51. Ibid., 269.

52. Both Joel Williamson and Deborah Barker maintain that this scene in the novel is based on a historical event from Faulkner's childhood, in which a black man, Nelse Patton, slit the throat of a white woman, Mattie McMillan (Williamson, *Crucible of Race*, 161; Barker, "Moonshine and Magnolias," 158). In *Sanctuary*, the interracial dynamics of this historical event are sublimated into the story of the "negro murderer's" act of violence against his wife. A very similar scene appears in Faulkner's next novel, *Light in August*, in which Joanna Burden is beheaded (Faulkner, *Light in August*, 465–66.)

53. Faulkner, *Sanctuary*, 347.

54. Though Sandburg does not note it, this song is a descendant of the nineteenth-century Anglo-Irish broadside ballad "The Unfortunate Rake." See Laws, *The British Literary Ballad*, 122; Goldstein, "The Unfortunate Rake: A Study in the Evolution of a Ballad."

55. Sandburg, *The American Songbag*, 228.

56. Goldstein and Narváez, "Producing Blues Recordings," 455.

57. Copeland, *Complete Recorded Works in Chronological Order, Vol. 1: 1923–1927.*

58. Faulkner, *Sanctuary*, 348.

59. Ibid., 349.

60. Ibid., 350.

61. Ibid., 351.

62. Ibid.

63. Freud, "Mourning and Melancholia," 250.

64. Faulkner, *Sanctuary*, 347.

65. Ibid., 219.

66. Ibid., 318.

67. Ibid.

68. Ibid., 257, 318.

69. Lewine and Simon, *Songs of the American Theater*, 188.

70. Armstrong, *The Complete Hot Five and Hot Seven Recordings.*

71. Faulkner, *Sanctuary*, 350.

72. Ibid., 349.

73. Copeland, *Complete Recorded Works in Chronological Order, Vol. 1: 1923–1927.*

74. On Faulkner's avowedly hostile attitude toward popular music, and evidence that this hostility was likely somewhat insincere, see Gussow, "Plaintive Reiterations," 58; Hamblin and Peek, *A William Faulkner Encyclopedia*, 260–62.

75. Faulkner, *Sanctuary*, 348.

76. Faulkner, "Introduction," vi.

77. Sandburg, *The American Songbag*, viii.

1. Westhoff, *Dirty South*, 6–7.

2. Quoted in ibid., 6.

3. Ms. Peachez, "Fry That Chicken."

4. Quoted in Westhoff, *Dirty South*, 3.

5. Ibid., 16.

6. Ibid., 17.

7. Richardson, *Black Masculinity and the U.S. South*, 200.

8. Sarig, *Third Coast*, 236.

9. Sparxxx, *The Charm*.

10. Big Boi, *Sir Lucious Left Foot*.

11. Richardson, *Black Masculinity and the U.S. South*, 199.

12. For a discussion of how Motion Family and other independent video crews have transformed music video production in the South, see Carmichael, "Motion Family, Decatur Dan, and Phil the God Lead Rap's Viral Offensive."

13. Yelawolf, "Pop the Trunk."

14. "Yelawolf—Pop the Trunk Lyrics."

15. Richardson, *Black Masculinity and the U.S. South*, 199.

16. "Yelawolf – Gadsden Alabama."

17. "YelaWolf Nervously Brings His Voice Home."

18. Yelawolf, *Trunk Musik*.

19. Willpower Omnimedia, "Yelawolf "I WISH" the REMIX Ft. CyHi Da Prynce and Pill."

20. "Big K.R.I.T. Defends Yelawolf."

21. Quoted in Westhoff, *Dirty South*, 6.

22. Big K.R.I.T., "'Hometown Hero' Remix."

23. Big K.R.I.T., "Happy Birthday Hip Hop."

24. "Yelawolf – Gadsden Alabama."

25. Ellison, "Living with Music," 236.

Bibliography

Abbott, Lynn, and Doug Seroff. "America's Blue Yodel." *Musical Traditions* 11 (1993): 2–11.

———. *Out of Sight: The Rise of African American Popular Music, 1889–1895*. Jackson: University Press of Mississippi, 2002.

Adams, James Taylor. "Bradley Kincaid and His Houn' Dog Guitar." *The Cumberland Empire* 1 (January 1932): 49–50.

———. "Preface." *The Cumberland Empire* 1 (January 1932): 5–6.

Adorno, Theodor W. "On Jazz." In *Essays on Music*, edited by Richard Leppert, translated by Jamie Owen Daniel and Richard Leppert, 470–95. Berkeley: University of California Press, 2002.

Allen, Theodore. *The Invention of the White Race, Volume 1: Racial Oppression and Social Control*. New York: Verso, 1994.

Amrine, M. F. "Letter to Dr. F. Lovell Bixby, Asst. Director, Bureau of Prisons, Dept. of Justice, Washington DC," July 6, 1934. John A. Lomax papers, Box 3d171, Folder 2. Center for American History, University of Texas at Austin.

Appadurai, Arjun. *Modernity at Large: Cultural Dimensions of Globalization*. Minneapolis: University of Minnesota Press, 1996.

Archive of American Folk Song: A History, 1928–1939, Compiled from the Annual Reports of the Librarian of Congress. Washington, D.C., 1940.

Armstrong, Louis. *The Complete Hot Five and Hot Seven Recordings*. CD. Columbia/Legacy, 2000.

———. *Hot Fives & Sevens*. Vol. 4. London: JPS Records, 1998.

Ballantine, Christopher. *Marabi Nights: Jazz, "Race" and Society in Early Apartheid South Africa*. 2nd ed. Scottsville, South Africa: University of KwaZulu-Natal Press, 2012.

Barker, Deborah. "Moonshine and Magnolias: *The Story of Temple Drake* and *The Birth of a Nation*." *The Faulkner Journal* 22, nos. 1–2 (Fall 2006–Spring 2007): 140–75.

Barker, Hugh, and Yuval Taylor. "Nobody's Dirty Business: Folk, Blues, and the Segregation of Southern Music." In *Faking It: The Quest for Authenticity in Popular Music*. New York: Norton, 2007.

Beastie Boys. *Licensed to Ill*. LP/cassette. Def Jam/Columbia, 1986.

Belden, Henry M., and Arthur Palmer Hudson, eds. *Folk Songs from North Carolina.* Vol. 3. Frank C. Brown Collection of North Carolina Folklore. Durham: University of North Carolina Press, 1952.

Big Boi. *Sir Lucious Left Foot: The Son of Chico Dusty.* CD. Def Jam, 2010.

Big K.R.I.T. "Happy Birthday Hip Hop (feat. Yelawolf)." MP3. Last King 2 (God's Machine). 2011.

———. "'Hometown Hero' Remix (Featuring Yelawolf)." 2010. https://www.youtube.com/watch?v=WRwEz9uYt1Y.

"Big K.R.I.T. Defends Yelawolf, Says Their Collaborative LP 'Country Cousins' Will Be Released." http://www.hiphopdx.com/index/news/id.21244/title.big-krit-defends-yelawolf-says-their-collaborative-lp-country-cousins-will-be-released.

Blind Willie McTell. *Blind Willie McTell, Complete Library of Congress Recordings in Chronological Order (1940).* CD. RST Records, n.d.

Blotner, Joseph. *Faulkner: A Biography.* 2 vols. New York: Random House, 1974.

Bluestein, Gene. *The Voice of the Folk: Folklore and American Literary Theory.* Amherst: University of Massachusetts Press, 1972.

Boetie, Dugmore. *Familiarity Is the Kingdom of the Lost.* New York: Dutton, 1969.

Brooks, Tim. *Lost Sounds: Blacks and the Birth of the Recording Industry, 1890–1919.* Urbana: University of Illinois Press, 2004.

Buhler, James. "Frankfurt School Blues: Rethinking Adorno's Critique of Jazz." In *Apparitions: New Perspectives on Adorno and Twentieth-Century Music,* edited by Berthold Hoeckner, 103–30. New York: Routledge, 2006.

Burgett, Paul. "Vindication as a Thematic Principle in the Writings of Alain Locke on the Music of Black Americans." In *Black Music in the Harlem Renaissance,* edited by Samuel A. Floyd Jr., 29–40. Knoxville: University of Tennessee Press, 1990.

Byrd, Rudolph P., and Henry Louis Gates Jr. "Jean Toomer's Racial Self-Identification: A Note on the Supporting Materials." In *Cane,* by Jean Toomer, lxvi–lxx. 2nd ed. New York: W. W. Norton, 2011.

Campbell, Olive Dame, and Cecil Sharp. *English Folk Songs from the Southern Appalachians.* New York: G. P. Putnam's Sons, 1917.

Cantwell, Robert. *Bluegrass Breakdown: The Making of the Old Southern Sound.* Urbana: University of Illinois Press, 1984.

———. *When We Were Good: The Folk Revival.* Cambridge, Mass.: Harvard University Press, 1996.

Carmichael, Rodney. "Motion Family, Decatur Dan, and Phil the God Lead Rap's Viral Offensive." *Creative Loafing Atlanta,* February 2, 2012. http://clatl.com/atlanta/motion-family-decatur-dan-and-phil-the-god-lead-raps-viral-offensive/Content?oid=4701562.

Carpio, Glenda. *Laughing Fit to Kill: Black Humor in the Fictions of Slavery.* New York: Oxford University Press, 2008.

Cash, Wilbur J. *The Mind of the South.* New York: Vintage, 1941.

Cockrell, Dale. *Demons of Disorder: Blackface Minstrels and Their World.* New York: Cambridge University Press, 1997.

Coltman, Robert. "Roots of the Country Yodel: Notes Toward a Life History." In *Exploring Roots Music: Twenty Years of the JEMF Quarterly*, edited by Nolan Porterfield, 135–42. Lanham, Md.: Scarecrow, 2004.

Copeland, Martha. *Complete Recorded Works in Chronological Order, Vol. 1: 1923–1927.* CD. Document, 1995.

Cruz, Jon. *Culture on the Margins: The Black Spiritual and the Rise of American Cultural Interpretation.* Princeton: Princeton University Press, 1999.

Davenport, Mortimer H. "Letter to Dr. F. Lovell Bixby, Asst. Director, Bureau of Prisons, Dept. of Justice, Washington DC," July 11, 1935. John A. Lomax Papers, Box 3d171, Folder 2. Center for American History, University of Texas at Austin.

Davis, Arthur P. "Growing Up in the Harlem Renaissance: 1920–1935." *Negro American Literature Forum* 2, no. 3 (Autumn 1968): 53–59.

Davis, Mary E., and Warren Zanes, eds. *Waiting for a Train: Jimmie Rodgers's America.* Burlington, Mass.: Rounder Books, 2009.

Davis, Thadious. "From Jazz Syncopation to Blues Elegy: Faulkner's Development of Black Characterization." In *Faulkner and Race: Faulkner and Yoknapatawpha, 1986*, edited by Doreen Fowler and Ann J. Abadie, 70–92. Jackson: University Press of Mississippi, 1988.

Douglass, Frederick. *Narrative of the Life of Frederick Douglass, an American Slave.* In *Narrative of the Life of Frederick Douglass, an American Slave* and *Incidents in the Life of a Slave Girl*, edited by Kwame Anthony Appiah, 1–113. New York: Modern Library, 2000.

Du Bois, W. E. B. *Darkwater: Voices from Within the Veil.* New York: Harcourt, Brace and Howe, 1920.

———. *The Souls of Black Folk: Essays and Sketches.* Chicago: A. C. McClurg, 1903.

———. "The Souls of White Folk." *The Independent*, August 18, 1910.

Duck, Leigh Anne. *The Nation's Region: Southern Modernism, Segregation, and U.S. Nationalism.* Athens: University of Georgia Press, 2006.

Duvall, John N. "'A Strange Nigger': Faulkner and the Minstrel Performance of Whiteness." *The Faulkner Journal* 22, nos. 1–2 (Fall 2006–Spring 2007): 106–19.

Early American Rural Music: Classic Recordings of the 1920's and 1930's. Vol. 8 of *Times Ain't Like They Used to Be.* Shanachie Entertainment, 2005.

Ebert, Roger. "Review of *Mandingo*." *Chicago Sun-Times*, July 25, 1975.

Ellison, Ralph. "As the Spirit Moves Mahalia." In *The Collected Essays of Ralph Ellison*, edited by John F. Callahan, 250–55. New York: Modern Library, 1995.

Ellison, Ralph. *Invisible Man.* New York: Vintage, 1995.

———. "Living with Music." In *The Collected Essays of Ralph Ellison*, edited by John F. Callahan, 227–36. New York: Modern Library, 1995.

Epstein, Dena J. *Sinful Tunes and Spirituals: Black Folk Music to the Civil War.* Urbana: University of Illinois Press, 2003.

———. "A White Origin for the Black Spiritual? An Invalid Theory and How It Grew." *American Music* 1, no. 2 (1983): 53–59.

Erlmann, Veit. *African Stars: Studies in Black South African Performance*. Chicago: University of Chicago Press, 1991.

Evans, David. "Black Musicians Remember Jimmie Rodgers." *Old Time Music* 7 (Winter 1972): 12–14.

———. *Tommy Johnson*. London: Studio Vista, 1971.

Faulkner, William. "Introduction." In *Sanctuary*, v–viii. New York: Modern Library, 1932.

———. *Light in August*. In *William Faulkner: Novels 1930–1935*, 399–774. New York: Library of America, 1985.

———. *Sanctuary*. In *William Faulkner: Novels 1930–1935*, 179–398. New York: Library of America, 1985.

Fauset, Arthur Huff. "Hail the Nordic Spiritual!" *Opportunity: A Journal of Negro Life* 7, no. 5 (1929): 163.

Favor, J. Martin. *Authentic Blackness: The Folk in the New Negro Renaissance*. Durham: Duke University Press, 1999.

Feder, J. Lester. "'Song of the South': Country Music, Race, Region, and the Politics of Culture, 1920–1974." (PhD diss., University of California, Los Angeles, 2006).

Filene, Benjamin. *Romancing the Folk: Public Memory and American Roots Music*. Chapel Hill: University of North Carolina Press, 2000.

Fleischer, Richard, dir. *Mandingo*. Dino De Laurentiis / Paramount Pictures, 1975.

Floyd, Samuel A., Jr. "Music in the Harlem Renaissance: An Overview." In *Black Music in the Harlem Renaissance*, edited by Samuel A. Floyd Jr., 1–27. Knoxville: University of Tennessee Press, 1990.

Ford, Karen Jackson. *Split-Gut Song: Jean Toomer and the Poetics of Modernity*. Tuscaloosa: University of Alabama Press, 2005.

Freud, Sigmund. "Mourning and Melancholia." In *The Standard Edition of the Complete Psychological Works of Sigmund Freud*, translated by James Strachey, 14: 243–58. London: Hogarth, 1953.

Frost, William Goodell. "Our Contemporary Ancestors in the Southern Mountains." *Atlantic Monthly* (March 1899): 311–19.

Gershwin, George. "Composer in the Machine Age." In *George Gershwin*, edited by Merle Armitage, 225–30. New York: Longmans, 1938.

Gilroy, Paul. *The Black Atlantic: Modernity and Double Consciousness*. Cambridge, Mass.: Harvard University Press, 1993.

Gitelman, Lisa. *Scripts, Grooves, and Writing Machines: Representing Technology in the Edison Era*. Stanford: Stanford University Press, 2000.

Goldstein, Kenneth S. "The Unfortunate Rake: A Study in the Evolution of a Ballad." In *The Unfortunate Rake (St. James Hospital)*. Folkways, 1960.

Goldstein, Kenneth S., and Peter Narváez. "Producing Blues Recordings." *Journal of American Folklore* 109, no. 434 (1996): 451–57.

Gordon, Eugene. "The Negro's Inhibitions." *American Mercury* 13, no. 49 (January 1928): 159–65.

Gordon, Robert. *Can't Be Satisfied: The Life and Times of Muddy Waters*. Boston: Little, Brown, 2002.

Graham, Maryemma. "The New Negro Renaissance." *Africana Age: African and African Diasporan Transformations in the 20th Century.* http://exhibitions.nypl.org /africanaage/essay-renaissance.html.

Gray, Michael. *Hand Me My Travelin' Shoes: In Search of Blind Willie McTell*. London: Bloomsbury, 2007.

Green, Archie. "Bradley Kincaid's Folios." *JEMF Quarterly* 13, no. 45 (Summer 1977): 21–28.

Greenway, John. "Jimmie Rodgers—A Folksong Catalyst." *Journal of American Folklore* 70, no. 277 (September 1957): 231–34.

Guralnick, Peter. *Searching for Robert Johnson: The Life and Legend of the "King of the Delta Blues Singers."* New York: Dutton, 1989.

Gussow, Adam. "Plaintive Reiterations and Meaningless Strains: Faulkner's Blues Understandings." In *Faulkner's Inheritance: Faulkner and Yoknapatawpha, 2005*, edited by Joseph R. Urgo and Ann J. Abadie, 53–81. Jackson: University Press of Mississippi, 2007.

———. *Seems Like Murder Here: Southern Violence and the Blues Tradition*. Chicago: University of Chicago Press, 2002.

Haden, Walter Darrell. "Vernon Dalhart." In *Stars of Country Music: Uncle Dave Macon to Johnny Rodriguez*, edited by Bill C. Malone and Judith McCulloh, 64–85. Urbana: University of Illinois Press, 1975.

Hamblin, Robert W., and Charles A. Peek. *A William Faulkner Encyclopedia*. Westport: Greenwood, 1999.

Hamilton, Marybeth. *In Search of the Blues*. New York: Basic Books, 2008.

Harkins, Anthony. *Hillbilly: A Cultural History of an American Icon*. New York: Oxford University Press, 2005.

"He Makes a Business of Ballads, as Told to Foster Adams." *Berea Alumnus*, April 1931.

Higginson, Thomas Wentworth. *Army Life in a Black Regiment*. Boston: Fields, 1870.

"The Houn' Dog Guitar." *Washington Post*, November 9, 1930.

"How the Jewish Song Trust Makes You Sing." In *Jewish Influences in American Life*. Vol. 3 of *The International Jew: The World's Foremost Problem*, 75–87. Dearborn, Mich.: Dearborn Publishing, 1921.

Humphrey, Mark A. "Holy Blues: The Gospel Tradition." In *Nothing But the Blues: The Music and the Musicians*, edited by Lawrence Cohn, 107–50. New York: Abbeville Press, 1993.

Hurston, Zora Neale. "Spirituals and Neo-Spirituals." In *Negro: An Anthology*, edited by Nancy Cunard, 359–61. London: Wishart, 1934.

Ignatiev, Noel. *How the Irish Became White*. New York: Routledge, 1995.

Ivey, Bill. "Border Crossings: A Different Way of Listening to American Music." *From Where I Stand: The Black Experience in Country Music*. Warner Bros. Records, 1998.

Jackson, George Pullen. "The Genesis of the Negro Spiritual." *American Mercury* 26 (1932): 243–49.

Jacobson, Matthew Frye. *Whiteness of a Different Color: European Immigrants and the Alchemy of Race*. Cambridge, Mass.: Harvard University Press, 1999.

"Jewish Jazz Becomes Our National Music." In *Jewish Influences in American Life*. Vol. 3 of *The International Jew: The World's Foremost Problem*, 64–74. Dearborn, Mich.: Dearborn Publishing, 1921.

Johnson, James Weldon. *The Autobiography of an Ex-Colored Man*. New York: Penguin, 1990.

————. "Preface to the First Edition." In *The Book of American Negro Poetry*, 9–48. Rev. ed. New York: Harcourt, 1931.

Jones, Loyal. *Radio's "Kentucky Mountain Boy," Bradley Kincaid*. Berea, Ky.: Berea College Appalachian Center, 1980.

————. "Who Is Bradley Kincaid?" *JEMF Quarterly* 12, no. 43 (Autumn 1976): 122–37.

Kincaid, Bradley. *Favorite Mountain Ballads and Old-Time Songs*. Chicago: WLS, 1928.

————. Interview by Dorothy Gable. Audio recording, November 1967. Bradley Kincaid Collection. Southern Appalachian Archives, Hutchins Library, Berea College.

————. Interview by Loyal Jones. Audio recording, April 24, 1974. Bradley Kincaid Collection. Southern Appalachian Archives, Hutchins Library, Berea College.

————. Letter to Elizabeth Gilbert, August 10, 1971. Bradley Kincaid Collection. Southern Appalachian Archives, Hutchins Library, Berea College.

————. "Modern and Up-to-Date History," n.d. Bradley Kincaid Collection, Southern Appalachian Archives, Hutchins Library, Berea College.

————. *My Favorite Mountain Ballads and Old Time Songs*. Vol. 11. 1940.

"Kincaid Says His Songs Are Not Hillbilly." *Dayton Journal*, May 1, 1943.

Koenig, Karl, ed. *Jazz in Print (1856–1929): An Anthology of Selected Early Readings in Jazz History*. Hillsdale, N.Y.: Pendragon, 2002.

Krehbiel, Henry Edward. *Afro-American Folksongs: A Study in Racial and National Music*. New York: G. Schirmer, 1914.

Kreyling, Michael. "Toward 'A New Southern Studies.'" *South Central Review* 22, no. 1 (Spring 2005): 4–18.

Laws, G. Malcolm. *The British Literary Ballad: A Study in Poetic Imitation*. Carbondale: Southern Illinois University Press, 1972.

Levine, Lawrence. "The Concept of the New Negro and the Realities of Black Culture." In *The Unpredictable Past: Explorations in American Cultural History*, 86–106. New York: Oxford University Press, 1993.

————. "The Folklore of Industrial Society: Popular Culture and Its Audiences." *American Historical Review* 97, no. 5 (1992): 1369–99.

Lewine, Richard, and Alfred Simon. *Songs of the American Theater*. New York: Dodd, 1973.

Locke, Alain. "Beauty Instead of Ashes." In *The Critical Temper of Alain Locke: A Selection of His Essays on Art and Culture*, edited by Jeffrey C Stewart, 23–25. New York: Garland, 1983.

———. "Foreword." In *The New Negro: An Interpretation*, edited by Alain Locke, xxv–xxvii. New York: Albert and Charles Boni, 1925.

———. *The Negro and His Music*. Washington, D.C.: Associates in Negro Folk Education, 1936.

———. "The Negro Spirituals." In *The New Negro: An Interpretation*, edited by Alain Locke, 199–210. New York: Albert and Charles Boni, 1925.

———. "The New Negro." In *The New Negro: An Interpretation*, edited by Alain Locke, 3–16. New York: Albert and Charles Boni, 1925.

———, ed. *The New Negro: An Interpretation*. New York: Albert and Charles Boni, 1925.

Lomax, Alan. *The Land Where the Blues Began*. New York: Pantheon, 1993.

Lomax, John A. *Adventures of a Ballad Hunter*. New York: Macmillan, 1947.

———. *American Ballads and Folk Songs*. New York: Macmillan, 1934.

———. *Cowboy Songs and Other Frontier Ballads*. New York: Sturgis & Walton, 1910.

———. *Cowboy Songs and Other Frontier Ballads*. Rev. ed. New York: Macmillan, 1938.

———. "Cowboy Songs of the Mexican Border." *Texas Magazine* 3, no. 5 (March 1911): 27–35.

———. "Half-Million Dollar Song." *Southwest Review* 31, no. 1 (Fall 1945): 1–8.

———. "Letter to Barrett Wendell," September 26, 1907. George Lyman Kittredge Papers, Houghton Library, Harvard University.

———. "Letter to Mrs. C. S. Prosser," May 15, 1913. Box 3d175, Folder 6. James Avery Lomax Family Papers, Center for American History, University of Texas at Austin.

———. "Letter to Mrs. Katherine D. Tucker, Keokuk, Iowa," May 28, 1912. Box 3d169, Folder 9. James Avery Lomax Family Papers, Center for American History, University of Texas at Austin.

———. "Letter to the Trustees of the Carnegie Foundation," January 14, 1908. Box 3d170, Folder 8. James Avery Lomax Family Papers, Center for American History, University of Texas at Austin.

———. *Negro Folk Songs as Sung by Lead Belly, "King of the Twelve-string Guitar Players of the World," Long-time Convict in the Penitentiaries of Texas and Louisiana*. New York: Macmillan, 1936.

———. "Self-Pity in Negro Folk-Songs." *The Nation* 105, no. 2719 (August 9, 1917): 141–45.

———. "'Sinful Songs' of the Southern Negro." *Musical Quarterly* 20, no. 2 (1934): 177–87.

Lomax, John A., and Alan Lomax. *Our Singing Country: A Second Volume of American Ballads and Folk Songs*. New York: Macmillan, 1941.

Lott, Eric. *Love and Theft: Blackface Minstrelsy and the American Working Class*. New York: Oxford University Press, 1993.

Malone, Bill C. *Don't Get Above Your Raisin': Country Music and the Southern Working Class*. Music in American Life. Urbana: University of Illinois Press, 2002.

————. *Singing Cowboys and Musical Mountaineers: Southern Culture and the Roots of Country Music*. Athens: University of Georgia Press, 1993.

Matthews, John T. "*As I Lay Dying* in the Machine Age." *Boundary 2* 19, no. 1 (1992): 69–94.

Maxwell, William J. *New Negro, Old Left*. New York: Columbia University Press, 1999.

Mazor, Barry. *Meeting Jimmie Rodgers: How America's Original Roots Music Hero Changed the Pop Sounds of a Century*. New York: Oxford University Press, 2009.

McDonald, Henry. "Muhammad Ali Receives Freedom of Great-grandfather's Irish Home Town." *Guardian*, September 2, 2009.

Melnick, Jeffrey. *A Right to Sing the Blues: African Americans, Jews, and American Popular Song*. Cambridge, Mass.: Harvard University Press, 1999.

Miller, Karl Hagstrom. *Segregating Sound: Inventing Folk and Pop Music in the Age of Jim Crow*. Durham, N.C.: Duke University Press, 2010.

Minstrel Songs, Old and New. Boston: Oliver Ditson, 1882.

Morrison, Toni. *Playing in the Dark: Whiteness and the Literary Imagination*. New York: Vintage, 1992.

Mphahlele, Ezekiel (Es'kia). *Down Second Avenue*. New York: Anchor, 1959.

Ms. Peachez. "Fry That Chicken." 2006. http://www.youtube.com/watch?v=rGrq W3nx5HM.

Muddy Waters: The Complete Plantation Recordings. CD. Chess, 1993.

Mullen, Patrick B. *The Man Who Adores the Negro: Race and American Folklore*. Urbana: University of Illinois Press, 2008.

Neal, Jocelyn R. *The Songs of Jimmie Rodgers: A Legacy in Country Music*. Bloomington: Indiana University Press, 2009.

Niles, Abbe. "Ballads, Songs, and Snatches." *The Bookman: A Review of Books and Life* 67, no. 5 (July 1928): 565–67.

————. "Ballads, Songs, and Snatches." *The Bookman: A Review of Books and Life* 68, no. 1 (September 1928): 75–77.

————. "Ballads, Songs, and Snatches." *The Bookman: A Review of Books and Life* 68, no. 3 (November 1928): 327–29.

————. "Ballads, Songs, and Snatches." *The Bookman: A Review of Books and Life* 68, no. 4 (December 1928): 457–59.

North, Michael. *The Dialect of Modernism: Race, Language, and Twentieth-Century Literature*. New York: Oxford University Press, 1994.

"Old Ballads Hit on Radio: One-Time Kentucky Mountain Youth Popular Over WLS Station." *News*. September 13, 1929.

Oliver, Paul. "Jimmy Rodgers." *Recorded Folk Music* 2, no. 2 (April 1959): 10.

————. *Songsters and Saints: Vocal Traditions on Race Records*. New York: Cambridge University Press, 1984.

Osbeck, Kenneth. *101 More Hymn Stories: The Inspiring True Stories Behind 101 Favorite Hymns*. Grand Rapids, Mich.: Kregel, 1985.

Palmer, Robert. *Deep Blues: A Musical and Cultural History of the Mississippi Delta.* New York: Penguin, 1982.

Paris, Mike, and Chris Comber. *Jimmie the Kid.* New York: Da Capo Press, 1981.

Pearson, Barry Lee, and Bill McCulloch. *Robert Johnson: Lost and Found.* Urbana: University of Illinois Press, 2003.

Pecknold, Diane. "Introduction: Country Music and Racial Formation." In *Hidden in the Mix: The African American Presence in Country Music,* edited by Diane Pecknold, 1–15. Durham, N.C.: Duke University Press, 2013.

Porterfield, Nolan. "Hey, Hey, Tell 'Em 'Bout Us: Jimmie Rodgers Visits the Carter Family." In *Country: The Music and the Musicians,* 13–39. New York: Abbeville Press, 1994.

———. "Jimmie Rodgers." In *Jimmie Rodgers: The Singing Brakeman.* CD. Bear Family, 1992.

———. *Jimmie Rodgers: The Life and Times of America's Blue Yodeler.* 2nd ed. Urbana: University of Illinois Press, 2002.

"Queer, Adj. 1." *OED Online.* Oxford University Press. http://oed.com/view/Entry/156236.

Radano, Ronald. *Lying Up a Nation: Race and Black Music.* Chicago: University of Chicago Press, 2003.

Ramazani, Jahan. *Poetry of Mourning: The Modern Elegy from Hardy to Heaney.* Chicago: University of Chicago Press, 1994.

Rampersad, Arnold. "Introduction." In *The New Negro: Voices of the Harlem Renaissance,* edited by Alain Locke, ix–xxiii. New York: Touchstone, 1997.

Ramsey, Guthrie P. *Race Music: Black Cultures from Bebop to Hip-Hop.* Berkeley: University of California Press, 2003.

Richardson, Riché. *Black Masculinity and the U.S. South: From Uncle Tom to Gangsta.* Athens: University of Georgia Press, 2007.

Rodgers, Carrie Williamson (Mrs. Jimmie). *My Husband, Jimmie Rodgers.* 2nd ed. Nashville: Vanderbilt University Press, 1995.

Rodgers, Jimmie. *Mississippi Delta Blues.* CD. Bear Family, n.d.

Roediger, David. *The Wages of Whiteness: Race and the Making of the American Working Class.* Rev. ed. New York: Verso, 1994.

Romine, Scott. *The Real South: Southern Narrative in the Age of Cultural Reproduction.* Baton Rouge: Louisiana State University Press, 2008.

Run DMC. *Raising Hell.* LP/cassette. Profile/Arista, 1986.

Russell, Tony. "Blacks, Whites, and Blues." In *Yonder Come the Blues,* 143–242. New York: Cambridge University Press, 2001.

Safford, Harold A. "Bradley Kincaid, a Kentuckian, Became a Noted Singer." *Kentucky Explorer* (November 1999): 82–83.

Sandburg, Carl. *The American Songbag.* New York: Harcourt, 1927.

Sarig, Roni. *Third Coast: OutKast, Timbaland, and How Hip-Hop Became a Southern Thing.* New York: Da Capo Press, 2007.

Sedgwick, Eve Kosofsky. *Between Men: English Literature and Male Homosocial Desire*. New York: Columbia University Press, 1985.

Sollors, Werner. *Beyond Ethnicity: Consent and Descent in American Culture*. New York: Oxford University Press, 1987.

———. "Jean Toomer's *Cane*: Modernism and Race in Interwar America." In *Jean Toomer and the Harlem Renaissance*, edited by Genevieve Fabre and Michael Feith, 18–37. New Brunswick, N.J.: Rutgers University Press, 2001.

Sparxxx, Bubba. *The Charm*. CD. Purple Ribbon/Virgin, 2006.

Szwed, John. *Alan Lomax: The Man Who Recorded the World*. New York: Penguin, 2010.

Tate, Claudia. *Psychoanalysis and Black Novels: Desire and the Protocols of Race*. New York: Oxford University Press, 1998.

Thurman, Wallace. *Infants of the Spring*. New York: Modern Library, 1999.

Toomer, Jean. *Cane: An Authoritative Text, Backgrounds, Criticism*, edited by Darwin T. Turner. New York: W. W. Norton, 1988.

———. *Cane: Authoritative Text, Backgrounds, Criticism*. Edited by Rudolph P. Byrd and Henry Louis Gates. 2nd ed. New York: W. W. Norton, 2011.

———. "The *Cane* Years." In *The Wayward and the Seeking: A Collection of Writings by Jean Toomer*, edited by Darwin T. Turner, 116–27. Washington, D.C.: Howard University Press, 1980.

Tracey, Hugh. *Music of Africa Series No. 2: Kenya*. LP. London Recordings, 1952.

———. *Sounds of Africa: Kipsigis, Kenya*. LP. International Library of African Music, 1950.

Turner, Darwin T. "Introduction." In *Cane*, by Jean Toomer. New York: W. W. Norton, 1988.

Unidentified group. *Judgment*, 1940. AFS 4074. American Folklife Center, Library of Congress.

Wagner, Bryan. *Disturbing the Peace: Black Culture and the Police Power After Slavery*. Cambridge, Mass.: Harvard University Press, 2009.

Wald, Elijah. *Escaping the Delta: Robert Johnson and the Invention of the Blues*. New York: Amistad, 2004.

Walker, Alice. "The Divided Life of Jean Toomer." In *In Search of Our Mothers' Gardens: Womanist Prose*, 60–65. San Diego: Harcourt Brace Jovanovich, 1983.

Walker, Kara. "The Art of War." Atlanta Cyclorama and Civil War Museum, Atlanta, Georgia, August 10, 2012.

Wallaschek, Richard. *Primitive Music: An Inquiry into the Origin and Development of Music, Songs, Instruments, Dances, and Pantomimes of Savage Races*. New York: Longmans, Green, 1893.

Waterman, Christopher A. "Race Music: Bo Chatmon, 'Corrine Corrina,' and the Excluded Middle." In *Music and the Racial Imagination*, edited by Ronald Radano and Philip V. Bohlman, 167–205. Chicago: University of Chicago Press, 2000.

Westhoff, Ben. *Dirty South: OutKast, Lil Wayne, Soulja Boy, and the Southern Rappers Who Reinvented Hip-Hop*. Chicago: Chicago Review Press, 2011.

Whisnant, David E. *All That Is Native and Fine: The Politics of Culture in an American Region*. Chapel Hill: University of North Carolina Press, 1983.

White, Newman Ivey. *American Negro Folk-Songs*. Cambridge, Mass.: Harvard University Press, 1928.

———. "Racial Traits in the Negro Song." *Sewanee Review* 28, no. 3 (July 1920): 396–404.

———. "The White Man in the Woodpile: Some Influences on Negro Secular Folk-Songs." *American Speech* 4, no. 3 (February 1929): 207–15.

Wilentz, Sean, and Greil Marcus. *The Rose and the Briar: Death, Love and Liberty in the American Ballad*. New York: W. W. Norton, 2005.

Will, G. F. "Songs of Western Cowboys." *Journal of American Folk-Lore* 22, no. 84 (June 1909): 256–61.

Williams, John Alexander. *Appalachia: A History*. Chapel Hill: University of North Carolina Press, 2002.

Williams, Raymond. *Marxism and Literature*. New York: Oxford University Press, 1978.

Williamson, Joel. *The Crucible of Race: Black-White Race Relations in the American South Since Emancipation*. New York: Oxford University Press, 1984.

Willpower Omnimedia. *Yelawolf "I WISH" the REMIX Ft. CyHi Da Prynce and Pill*, 2010. http://vimeo.com/9365855.

Wolfe, Charles K. "A Whiter Shade of Blue." In *Nothing But the Blues: The Music and the Musicians*, edited by Lawrence Cohn, 233–63. New York: Abbeville Press, 1993.

Wolk, Josh. "Gay '90s." *EW.com*. http://www.ew.com/ew/article/0,,84865,00.html.

Work, John W., Lewis Wade Jones, and Samuel C. Adams Jr. *Lost Delta Found: Rediscovering the Fisk University–Library of Congress Coahoma County Study, 1941–1942*. Edited by Robert Gordon and Bruce Nemerov. Nashville: Vanderbilt University Press, 2005.

Wright, Richard. "Blueprint for Negro Writing." *New Challenge* 2 (Fall 1937): 53–65.

———. *Uncle Tom's Children*. New York: Harper Perennial, 2008.

Yelawolf. "Pop the Trunk." Motion Family, 2010. http://vimeo.com/8773675.

———. *Trunk Musik*. Ghet-O-Vision, 2010.

"Yelawolf – Gadsden Alabama." http://www.dailymotion.com/video/xieone_yelawolf -gadsden-alabama_music.

"YelaWolf Nervously Brings His Voice Home." *GadsdenTimes.com*. http://www .gadsdentimes.com/article/20100625/news/100629912.

"Yelawolf—Pop the Trunk Lyrics." *Rap Genius*. http://rapgenius.com/Yelawolf-pop -the-trunk-lyrics.

Žižek, Slavoj. *The Sublime Object of Ideology*. London: Verso, 1989.

Index

The New Southern Studies

Finding Purple America: The South and the Future of American Cultural Studies
by Jon Smith

The Signifying Eye: Seeing Faulkner's Art
by Candace Waid

Sacral Grooves/Limbo Gateways: Travels in Deep Southern Time, Circum-Caribbean Space, Afro-creole Authority
by Keith Cartwright

Jim Crow, Literature, and the Legacy of Sutton E. Griggs
edited by Tess Chakkalakal and Kenneth W. Warren

Sounding the Color Line: Music and Race in the Southern Imagination
by Erich Nunn